the cross & the flag

Clouse · Linder Pierard

CREATION HOUSE
Carol Stream, Illinois

FIRST EDITION

Library of Congress Catalog Card Number 72-85415

CONTRIBUTING AUTHORS

Robert G. Clouse is Professor of History at Indiana State University, Terre Haute, and also is an active Brethren minister. He received the B.A. from Bryan College, the B.D. at Grace Theological Seminary, and the M.A. and Ph.D. at the University of Iowa. He is a student of millennial and utopian thought and militarism in modern history. He is a coeditor of *Protest and Politics* (1968), and has contributed chapters to *Puritans, The Millennium and the Future of Israel* (1970) and *Christ and the Modern Mind* (1972).

Ozzie L. Edwards is Assistant Professor of Sociology at the University of Michigan, Ann Arbor. He holds a B.A. from Wheaton College, the M.S.W. from the University of California at Los Angeles, the M.A. from California State College at Los Angeles, and the Ph.D. from University of Wisconsin. He is a specialist in ethnic studies, American minorities, and human ecology, and earlier served on the sociology faculty of the University of Illinois, Chicago Circle. He is a Contributing Editor of *The Other Side* and is author of a chapter in *Birth Control and the Christian* (1969).

George Giacumakis, Jr. is Chairman of the Department and Associate Professor of History at California State College at Fullerton. He gained the B.A. degree from Shelton College, and the M.A. and Ph.D. in Mediterranean and Near Eastern Studies at Brandeis University. He has written *The Akkadian of Alalah* (1970), and contributed articles to *The Biblical World, International Standard Bible Encyclopedia,* and *Zondervan's Pictorial Encyclopedia.* He is active in California Republican politics, and is an elder in the Evangelical Free Church of America.

47714

3

Nancy A. Hardesty is Assistant Professor of English and Chairman of the Division of Languages and Literature, Trinity College, Deerfield, Illinois. She holds the B.A. from Wheaton College, Illinois, and M.S. in journalism from Northwestern University, and has pursued graduate work in religion and theology at the University of Chicago and Temple University. She previously served as editorial assistant for the *Christian Century* and was assistant editor of *Eternity* magazine. She is coauthor of the forthcoming book *The Christian Woman's Liberation.*

Paul B. Henry is Assistant Professor of Political Science at Calvin College, Grand Rapids, Michigan. He obtained the B.A. from Wheaton College, Illinois, and M.A. and Ph.D. from Duke University, all in political science. He was formerly a Peace Corps Volunteer and Legislative Assistant to Congressman John B. Anderson of Illinois, and currently is Vice-President of the Kent County Young Republicans. He is coauthor of *The Dynamics of American Politics* (1972) and has contributed articles to *Christianity Today* and *Christian Life.*

Thomas Howard is Associate Professor of English at Gordon College, Wenham, Massachusetts. He was awarded the B.A. degree by Wheaton College, Illinois, the M.A. at the University of Illinois, and the Ph.D. at New York University. He was formerly English master at Kingsmead School in England and then at St. Bernard's School in New York City. He has written two books, *Christ the Tiger* (1967) and *An Antique Drum* (1969), and his articles have appeared in numerous magazines and journals, both religious and secular.

James E. Johnson is Professor of History at Bethel College, St. Paul, Minnesota. He received the B.A. from Syracuse University, the M.A. from the University of Buffalo, and the Ph.D. at Syracuse. He formerly taught at Syracuse and Youngtown Universities. He is author of *The Scots and Scotch-Irish in America* and *The Irish in America* (1966), and he contributed a chapter to *Protest and Politics* (1968) and articles to various historical journals. He is currently working on the history of the child-welfare movement.

Robert D. Linder is Associate Professor of History at Kansas State University, Manhattan. He earned the B.S. from Kansas State Teachers College, the B.D. and M.R.E. from Central Baptist Theological Seminary, and the M.A. and Ph.D. from the University of Iowa. For two years he taught at William Jewell College. He is author of *The Political Ideas of Pierre Viret* (1964), coeditor of *Protest and Politics* (1968) and *Calvin and Calvinism* (1970), and editor of *God and Caesar* (1971). A prominent figure in Kansas Republican politics, he currently serves on the Manhattan city commission and was mayor in 1971-72.

Lee Nash is Professor of History at Northern Arizona University, Flagstaff. He holds the B.A. from Cascade College, the M.A. from the University of Washington, and the Ph.D. from the University of Oregon. He served for thirteen years at Cascade College, the last five years as Dean. He is interested in American intellectual and cultural history and has published widely in historical and religious journals. He is the United Methodist "Good News" renewal leader for Northern Arizona, and in 1972 was elected as a delegate to the Arizona Democratic Party State Convention.

Richard V. Pierard is Professor of History at Indiana State University, Terre Haute. He studied at Los Angeles Baptist and Westmont colleges, and he received the B.A. and M.A. from California State College at Los Angeles, and the Ph.D. from the University of Iowa. He was a Fulbright scholar at the University of Hamburg, Ger-

5

many, and has served as a visiting lecturer at the German
Bible School of Greater Europe Mission. He is a coeditor
of *Protest and Politics* (1968) and author of *The Unequal
Yoke* (1970), and has published numerous articles.

Earl J. Reeves is Professor of Political Science and Director of Urban Studies at the University of Tulsa. He holds
the B.A. and M.A. from Wichita State University, and the
Ph.D. from the University of Kansas. He previously taught
at the University of Nebraska, Omaha, and University of
Missouri, St. Louis. He has published several research studies and articles in the area of public administration. He
was formerly Vice-President of the Berkeley, Missouri,
city council and now serves on several civic bodies in Tulsa.
He is an active United Presbyterian layman.

CONTENTS

PREFACE

Evangelical Christians often have rendered unto Caesar that which is God's.

We cite Romans 13 as proof that the State always demands our total and unquestioned allegiance. But we neglect Revelation 13, which pictures the State as a beast, or Revelation 18, which prophesies the downfall of any nation that becomes a modern Babylon, corrupted by its wealth, materialism, and injustice.

We point out that Peter has written, "Be subject for the Lord's sake to every human institution, whether it be to the emperor as supreme or to governors . . ." (1 Pet.2:13 RSV). But we neglect to recall that, after one of his arrests by authorities, Peter also said, "We must obey God rather than men." (Ac. 5:29).

Further, while we are quick to condemn any person who upsets social normalcy, we forget the words used in the Bible to describe the apostles: "These men who have turned the world upside down have come here also, and Jason has received them; and they are all acting against the decrees of Caesar, saying that there is another king, Jesus" (Ac. 17:6-7).

When Christ told us to "render unto Caesar that which is Caesar's," he did not mean that we should give Caesar anything he asks for. Caesar may deserve the coins that he already owns; but God deserves our total allegiance if He truly is the owner of our lives.

A look at the life of our Lord does not justify the picture of one who unquestionably abides by the wisdom and wishes of those holding power in society. Christ upset the status quo of his day. He even called Herod a "fox" (Lk. 13:32), named at least one Zealot (political revolutionaries against Rome) as a disciple (Simon the Zealot—Lk. 6:15), and was certainly viewed by the Roman authorities as a potential political threat, or "The King of the Jews." So a serious study of God's Word will not always allow us to view the State, and its rulers, with uncritical acceptance and automatic approval.

Yet, at the same time, the Scriptures will not let us conclude that government is inevitably an evil institution that should be ignored, distrusted, and disobeyed. We are instructed to honor and pray for those in authority, and the Bible makes clear that there is a design of a positive role for government to play in the working of God's will for all mankind. All authority, according to the New Testament, is ultimately under the rule and judgment of Christ.

Where should the Christian turn, then, in order to discover how to act toward contemporary political and social issues?

Unfortunately, our culture and many evangelical churches have given little guidance to us in the past. We have taken the Constitutional doctrine of separation of Church and State, and converted it into a practice of separating the world of faith from the world of politics. The result is clear: our political system is threatened by a vacuum of moral values and the evangelical church is threatened by a vacuum of social relevance.

Evangelicals point out very correctly the dangers of reducing faith to nothing more than allegiance to a program of social reform. But we fail to preach and live the whole Gospel when our attitudes and relations with fellow men, which includes "politics" at some level, are not guided by our faith in Christ.

Our first responsibility is to restudy God's Word on these issues. In the past, we often have come to the Scriptures with our preconceived, culturally-molded notions about political issues, seeking to find proof texts that justify our prejudices. If we are against welfare, for instance, we point out that Jesus said we would always have the poor with us, but we fail to examine either the context of that passage or what else the Bible has to say about the disadvantaged and dispossessed in the world. If we regard the Word of God as the authority over our lives, then we must study with open minds what it may say to our perspectives on contemporary problems.

Of course, we cannot always expect to find specific answers to every problem, or a concrete blueprint for our action, directly from the Scriptures. It is often said, for instance, that Jesus never marched in any demonstrations. But Jesus never wrote his congressman either.

We can find, however, general principles, priorities and attitudes from the Scriptures and the life of Christ that are directly applicable to our lives in present situations. The essays in this volume represent clear evangelical thinking that attempts to make this application of faith to contemporary affairs. The authors are thoughtful Christians who have drawn upon interpretations of the Scriptures as they examine modern problems. Doubtless, their approach will stimulate us all to more serious thinking about these questions, and to a deeper study of God's Word.

Peter instructs us to give honor to everyone: love to the brotherhood, reverence to God, honor to the sovereign (1 Pet. 2:17, free trans.). In our time, it is essential that evangelicals discern the difference between the reverence, or "fear" that is due only unto God, and the "honor" that is due to the sovereign. Only then will we know how to render unto God all that is His.

— *Senator Mark O. Hatfield*

1

Introduction

Television viewers across the country were treated to a rare spectacle on December 20, 1971—or was it really so unusual? The occasion was a football game, the Liberty Bowl at Memphis, Tennessee. During the half-time intermission the 30,000 spectators, many of whom were drunk, waved tiny American flags while the University of Arkansas band formed a cross on the playing field. As the band played "Silent Night, Holy Night," a group of scantily clad baton twirlers bumped and ground to the rhythm. In addition, contingents of Boy Scouts, sailors, and marines went through various exercises, all courtesy of the Freedoms Foundation at Valley Forge, Pennsylvania, sponsor of this patriotic circus. What an obscene perversion of two revered and meaningful symbols: the cross and the flag!

This travesty should have outraged every believing Christian, but it passed largely unnoticed for reasons that are not difficult to understand. The spiritual foundations of Christianity in the United States have been eroded by a number of factors having little to do with a biblically based religion, and they have transformed what historically was a forward-looking, action-oriented faith into a largely defensive, culture-bound one. Since this situation has been particularly vexing to many younger theologically conservative Christians, the factors producing it need to be brought to the attention of all believers so that remedial action can be taken. [1]

One of these is a persistent, uncritical alliance between conservative Protestantism and conservative political, economic and social interests which at times is so pronounced that some have come to feel that evangelical Christianity is enslaved by the political far right. Nothing has so distorted evangelical social ethics as this identification with political and social conservatism. Too many Christians have lost interest in changing the world because they like it as it is. As they become increasingly committed to preserving the status quo, they often unconsciously tie themselves to those very forces which have a vested interest in maintaining social injustice.

Other professing Christians have sold out completely to the current socioeconomic establishment and support it under any circumstances as if God and government were synonymous terms. A good example of this kind of mentality was the reaction of Dr. Bob Jones, Jr., president of Bob Jones University, to the news of the killing of four Kent State University students by National Guardsmen during the campus unrest of May, 1970. He is reported to have exclaimed: "Those young people got exactly what they were entitled to. I'm all for the police shooting to kill when anyone is in mob violence attempting to destroy property and attack law enforcement officers. More power to them."[2]

A second difficulty is that conservative believers many times give very simplistic attention to social and political problems. They say that "Christ is the answer" to all problems of human existence. When a man's life is changed through the new birth, he will naturally be concerned about the needs of his fellowmen. When men turn to Christ, problems such as racial discrimination, poverty and hatred among nations will either wither away or at least eventually take care of themselves. They argue that the early Christians never mounted political crusades for the underprivileged masses, but nevertheless they turned the world upside down for God and their legacy today is the most advanced civilization in human history.

A third matter of concern is the emphasis placed upon solely personal problems while social ones are overlooked. To cite one example, a prominent Evangelical recently wrote that the love of God in the New Testament "appeals to individuals, challenges individuals, and works through individuals." For the church to "turn from witness to individuals to attempts to reshape society through the state means it will be "trying to play God."[3] Evangelicals are quite willing to attack individual sins, such as the sale of alcoholic beverages, prostitution, gambling and pornography, but social and economic evils are blithely ignored. Such Christians regard laws to enforce personal morality as desirable because they seemingly bring people closer to God. However, legislation and other positive actions which attack social sins like poverty, racism, poor housing, disease, militarism, war and environmental pollution are rejected as "mixing politics with religion." What this means is that the conservative Protestant all too often sides with those opposed to purposeful change and manifests a shockingly calloused indifference to social questions.

The failure of much of Evangelicalism to leap over the wall of individual piety and to demonstrate a capacity to criticize the secular order has stunted the gospel witness and forced many concerned Christians to abandon the normal structure of the church in order to struggle for social justice. Two recent works by evangelical scholars have underscored the abysmal failure of conservative Protestantism in this respect. Baptist Vernon C. Grounds states: "An evangelical cannot deny that, historically, his faith has been complacent, compliant, and compromising, an uncritical

15

ally of whatever authority might happen to be in power." [4]
Mennonite Calvin Redekop notes that Christianity preaches
one thing but lives in a completely falsified objective
reality. The result is a general cynicism about the faith which
has been pointed up by an atheist who allegedly said: "I
think Christianity has the answer to the world's problems.
Why doesn't somebody try it?" [5]

What is desperately needed are alternative stances to
social and political problems that will free Evangelicals from
the stigma of the status quo and reaction. Both on the individual and corporate levels they must become involved in
confronting current social evils and transforming structures
that perpetuate injustices. Sherwood Wirt, editor of *Decision*
magazine, appropriately reminds the people of God that
they are not to move in some special orbit but in "the mainstream of life." [6]

On the other hand, socially concerned Christians must
guard against a simplistic alliance with the extremists of
the left. They must maintain a degree of independence with
respect to all groups, movements, and organized agencies.
Sociologist David Moberg properly warns believers that if
they become too rigidly linked with any associations, they
may lose their "opportunity to help correct the sins of that
group." He advises the church to stand up for the weak,
poor, and exploited but not "become the voice for revolutionary groups which try to use the church to promote their
selfish ends." [7] In short, the Christian must "hang loose"
and take care to discharge his stewardship responsibilities
faithfully in accordance with biblical precepts.

Also required is a balance between the theological
perspective and practical action. The conservative view that
converting individuals to Jesus Christ is the answer to social
and political problems of the world is as much a form of
utopianism as liberal ideas of establishing the kingdom of
God on earth. What Evangelicals should do is emphasize
that their faith is unique because it ministers to the whole

man, including his inward mystical nature and his outward social needs. Carl F. H. Henry insists that a Christian doctrine of society must stress both the demand of God for personal righteousness and universal social justice, and God's gracious provision for a new man and a new society on the basis of redemptive grace. [8]

The Christian who argues for balance and moderation in a day when extreme positions are the vogue is likely to find himself caught between crossfire from both the right and the left, from the pietist and the activist. Unfortunately we are living in a polarized age where the vital witness of the Christian church is muted. As Myron Augsburger, president of Eastern Mennonite College, pointed out at the 1970 Inter-Varsity Christian Fellowship Urbana conference, "Because we are polarized, we have come to the place where the activist is limited because he cannot back up his action with deep devotional commitment to Christ and the pietist is limited because he is insecure, ineffective, and irrelevant when it comes to involvement in society." [9]

The Christian, however, need not simply straddle the fence or hug the middle of the road but instead demonstrate there is a third alternative to the polarities of activism and pietism. A pure social gospel is nothing more than humanism overlaid with a thin veneer of Christianity, while a gospel concerned only with saving souls and preparing people for the afterlife is, to use a shopworn cliche, "so heavenly minded that it is no earthly good." It is imperative that evangelical Christians in the 1970s return to the biblical synthesis of deep personal faith in Christ and genuine concern for other people. Such a stance is no compromise—it is the classical tradition of the church.

Since this book is designed to speak to evangelical Christians, it is advisable at this point to define the term *Evangelical*. Harold Ockenga, one of the foremost representatives of the position in the United States, wrote in *Christianity Today* that an Evangelical is one who holds to the fundamental doctrines of historic Christianity—the deity of Christ, the fallen condition of man, Christ's atonement for sin, salvation through faith alone without the assistance of good works, and regeneration by the Holy Spirit. Also, he stands firmly on the premise that the Bible is the inspired, authoritative Word of God and the norm of judgment in faith and practice. Evangelicalism and fundamentalism also adhere to the same position doctrinally, although they differ somewhat on their attitudes toward participation in modern life. 10 Perhaps, then, one can say that all Evangelicals are characterized by an emphasis upon biblical authority and individual spiritual rebirth through faith in Christ. Since these are also the basic tenets of historic Christianity, the adjectives "orthodox," "biblical," and "conservative" can be used interchangeably with "evangelical" without distorting the meaning in any way.

Why do conservative Christians tend to shy away from political and social involvement? For one thing, the doctrine of sin intimates that the world is corrupt and evil and no effort on their part will make any difference. Therefore, some Christians feel that to suggest a more equitable society can be built in a fallen world is to advocate "humanism."

Eschatological teachings also deter political and social involvement, especially for many premillennialists. Human suffering is a sign of the times, a necessary prelude to the second coming of Christ. Since conditions in the world will become increasingly worse as the Lord's return approaches, all efforts to deal with social problems are futile. Those who hold this view believe that it is far better to concentrate on the spiritually productive tasks of winning souls and the moral reform of individuals in preparation for Christ's kingdom.

Particularly significant is the emphasis many well-meaning Christians place upon the exclusively spiritual nature of God's work in the world. They claim that Jesus died to save

18

individual persons from eternal loss, and every Christian is duty-bound to win souls, to snatch them as "brands from the burning." Believers are to separate themselves from the sinful world which stains all those who come in contact with it. The kingdom of Christ is not of this world (Jn. 18:36), and thus secular society is of no concern to His people. The Christian must devote his full effort to evangelism and other spiritual activities—prayer, Bible reading, meditation, confession of sins, and seeking the filling of the Holy Spirit.

Others are willing to accept the idea of practicing Christian social concern so long as it is restricted to believers. They teach that the primary function of Christians is to preach the gospel, and the only social dimension of their ministry is caring for believers in need. There is simply no time for extensive action programs. Baptist theologian Paul Benware effectively summarizes this position on social involvement in a recent article which enumerates the following "basic principles":

> (1) Christian social work is primarily an individual responsibility. (2) Christian social work is to be directed towards alleviating the needs of fellow Christians. (3) The organizational church is to work only for the betterment of born-again persons. (4) There is no indication anywhere in the New Testament that the church can align itself formally or informally with society in order to bring about social change. (5) Individual Christians are first to help believers, but are also directed to use some of their remaining resources as occasion permits to help the unbeliever for the glory of God. 11

These factors are more or less theological in their formulation, but there are other reasons for this reluctance to become involved in politics and social action as well. A recent empirical study of the evangelical Christian subculture made by a reputable psychiatrist found that conservative Christian society tends to produce a "fundamentalist personality," characterized by "closed mindedness" and a noteworthy lack of humanitarian concern. The author, an Evangelical himself, stresses that it is not religion per se that brings about this situation but rather membership in a religious culture that has isolated its members from involvement in the community at large. [12]

Moberg calls attention to a growing conformity to worldly standards on the part of Evangelicals who are rising in the social class structure. They have gradually accommodated their religious beliefs to materialistic patterns of personal and family life and have come to identify themselves with the interests of wealth and power in society. [13] It seems obvious that in their zeal to separate from "sin" and keep the gospel "pure," many conservative Evangelicals fall victim to other sins—the lack of Christian compassion and the failure to love their neighbors as themselves.

These positions, however, quickly crumble when they are subjected to biblical scrutiny. In fact, the social obligations of the Christian are so self-evident in the Scriptures that one wonders if many Evangelicals really take the Bible seriously. Noted theologian John Warwick Montgomery is fully justified in saying that an effort to prove that Christians should have social concern "would be tantamount to a statistical survey demonstrating that all husbands are married, or a search purporting to discover who is buried in Grant's tomb." [14] How, then, do these explanations for noninvolvement fall short of the divine standards?

The emphasis upon the sinfulness of the present world overlooks the fact that it is God's creation and still belongs to Him even though it may temporarily lie under enemy occupation. He made the world, rules over it, and loves it. The Scriptures declare clearly that "everything created by God is good," and we should accept it with gratitude (1 Ti. 4:4, RSV). Through His all-embracing providence the world is sustained (Ps. 104), and nothing so reveals God's continuing love for the earth as His practice of bestowing life-giving sunshine and refreshing rains, regardless of the spiritual state of the men benefiting from them, whether they be "just" or "unjust." (Ac. 14:17; Mt. 5:45). Further, man is also a creation of God, made in the divine "image" and "likeness" (Gen. 1:26), and thus is of infinitely greater worth than other creatures. This implies that man occupies a unique place in the creation and that he is to participate in the working out of the divine purpose in the world. When man sinned and fell, God's concern for him was so great that He sent His only Son to die for the redemption of humanity. Christians must reject any type of Manichean heresy that holds that God's world is evil and that they will be soiled if they come in contact with it.

With respect to the future, very few Evangelicals believe that the implementation of social solutions will lead to a perfect society. But they do realize that what death is to the individual person, the second coming is to the entire human race. As they continue in their daily activities, even though death is inevitable, so likewise the return of Christ should find every believer faithfully working for Him both in the spiritual and social realms. The Bible does not teach a supernatural social ethic but rather that God uses human means to accomplish His purposes. Just as Christians should witness for their Lord to win souls, so they should try to combat the injustices of society. As C. S. Lewis put it, a belief in the second coming does not preclude:

> Sober work for the future within the limits of ordinary morality and prudence. . . . For what comes is judgment: happy are those whom it finds laboring in their vocations, whether they were merely going out to feed the pigs or laying good plans to deliver humanity a hundred years hence from some great evil. The curtain has indeed now fallen. Those pigs will never in fact be fed, the great campaign against white slavery or governmental tyranny will never in fact proceed to victory. No matter; you were at your post when the inspection came. [15]

21

The view that God's work is only spiritual is another dangerous teaching that orthodox Christians should avoid. God clearly indicates that justice in mundane affairs is very important to Him (Amos 5:24). He established the institution of human government so that man could live in a just and orderly relationship with his fellows. The Old Testament prophets spoke frequently of social justice, as, for example, in the many references to widows and orphans or the jubilee principle in Leviticus 25, all of which reveal God's interest in those who are in a socially weak position. The divine concern is expressed not in terms of paternalism but of justice (Ja. 5:1-6).

Moreover, in His ministry Jesus never distinguished between the "religious" and the "social." He fed the hungry, healed the sick, and raised the dead. In Matthew 25 He underscored the importance of such people-oriented deeds as giving nourishment to the starving, caring for the sick, rehabilitating prisoners, clothing the destitute, and housing refugees, and specified that such activity by His disciples was equivalent to devotion to Himself. In fact, Jesus placed the needs of earthly man above religious and ceremonial considerations, as exemplified by His defiance of Sabbath customs (Mk. 2:23-28) and His treatment of the woman taken in adultery (Jn. 8:3-11).

The Lord stressed that His disciples were to be servants of humanity (Mk. 10:43-44). They were to be "salt" and "lights" in the world (Mt. 5:13-16). In the prayer for His followers just before His arrest, Christ asked not that they be taken from the world but instead kept from evil in it (Jn. 17:15). This strongly conveys the idea that believers are not to live in monastic isolation from the everyday world, but rather to be engaged in bringing God's judgment and Christian values to bear upon its structures and practices.

The position that Christian social concern is limited to those in the "household of faith" flies in the face of the directive to love our neighbors as ourselves (Lev. 19:18, RSV). In order to show that neighbor love extends beyond the confines of one's own group, Jesus gave the story of the good Samaritan as a response to the question, "Who is my neighbor?" (Lk. 10:29-37). Although Galatians 6:10 does mention doing good to the household of faith, the first clause of the verse clarifies the necessity to "do good to all men."

The development of a close-minded evangelical subculture is a direct outgrowth of a misguided and misplaced emphasis on separation from the world. Many Christians misunderstood what the world was and misinterpreted the passages about not loving the world and separating from evil, and the result was the formation of an evangelical ghetto with its corresponding mentality. Recognizing Christ's commands to be involved in human affairs and then acting upon them is undoubtedly the best therapy for this malady.

The identification with the wealthy and their values is related to the previous point. When the Bible says "love not the world, neither the things that are in the world" (1 Jn. 2:15), it refers to the worldly value system. James 2 and 5 serve notice to the wealthy that their practices do not always harmonize with the law of God, and the congregation that shows favoritism to the rich and powerful stands under the judgment of God. Those who are climbing the status ladder should not forget the divine command, "Be not conformed to this world" (Ro. 12:2). That definitely means one must avoid an uncritical acceptance of the standards of the age.

This brief summary of biblical teaching on the subject should be more than enough to convince even the most hesitant Christian that he ought to engage in confronting and solving contemporary political and social problems. However, what are the prospects that such will occur? Until recently those who preached this were little more than isolated voices in the wilderness of culture-bound apathy and otherworldly indifference, but encouraging signs of change are now evident. Carl Henry's recent call for Christians to go beyond a mere ministry to victims of social injustice and seek hopeful ways of remedying and eliminating the causes of that social injustice" 16 is being echoed over and over again in evangelical circles. In his best-selling book, *World Aflame*, Billy Graham forthrightly and unequivocally declared:

> We as Christian citizens have no right to be content with our social order until the principles of Christ are applied to all men. As long as there is enslaved one man who should be free, as long as slums and ghettoes exist, as long as any person goes to bed hungry at night, as long as the color of man's skin is his prison, there must be a divine discontent. 17

The tremendous enthusiasm for political and social involvement manifested at the U. S. Congress on Evangelism in 1969 and the IVCF Urbana missionary convention in 1970, and the growing participation by evangelical Christians in the quest for racial justice, all bear testimony of far-reaching attitudinal changes taking place in evangelical circles.

Nevertheless, a long road lies ahead. A majority of conservative Christians still seem to be apathetic and often even hostile to the idea of social involvement. A recent letter to the editor in *Christianity Today* by a wealthy, nationally known Christian businessman should serve to remind Evangelicals that they still have much progress to make. The writer declares:

> As a human being, I want to see justice to all; but it would be silly in my opinion, to expect justice in a world dominated by wickedness. In this world, I may get a different kind of injustice than a black person, but I could recite a long list of what I consider personal injustices. . . .I can thank God not only for the new life in Christ but for the injustices and other trials that have come to me, knowing that tribulation works patience and that it is through troubles that we find the greater blessing of Christ. 18

A different problem is that of those who consciously choose to be noninvolved, above all, the so-called "Jesus People." Their emphasis on Jesus, the Bible, and love, and their youthful zeal and spontaneity have brought a breath of fresh air into many staid and indifferent orthodox churches. But, it seems that their whole experience is a mystical, internal one—the life of the spirit and communion with God—and that their concern does not reach beyond the confines of their individual personalities and communal groups to the world at large. It is fine to be "high on Jesus" but what about the outside world? If the Jesus Movement fails to relate to those outside and show that the Christian faith can make a difference in society as a whole, it will prove to be nothing more than a passing fad.

The essays in this book are designed to help theologically conservative Christians bring their faith to bear on the issues of the day. Although most of the contributors are not professional theologians as such, they are specialists in their various disciplines and deeply committed Evangelicals who have grappled with the problems of relating their faith to the world in which they live. It goes without saying that the viewpoints expressed in these essays are those of the individual writers and do not necessarily reflect the views of the editors or of the other contributors.

The editors have selected a series of significant issues about which they hope to sensitize their fellow Christians. The treatments are not exhaustive nor will they identify and perpetuate supposedly "Christian" elements within the Western cultural tradition. Instead of trying to set up a new political, economic, and social orthodoxy, the authors intend merely to examine the ramifications of these topics, suggest some viable alternatives, and encourage Christians to do some serious thinking about them. It is hoped that ministers and lay leaders alike will find this book suitable for use in the Sunday school classes, adult discussion groups, and young people's fellowships of their churches. The work is also designed to appeal to students and campus Christian organizations, for it is on the college and university campuses that much of the searching, critical rethinking of the naively held cultural assumptions of Western Evangelicalism is taking place today.

The evangelical Christian community is a large and potentially powerful force in modern society, one that cuts across denominational, occupational, and social class lines, and it could accomplish a great deal of good for mankind today if only it would act. Perhaps the following course of action recommended by J. N. D. Anderson will be of value as a beginning: First, preach the gospel and the radically changed lives of men who turn to Christ will soon become evident in every aspect of public and private life. Then, Christian social principles must be proclaimed to others, both from the pulpit and through the lives, lips, and pens of those who embrace the faith. Finally, Christians should work to see that laws are enacted which put these principles into effect in contemporary society. [19]

The problems raised by the interrelationships of those needs and values represented symbolically by the cross and the flag will remain for some time to come. Evangelical Christians must respond to the issues of the 1970s and reinforce their faith with actions if they expect it to remain a relevant force. Will they plunge into the fray or will they resign themselves to a place on the sidelines? The answer for the most part lies with those of you who now read these pages and reflect on the ideas presented in this volume.

2

The Christian and Political Involvement in Today's World

PRACTICAL POLITICS: DOES CHRISTIAN FAITH MAKE A DIFFERENCE?

Seven men of various ages, backgrounds, and races sat at a table in the chambers of the local city council discussing the latest crisis in municipal government in a medium-sized community in the Western United States. The issue was whether or not to ask the city manager to resign from the position which he had held for the past twelve years. Five of the seven councilmen had been swept into office in the previous election several months before by promising to introduce much-needed reform and change on the local scene.

Several of the new men on the council were evangelical Christians, as was one of the holdover members of the governing body. But, interestingly enough, not all of the Evangelicals were on the same side in this particular political dispute. At stake was control of the city's government. For years the local power structure had guarded its interests and had its way by maintaining a majority on the city council through various means and maneuverings. Now, for the first time in decades, the community's economic elite no longer commanded this majority, and the city manager, long sensitive and attentive to their demands, was in danger of losing his job. How would the Evangelicals on the council react to this move to oust the city manager from office?

The proverbial generation gap seemed to be a factor. The younger Christians on the council sided with the other reformers and called for the city manager's release on grounds of incompetency and an apparent lack of a sense of responsibility to the direction of the local governing body, the point upon which the whole concept of the manager-council form of government was posited. However, the older evangelical Christian on the council sided with the local power elite and warned the board's majority of the perils of attempting to resist the obvious desire of the local power elite to retain the city manager in office.

The exchange between the two sides became heated. In the course of the discussion one of the younger members of the council, an active Evangelical churchman, commented that he had been warned of "reprisals" if he voted to remove the city manager. The older Christian on the governing board who was in favor of retaining the city manager, a man who had served on the committee which had sponsored a Billy Graham crusade in the community only a few months before, blurted out at this point: "If reprisals come, you will get exactly what you deserve. The people who count in this community want this man kept in office and you are going against their wishes. You will get what you deserve!"

How is it that apparently sincere Christian men found themselves on opposite sides of this extremely important issue—an older Evangelical defending the local establishment and the status quo, the other younger believers advocating reform and change? Why is it that in another city not far away a prominent Christian businessman violated a local city ordinance by constructing a grotesque off-site sign advertising his place of business some blocks away while at the same time growling his defiance to the municipal governing body "to do something about it if you dare"? Why is it that in still another town in the same area a building contractor who professed Christ and was active in a local church known for its gospel witness, opposed a public housing project because "it would hurt my business"? [1]

Turning to the national scene, evangelical Christians in politics at that level have encountered even more perplexing dilemmas as they have attempted to relate their faith to the task of governing the country. For example, one nationally prominent Christian in high office expressed doubt about the wisdom of running for reelection after a number of disheartening and disconcerting experiences during his first term in office. One of the ironies of the situation is that this particular man is unusually qualified for high office, perhaps even for the presidency of the United States, yet his chances of remaining in his present position and of someday running for the office of President appear to be in doubt at the present time.

This individual is contemplating not announcing for reelection for a number of reasons. For one thing, he does not have enough money. He has crossed the fabled "fat cats" of his party's establishment too often, and it has been widely reported that they will withhold substantial amounts of funds from his campaign should he choose to run again. Some of the extremists in his party have gone so far as to encourage primary opposition to this particular officeholder, even though he is an incumbent. This Christian in politics is not a rich man, nor even a fairly affluent one. When he makes a substantial part of his income from the lecture circuit during the year, the secular press takes swipes at him, implying that this practice is inherently wrong, or at least questionable. All of this opposition from within his own party and the occasional harassment of the press have become exceedingly wearisome.

29

Moreover, he has received a great deal of abuse from so-called fellow Christians. A number of Evangelicals have denounced him and even questioned the genuineness of his Christian profession and his loyalty to the United States because he has opposed the Vietnam War and because he has not uncritically supported the President and the Pentagon in their every wish and command. Men in political life in a democracy can expect considerable abuse because of the inherent nature of the democratic political process and the growing complexity of issues. However, there is nothing more discouraging to a Christian in politics than to be scorned, criticized, and vilified by fellow believers who somehow equate piety with patriotism, Christianity with the flag, and unquestioning obedience to high powers with the will of God. Modern democratic political life is exhausting and burdensome enough without the added weight of this sort of vituperative criticism. And it often turns out that the evangelical Christian in political life has a built-in disability because non-Christians many times write him off without a hearing because of his commitment to Christ, while being a believer does not guarantee him the "Christian vote" by any means—if there is such a thing.

The time which a Christian commitment to politics requires is a third major factor in his reluctance to run again. A call to politics does not mean neglecting other aspects of the Christian life such as church and family. However, the Christian public servant experiences a certain weariness of the flesh when deprived of so many of the normal relationships of life because of politics. He constantly must assess and reassess his situation in order to make a judgment about the value of what he is doing. He must be convinced that his contributions to public life are worth the sacrifices which he invariably must make in order to hold elective office. This particular individual has said on several occasions that one of the things which bothers him most about his political career is that it requires so much time away from his family. It is a matter of priorities. [2]

POLITICS: MORAL OR IMMORAL?

Can democracy in America survive if Christian men like this one find it impossible to continue to participate in public life because of defects in the political system and imperfections in American Christianity which *can* be corrected but which no one seems willing to change? This question along with the ones previously raised and others closely related to them, deeply affect all Christians in democratic nations because they live in societies closely shaped by political decisions. In view of growing doubts about the morality of politics, the apparent lack of consensus concerning the nature of the political involvement of Christians and the uncertain trumpet of evangelical social concern, it is vital that the question of the evangelical Christian and political involvement in today's world be discussed. First, this essay examines three fundamental ways of viewing politics. Second, some reasons are advanced as to why Christians should be involved politically. Finally, a few meaningful conclusions about Christian political and social concern are made, based upon these remarks and the current world situation.

People tend to look at politics in three basic ways. Each of these views has extraordinary and far-reaching implications for the Christian. First, there is the feeling that politics is immoral. This view is commonly expressed in the oft-heard phrase "politics is dirty" and seems to be the traditional American way of looking at political affairs. In other words, there seems to be a deep-seated feeling among many Evangelicals and perhaps most Americans that "politics is dirty." A recent Gallup Poll revealed that two out of three Americans believe that Congressional misuse of public funds is fairly common. Members of a PTA group in a large suburban high school were asked not too long ago to check in order of preference the occupations they wanted their children to enter. Among those listed, medical doctor, dentist, and lawyer were at the top. Elected public official was near the bottom. This certainly says something about what they thought of those in elective public office. 3

Even jokes reveal something of what Americans think of politics and politicians. One story is that on a recent visit to Chicago, the mayor of that city invited the President and Vice-President to take a cruise on Lake Michigan on his own private yacht. However, several miles from shore something suddenly went wrong and the craft began to sink. It was then that they realized that the yacht had on board only a single one-man life raft. The President argued that he should be the *one* to use the raft since he was obviously the most important individual aboard. The Vice-President pleaded that he should be the *one* to use the life raft because he had not yet had a chance to demonstrate what he could do for the country. The mayor objected to both lines of reasoning and said that since America was a democracy, they should vote on it. They agreed, and Mr. Daley won 29 to 2! 4

Others believe that politics are neither moral nor immoral but amoral, or at least outside the realm of moral judgment. This view was articulated first in modern times by Niccolo Machiavelli in his political treatise entitled *The Prince*, and was widely disseminated throughout the Western world. According to this outlook, *power* is all that counts, and power is the only meaningful end of politics. Machiavelli ignored the issue of the end of the state in extrapolitical terms and confined his inquiries to the means that are best suited to acquire, retain, and expand power. What is done in the name of the state is not "right" or "wrong" because the state is an autonomous system of values independent of any other source. As Machiavelli himself stated, in the action of rulers, "The end justifies the means."

In the modern Christian world, the Machiavellian-relativistic approach has been appropriated by conservative advocates of situation ethics who, for example, argue that killing for the state is of a different order than killing as a private citizen. In the thinking of some Christians who accept this point of view, the activities of the state lie beyond the pale of judgment by Christian moral and ethical standards. 5

The third position concerning politics, which has been the traditional Christian view, is that political acts are not amoral or outside the bounds of conventional morality, but either moral or immoral; or to put it another way, that all political acts have moral content. In fact, this concept goes back beyond the beginnings of Christianity to the ancient Greeks who believed that politics meant the formation and implementation of public policy for the public good. In other words, the Greeks did not divorce politics from ethics but rather saw politics as ethics applied on a community-wide scale. Therefore, the same virtues demanded of the citizen were demanded of the state. They recognized no difference between public and private virtue. In the ancient world this close union of ethics and politics was reinforced by the teachings of the New Testament and became the basis for Western thought on the subject until Machiavelli in the sixteenth century. Since that time there has been a division over the point among political thinkers in the West, but this remains the Christian view; and the majority of Christians still believe that since society is made up of individuals it can collectively make decisions which have moral meaning and implications. 6

CHRISTIANS: POLITICAL SPECTATORS OR PARTICIPANTS?

If politics, in fact, is moral or immoral, then it is clear that the Christian living under any regime has a certain interest and stake in it. But in a democratic system of government such as that of the United States, Canada, or Great

33

Britain, political involvement becomes even more imperative, perhaps even inescapable, for the Christian believer. There are a number of reasons why Christians should be involved in politics, especially in a democracy.

First, there is the argument from creation and providence, a view which has been articulated at length in a well-reasoned presentation by British Evangelical J. N. D. Anderson in his helpful book, *Into the World*. Anderson suggests that the Christian idea of holiness is "the life-and-death involvement of the soldier, whose mission it is to liberate enemy-occupied territory and restore it to the sway of its proper King." He sets forth some broad principles that make involvement imperative for the Christian. First, God created man in His own image and after His likeness, and this gave man his original worth. When man fell into sin, Christ died for him, thus indicating the value which he still had in God's eyes. In the incarnation, God Himself became truly man and experienced all that is humanity— joy, sorrow, hunger, thirst, weariness and refreshment, temptation, taxation, government, suffering, and even death itself. Also, God made the material world and has a purpose for it as such. Man can give glory to God by using created things rightly, that is, in accordance with the Creator's revealed will. Moreover, in the new creation all things will be summed up in Christ as Head, for His cross had reconciled not only the world of men but also the whole material and spiritual universe.

Furthermore, Anderson reminds Christians that this present world is still under God's government and is very much the object of His love and concern. Christ taught that one should love and serve his neighbor; the prophets passionately proclaimed God's demand for social justice, and the apostles stated unequivocally that human institutions such as the family and the state are ordained by God and designed to fulfill particular functions and purposes for the welfare of man. In addition, Christ emphasized to His followers that they were to be the "light" and "salt" of society, and He prayed that they would be kept from evil as they did their work in the world. Thus, Christians should affirm in no uncertain terms that this is God's world and that He is the sovereign Lord of the universe and not merely the personal solace of individuals. 7

Second, there is the difficulty in separating political issues from moral issues. At this point Christianity and politics are almost inextricably intertwined. It may be possible and highly beneficial to separate the institutions of church and state. However, it seems to be virtually impossible and for the most part undesirable to separate Christianity and politics. In the first place, nearly everyone takes certain presuppositions with him into the decision-making processes he exercises on a day-to-day basis, including the political decision-making process. It is impossible for the genuine Christian to compartmentalize his faith and seal it off from the rest of life, including his activities as a citizen of a political unit.

Moreover, every believer is involved in society and its problems by virtue of living in the world today. Even the expression of a Christian's spiritual life and his articulation of the gospel are shaped by the language, laws, and customs of the surrounding political community and cultural group. Society establishes patterns of relationships and rules for activities which must be observed by Christians under penalty of law. Christianity never has been and can never be "purely personal" because it has to do with mankind. The gospel is preached and lived in a political context which profoundly affects its outward expression.

And finally along this same line, most political questions have moral and spiritual dimensions which cannot be ignored by the Christian. This is true of nearly all of the most warmly debated issues of present-day America: war and peace, social justice, racism, militarism, separation of church and state, welfare, population control, pollution, poverty, civil rights, prison reform, treatment of the mentally ill, drug abuse, and so forth.

Third, it is hardly possible for a Christian in today's world to remain politically neutral. Those believers living in a democratic society who insist on remaining on the sidelines in effect are saying two significant things. Certainly their action implies that their spiritual message is totally irrelevant to practical problems except, perhaps, as it might change men's basic motivations and aspirations. This is important and has certain political implications as well. However, to remain aloof from politics in a democracy is to deny implicitly the statements of many Bible passages which indicate, either directly or indirectly, that Christians must be actively concerned about political issues and other societal problems.

Moreover, the pose of political neutrality through inaction conveys, by implication, an endorsement of the status quo. This may place politically neutral Christians in the camp of those who want to preserve the best in a social and political system, which may be well and good. However, it also puts them in the position of seeming to bless or sanctify evil leaders, institutions, and practices instead of exposing and condemning the works of darkness. Approval of the status quo in many cases is tantamount to approving the vested interests of power and wealth, strongly suggesting that such persons and organizations are always morally right in political controversies. In other words, a truly Christian concern of individual persons necessitates caring for these same people as members of large-scale organizations and participants in widely diffused institutions such as government. How can Christians be neutral on political issues involving neighbor love and human welfare? [8]

Fourth, there is the obvious need for more Christians—or at least more Christianity—in government. I would go so far as to argue that unless Christians in America decide to become more involved in political issues, the time may come when it will be impossible for them to do so. If the United States is in trouble politically, morally, and religiously, then professing Christians in the land must assume major responsibility for the present state of affairs. If there is corruption in government and if the so-called "military-industrial complex" is manipulating things for its own selfish ends, then where are the Christian voters and politicians? And where have they been all of these years? If the personal morality and alleged improprieties of some national leaders like Edward "Ted" Kennedy, Ronald Reagan, Martha Mitchell, William O. Douglas or the late Mendel Rivers offend Christian sensitivities, then believers had better start working to get some Christians elected. 9

There is an old saying: "All that is necessary for evil to triumph is for good men to do nothing!" Commenting on this adage, Senator Mark O. Hatfield says: "This is precisely where we find ourselves today in the matter of Christian ethics and political morality. For too many political generations too many good men have done nothing. They have stood by as neutral observers while the contest was fought in the political arena. This is true in the local community, it is widespread on the state level, and it is certainly the the case in national politics." 10

What happens when good men stand by and do nothing over a long period of time? Nazi Germany in the 1930s and early 1940s and East Germany today are examples of this kind of inaction on the part of Christians and other responsible people. The two groups which could have spoken out against Hitler with the greatest effect in his years of rise to power were the intellectual community and the Christian churches. However, most German Evangelicals rationalized their obedience to the Nazi regime under the shibboleths of patriotism and subsumed their moral responsibilities under the rubric of Romans 13. Much the same thing has happened in the Communist state of East Germany. The result has been the death of freedom and justice in each of these totalitarian regimes and, in the case of Hitler, six years of the holocaust and madness of World War II.[11] Can such a thing happen in the United States? It seems patently clear that the need for Christian participation in politics in America at the present is not only great but absolutely crucial!

Fifth, Christians should participate in politics because the form of government under which they live *does* make a difference. In modern times, Christians have existed under totalitarian regimes, absolute monarchies, limited monarchies, democracies, and dictatorships of various sorts. Although none of these governments could or can separate man against his will from the love of Christ, the political system does make a difference in the implementation of the Great Commission, and most nondemocratic forms of government bring with them certain disabilities for believers, including political ones.

These are critical days for the survival of democracy in the United States. There are forces abroad which could destroy all of the positive things for which America stands, including both the Constitution with its highly important Bill of Rights and the guarantees of "life, liberty and the pursuit of happiness." [12] There are also those extremists who would wipe out the last forty years of progress toward social justice in the country. There are alarming dehumanizing trends in American society which will continue and accelerate unless greater numbers of Christians become more politically aware and active. Democracy is not a perfect form of government but Christians should think twice before standing idly by and watching it destroyed by the radicals of the right and left.

Sixth, it is a sin not to participate in the political process when a Christian in good conscience and without compromise can do so. It is a sin not to be concerned about the needs of suffering mankind, and it is selfish to say that Christians must keep "pure" in God's sight by avoiding "worldly problems." Lack of Christlike compassion is a symptom of spiritual death. Wrapped up in selfish pursuits, sometimes even using church participation to advance socially, many professing Christians assume that the essence of spirituality lies in church activities. As David Moberg puts it, "Clinging to the husks of religious conformity, they have lost the kernel of true religion." 13

Too many so-called Christians are not really concerned about anyone but themselves, and certainly not about the political process. Most American Evangelicals realize that at the heart of the matter is the spiritual dimension, the willingness of the believer to be used of God—even in politics. If a man has a genuine encounter with God, his life will be transformed from self-seeking and self-aggrandizement to concern for other people, which will express itself in political and social involvement. The Scriptures call for social concern, and one of the greatest avenues of social action open to American Christians today is that of political participation. As Earle E. Cairns, Charles I. Foster, and Timothy L. Smith have pointed out in their various works on Christianity and social issues, the role of reformer has come easy and naturally for believers in previous eras. 14 What about Evangelicals today?

Seventh, last, and perhaps most importantly, Christian men and women can come to the responsibilities of public office and public trust with certain advantages and spiritual resources which enable particularly effective political participation. Politics in a dynamic, volatile, and democratic country like America or Great Britain can be terribly draining spiritually, psychologically, emotionally, physically and financially. Any individual in public life, from city council to Congress of the United States, pays a price for his position of dubious eminence. Moreover, in a democracy some of the best politicians are the most controversial. Christian men in political life, such as Senator Mark O. Hatfield of Oregon, former Senator Frank Carlson of Kansas, Congressmen John B. Anderson of Illinois, Jim Wright of Texas, and Fred Schwengel of Iowa, Governor Warren Hearnes of Missouri, and Lieutenant Governor Paul Simon of Illinois, to name a few, have testified that their Christian faith has served to bolster and renew them on many occasions after hard political battles.

But beyond this, the Christian involved in politics at any level and in any manner possesses the proper motivation for participation. As the Bible points out in 1 John 4:7-12, Romans 12:9-21, and many other places, love for God means love and concern for one's fellowmen. Therefore, a Christian should be ready to participate in public affairs which so decisively shape the lives and determine the welfare of his fellows. In other words, public concern should flow naturally out of Christian concern! One of the most effective ways a Christian can assist his neighbor is through joint action of the total community, that is, governmental action. To be certain, love cannot be legislated; but good laws go a long way toward insuring decency and justice. Or, as Christian solon John B. Anderson said recently:

> A legal guarantee of civil rights for all Americans regardless of race or color may not put an end to hatred and distrust between black and white—we may not be able to legislate love between different colored children of God—but certainly civil rights ought not to be denied any man because of his race, for equality before the law is a right deriving from the fact of humanity. Was the divine breath of life that made man a living soul either black or white, yellow or brown? [15]

In addition, a biblically oriented individual should have the capacity to rise above the level of self-interest which debases so much of public life. This is because he understands the paradox involved in losing and finding one's life (Mat. 16:24-25). Also, the believer has constant recourse to prayer, a mighty resource which others use only sparingly or not at all. Political decisions at even the most elementary level can be extremely difficult. It often takes at least "divine wisdom" to deal with some of today's pressing political and social issues. Furthermore, a Christian has a perspective which allows him to fulfill his duties as a citizen, knowing that his efforts are within a divine order of things that gives hope and meaning to all of life (Ro. 8:26-28).

Finally, the genuine Christian in politics can and should bring with him into the fray his evangelical social conscience. Sherwood Wirt's remarks on the Christian and political and personal involvement are particularly relevant:

> If there is poverty, he should be taking a lead in seeking to eradicate it. If there is injustice, he should be an Amos, pointing it out. If there is corruption, he should be helping to turn the rascals out. If there is waste, he should be acting the role of the good steward. It is in this role, rather than in the stance of the pristine rugged individualist, that the evangelical Christian can make his best contribution. [16]

WILL CHRISTIANS BALANCE THE SCALES OF GOVERNMENT?

The foregoing remarks have made clear the need, opportunities, and possibilities for Christian political involvement. There are, however, some additional observations that should be made at this point. First, there is a pressing need for balance in the approach of the Christian to the totality of life, especially in relation to political activity. By this is meant a balance between Christ's emphasis on individual salvation and His stress on community responsibility as well as a balance in political participation as Christians. The noted historian Christopher Dawson once observed, "Men today are divided between those who have kept their spiritual roots and lost their contact with the existing order of society, and those who have preserved their social contacts and lost their spiritual roots." [17] According to the Bible, neither of these predicaments of modern man is Christian because the believer keeps both his spiritual roots and his

41

contact with the existing order of society as he proclaims a complete gospel for the whole man. [18]

Once the redemptive gospel was a world-changing message, but in the twentieth century it has too often been narrowed to a world-resisting creed by an embarrassing divorce between the need for personal salvation and the necessity for social involvement. Evangelist Billy Graham recognized the social implications of the gospel when he wrote in his 1953 best seller, *Peace with God*: "Jesus taught that we are to take regeneration in one hand and a cup of cold water in the other. Christians, above all others, should be concerned with social problems and social injustices." [19]

There is no reason why Evangelicals should keep worrying about the fact that the theological liberals have been preaching a so-called Social Gospel for the last two generations. After all, historic Christianity proclaimed the social dimensions of the gospel as a matter of course for hundreds of years before the advent of modern liberal theology; and one must remember that a movement as sterile as theological liberalism must have some rationale for its continued existence.

On the other hand, Evangelicals as twice-born individuals must be more concerned with the whole gospel, with individual regeneration *and* the cup of cold water for the unfortunate and needy. If anyone is really a follower of Jesus Christ, let him heed what the Lord said about service to mankind as well as what He taught about being born again. Let Christians keep the gospel in proper balance as Christ intended.

Moreover, the gospel imperative will lead Christians in political life to avoid extremes and extremism. Obviously there are no specific Scripture verses that warn Christians in politics to shun the radical right and the radical left, nor may the radical implications of commitment to Christ and the revolutionary aspects of the gospel be denied. On the other had, the essence of the gospel makes it clear that a Christian in public life will be an independent, a humanitarian, a reconciler, a healer, a bridge-builder. This does not mean that he will be spineless and without conviction, unwilling to take a clear-cut stand on important issues. Rather, it implies that in all of life, and especially in politics, the believer needs to be "as wise as a serpent and as harmless as a dove." [20] Or, as it might be paraphrased today, the Christian politician needs to possess a "tough mind and a tender heart."

A Christian cannot embrace the rhetoric, methods, and goals of the political extremists without degrading the gospel. It is not easy to be independent, moderate, and nondoctrinaire in American politics today; in fact, to act in this manner is to be a "radical" in the best sense of that term. Men and women of this persuasion are desperately needed if democratic nations are to avoid the most dire political consequences and the kind of polarization which often leads to a totalitarian regime.

It is especially important to note what implications political involvement by the present generation has for the future. For one thing, it has nothing to do with the United States being a "Christian nation." Actually there is no such thing as a "Christian nation" or a "Christian government," and there has never been such in the United States. On the other hand, Christians have served as the leaven of political life and institutions in America and elsewhere for a long time. Their influence has been extensive and important for the development of Western democratic ideas and practices.

But recent developments in the United States and other countries make it obvious that these are unusual days. The affairs of the nation and the world are confused, chaotic, and constantly changing. Some individuals in places of leadership assure the public that nothing much is wrong with the system and people of America, and that only a small minority of malcontents are responsible for the unrealistic and exaggerated criticisms of the government's practices. There are claims that most Americans, the now-famous "silent majority," have unquestioning faith and confidence in the present political regime. Unfortunately, this is not the case. Disillusionment is widespread, increasingly questions about the future are being raised, and more than only young people are beginning to express concern for America's political health.

A recent Gallup study of political attitudes in the United States revealed that the majority of the people in the country feel that the nation has lost rather than gained ground in the past five years. This is especially significant because since World War II only once before in such a survey have a majority of a nation's people felt that their country was falling behind rather than moving ahead, and that was the Philippines in 1959. The recent Gallup Poll also indicated nearly one out of every two Americans believes that national unrest is serious enough to lead to a real breakdown of governmental processes. Furthermore, the majority of those asked said they did not see this unrest as merely the result of troublemakers but as related to the present quality of leadership in the nation and the current performance of its institutions. [21]

What will be the role of the Christian believer in the midst of the present crisis and turmoil? How can Evangelicals help to shape the political future? It is rather obvious that the answer to this question lies largely in the hands of those believers who are now between the ages of eighteen and fifty, the leaders of the Christian community during the next three decades. They might well take heed to what has happened in the past to other nations when Christians failed to participate in politics when they had the opportunity. Nazi Germany has already been mentioned as an illustration of the political failure of Christians, especially Christian intellectuals. Beyond Hitler's Germany stands East Germany today where it is difficult for a genuine Christian to participate actively and fully in the political life of the state, no matter how much he might love his country. The German Christians failed to use what opportunites they had to oppose totalitarian tendencies, both before 1933 and shortly after 1945, and the Christians of East Germany are now paying the price for their past political sins. [22]

Another instance of the ineffectiveness of Evangelicals in politics is Northern Ireland. Ulster is a heavily Christian land, with a majority of its population of one and a half million claiming affiliation with an evangelical church of some denomination. Yet the country lives daily in the grip of fear and terrorism, and teeters dangerously on the brink of all-out civil war. The supreme irony of the situation is that the Rev. Ian Paisley, leader of the Protestant extremists in Northern Ireland, maintains his position by skillfully blending together the gospel, bigotry, and conservative politics. Although it is not altogether their fault, moderate Irish Evangelicals have failed thus far in achieving a just and Christian settlement of the problems which today are tearing that beautiful land apart. [23]

The frightening thing about Germany and Northern Ireland is that the seeds for the development of both kinds of political aberrations are present today in America. Extremists of the right and left are intensifying their attacks on established political institutions and the elected leadership. At the same time, ironically enough, totalitarian trends also are evident in some government programs and policies aimed at combating the extremists. There are just too many uncomfortable parallels between the political developments in Germany in the 1920s and early 1930s and the present political climate in the United States.

At the same time, the American racial crisis continues, some even say worsens day by day. In many ways the current situation in Northern Ireland resembles the racial unrest in the United States. In both countries, there stand two distinct communities of different national origin segregated by long years of separate schools, social life, customs, and churches. In both places, the majority long has denied the minority basic civil rights, and complex historical developments leading up to the present are finally coming to a head and producing exremely dangerous situations. And in both countries strong evangelical Christian communities, for the most part, have stood idly by and been political spectators, leaving the field to the extremists; or worse yet, they have yoked themselves to conservative politics and the status quo in an attempt to maintain the oppressive policies of the past.

Whither America and Christianity in America in the last decades of the twentieth century? Once again, these are critical days for the world and for the Christian faith. There is a tremendous need for quality leadership at every level of life, including the political.

Shortly before His ascension into heaven, Jesus gave the Great Commission to His followers: "But you are to be given power when the Holy Spirit has come to you. You will be witnesses to me, not only in Jerusalem, not only throughout Judaea, not only in Samaria, but to the very ends of the earth!" (Ac. 1:8, Phillips). The witness of the believer in politics can and should be as "Christian" and as important as his witness in any other area of life. The Christian who takes an active part in the political life of his neighborhood, his community, his state, or his nation is doing God's work just as truly as a pastor or missionary who seeks to win the lost to Christ. Who else is better equipped to restore stability, honesty, justice, compassion, peace, and sanity to the socio-political world than a man or woman imbued with the Spirit of God and ruled by the precepts of the Bible?

3

The Evangelical Christian and the American Civic Religion

GOD, MOTHER, AND APPLE PIE

If you want to arouse knowing chuckles and arch smiles in a group—say in New York—that thinks of itself as comprising intelligent contemporary types, you may do so quite handily by suggesting that we all suddenly reassert our loyalty and devotion to God, Mother, country, apple pie, the flag, the Boy Scouts, and the *Saturday Evening Post.* "Ah yes," the response will run. "The dear old flag. And Mother. Dear, dear. Gingham frock, apron, hair in a bun, flour up to the elbows. Main Street. The Fourth. Help a little old lady. Amazing Grace. Those were the days." [1]

The reaction you will start by a ploy like this will tend to be amused, incredulous, and patronizing. It would be as though you had trotted out a puppy in a wicker perambulator, or had told everyone you were starting a campaign to stamp out sin. "Such engaging jokes you devise, my dear."

Now, to increase the piquancy of your experiment, suggest exactly the same list, and call for the same devotion in an entirely different group; say, of Moms and Dads from somewhere—just a random sampling from here and there, and from this and that line of work. They might be the sort of people you come across at a shopping mall, perhaps, and on

47

Trailways buses, and who come to Disneyland and Radio City Music Hall and Easter sunrise services. You will either draw a blank from your experiment ("We missed the punch line"), or some enthusiasm ("Hurrah! It's about time somebody stood up and spoke out for the old things! All together now, 'O beautiful for [sniff] spacious skies . . .'").

Both of these groups will have been made up of Americans. And their reactions (admittedly, perhaps, a bit fancifully imagined here—but not *that* far afield) furnish an interesting glimpse of a hiatus in contemporary consciousness that may or may not be bridged or filled in as time goes by. No one really knows what the contour of national sensibility will be in 2001—supposing, of course, that there is a national entity to have a sensibility at all.

But why the two different reactions to your list? What *are* those items, separately and collectively, that they seem to be words to conjure with? Clearly it is not a neutral list, as another one that followed similar categories might be— say, Jupiter, sister, county, spinach, handkerchiefs, the Red Cross, and *The Daily News*. What is conjured in the first list? And what is there about it that divides? If your two groups were brought together at this point, the chuckles and waving hands might shortly turn to shouts and fisticuffs.

It is a list of ingredients for the American image or, more precisely, the traditional American image. In the century and a half between the founding of the nation and a point shortly after World War II, a national imagination grew and matured, and luxuriated in its own vigor and color and ebullience. It was a new thing on the global scene and therefore something of a wonder. Persia and Switzerland and China and France and England—these had all been around for centuries. Their imagery was old, mellow, well-worn, while ours was new, conscious, brittle.

But it also was uncertain. Who *were* we, in fact? And what, exactly, were we doing? Where did we imagine we

48

were headed? These are the concerns, probably only semi-conscious, that bubble up into any national imagery, and that give flavor and hue and shape to national existence. Undoubtedly ours, like everybody else's, emerged from the kinds of answers we were giving to those questions. And so during the late eighteenth, through the nineteenth, and into the twentieth century, our national imagery developed and our national sensibility took shape. It would take the combined efforts of political philosophers, anthropologists, psychologists, sociologists, historians, and even poets to pin together all the relationships among the events that produced that imagery and sensibility. But it emerged—no doubt about that. And, it had an unmistakable shape and color about it.

We got a flag—who doesn't know that story? And some good wife must have started putting apples instead of gooseberries or pork into pies and *that* took hold. And somebody thought of calling the high street, Main Street. And the Boy Scouts, although not of American origin, somehow seemed to be an ideal of American boyhood. And the good old *Saturday Evening Post* articulated and celebrated it all for us. What high promise for glory and longevity!

And, to add to the bargain, we were, of course, a Christian country. God was there in the list, and everyone assumed that it was the Christian God. A Christian country then. "Ah. To be sure. Yes . . . um. Well, of course, we *are*! Were, that is. Not officially, of course. But to all intents and purposes. The point being . . . ."

Precisely, the point is that our bluff has been called, and we are left mumbling and puffing and casting about for firm data to shore up the old assumptions against the assault.

For there has been an attack against the whole image and especially the religious suppositions that accompanied it. In our recent history (certainly since 1950) major questions, not to say doubts, about the nature of our national identity have broken into public consciousness. Let it be emphasized that this has been the breaking into *public* consciousness of these doubts, since historians could itemize for us the step-by-step sequence of ideas, events, and movements—law suits, tracts, committees, rallies, new ingredients in the melting pot—that bespoke the advent of some such major reckoning long before everyone was talking about it.

Under fire was the nature of the answers that we had been giving to those questions that lay in the subconscious of the the nation: Who are we? What are we doing? Where are we going? The answers we had come up with were no longer adequate, we were told. That is *not* America, the objection went. Or, if it is, it is a grotesquery and we must redo the whole thing.

The assault was a two-pronged one. One prong was official, and the other was popular. The one found its champion in the Supreme Court. The other sprang up in the always warm and fecund matrix of the undergraduate world and spread into the realms of journalism, academe, politics, and finally, general national concern.

AMERICA—THE CHRISTIAN NATION

But before we analyze the assault and where it has left us and what is to be expected now, we ought to note how it was that we arrived in such a vulnerable position. That is, how did we ever suppose America to be a *Christian* nation? How did *God* get into the list of national tokens, along with pie and the flag? 2

Of course, it is nothing notable for a nation to invoke God, or the gods, as a sort of backdrop for its national imagery, or as a supporting genius for national enterprises. Many political entities, especially those that existed before the advent of the modern secular state, have done this—among them Greece, Rome, Spain, England, and Russia. The questions here are: What is noteworthy about America's invocation of God, the Christian God? How did this come about? What ironies, not to say contradictions, were written into it from the start?

50

The historical answer is not a difficult one to discover. In a sense, the identity between America and Christianity came about by default, since no one really challenged the correctness of the view that history seemed to supply.

Events *did* seem to support this idea. After all, were the fathers not religious men on a godly quest? And were they not just generally religious, but Christian—rigorously, emphatically, heroically so? The early seventeeth-century settlements were unmistakably Christian in structure, ethos, and confession. Anglican Puritans, Nonconformist Congregationalists, Quakers, and Roman Catholics all came to America, and even in those colonies whose origin was not religious in nature there was no official challenge to Christian assumptions. There was nothing unique about this, of course, since, aside from the alien Islamic presence, there had been no alternative in the Western world to Christianity for a millennium and a half. *All* states were Christian, from the Holy Roman Empire, to France with her "Most Christian King," to England whose ruler held the title "Defender of the Faith." The French Revolution with its doctrine of liberty, equality, and fraternity had not yet replaced Christian dogma as the working assumption of society.

In the early decades in America this was possible since not many people lived here yet, and those who did settle in a place tended to subscribe to the accepted viewpoint of the locale, to shape society according to religiously agreed-upon rules. If one had a strong notion as to the nature of human society and the extent to which the governor was God's rod on earth, and the minister his oracle, the political organization reflected this. Virtue was held, quite unabashedly, to be the end of man (an ancient and widespread notion, actually, and one hardly unique to the Christian outlook), and the purpose of society was to furnish the conditions under which virtue could be cultivated and guaranteed. Looking back at this from the perspective of the twentieth century, the mind boggles at the rigor with which the religious ends of society were pursued.

But we must not make the mistake of believing that this was a new, much less an outrageous, thing for states to do. The states of antiquity and of medieval times also demonstrated a religious character. The particular ideas that our own age had of "freedom" and pluralism are late arrivals and do not really give us a useful vantage point from which to pass judgment upon religious societies. One reads of people being placed in the stocks for activities that strike us as being entirely harmless or, in any case, matters of private conscience. The contemporary response to this is, however, conditioned by a set of notions that would have seemed as odd to the culprits as to the judges. The question of society's *right* to insist on a Christian ethos was never really hotly debated.

The changes of time sweep away, or at least erode, the fervor and purity that mark the ideas and visions of states, institutions, and enterprises in their early stages. Coming to terms with time presents ambiguities with which no idea ever really successfully copes. The sheer wear of passing years seems to grind things down, to say nothing of the complexities that arise (new generations, more people, different people, new myths, new situations) and demand accommodations that nobody had thought of in the beginning. How many early Communists, for example, would be pleased with the variation on the Marxist theme visible in Soviet Russia today? Or what Christian will regard all of church history as a reflection of New Testament ideas?

Of course, there *was* no clear idea of an "America" in the seventeenth century. The colonies pieced themselves together bit by bit, and shuffled into place, and it was only in a rather random fashion that any self-consciousness was acquired. It was the American Revolution that cemented things effectively and finally.

At the time of the revolution the situation was by no means what the Pilgrim fathers, William Penn, Lord Baltimore, or the Virginia planters had visualized. Many of them had come here for "freedom" of one sort or another, and it was undoubtedly as candid a hope for freedom as human beings could muster. For the more austerely religious of the colonists, of course, it meant freedom to do things *our* way, not *yours*. But as time passed, a substantial measure of freedom of conscience and religious exercise had evolved. And, in that atmosphere of freedom, ideas at variance with the earlier Christian consensus appeared and flourished, so that by the time the colonies were drawn together in the revolution, the cement was largely a political one, and hence the appeal was to an imagery of nationhood, patriotism, and common political cause. A religious plurality was assumed—tacitly if not articulately, semiconsciously if not consciously. The struggle was not now between Calvinism and Arminianism, or Presbyterianism and Congregationalism, or Anglicanism and Roman Catholicism. It was between political entities—the colonies versus the mother country.

With the winning of independent, sovereign status, the founding fathers consciously proceeded to put together a nation at the epocal conclave in Philadelphia from which emerged the Constitution of the United States of America. When one reads about it, he is impressed that what ruled in those deliberations was a hard, cool, lucid *intelligence*—lofty and idealistic, yes; but also earthy and unsentimental. They were *rational* men.

Rational is the key word here, for they were "typical" eighteenth-century men. We call that era the Age of Reason, and not without good cause. The sixteenth and seventeenth centuries had witnessed an enormous shift in the Western world view from the populated, animated, personal universe of antiquity and the Middle Ages, toward the vacuous, mechanical, depersonalized universe of modernity. *Toward*, that is, since the old visions of titans and gods and angels, and of divine and demonic traffic all through the cosmic map did not vanish in a moment, or even a century. But the intellectual outlook began to shift toward what we now have, with the advent of the analytic, inductive (i. e., "scientific") method of approaching data. Francis Bacon was the great popularizer for the English-speaking world of the new methodology. The idea was to abandon the old scholastic method of the medieval School-men—that elaborate intellectual pursuit of metaphysical questions of being and essence to exhausting lengths—and to focus our attention and efforts instead upon the world around us. For us to *observe* and *experiment*, and then draw modest conclusions from our tests is the true task of human intellect. God has given His creature, man, a rational faculty which tunes him to nature and enables him to perceive the causes of and correspondences between things.

Bacon did not consider the new science antireligious. On the contrary, the new methodology freed man from the tyrannical clutter of mere metaphysics, and set him on a course toward real progress in advancing the frontiers of useful knowledge. It was not at all to imply an assault on *faith*. The whole enterprise proceeded upon an acceptance of the Christian creeds, and in fact some of the scientists of the seventeenth century went to great pains to assure everyone—and themselves undoubtedly—of their religious orthodoxy. The point was that there were seen to be two distinct realms of data—the one we approach by faith that tells us of God and redemption and beatitude, and the other we approach by reason that is based upon our physical environment on the planet earth. Neither threatens the other, but we must be careful to keep each in its own bailiwick.

Traditionally minded people, a category which included nearly everybody and most certainly orthodox Christians, entertained fears about the effect of this new methodology. It seemed to be eroding the foundations of faith, despite assurances to the contrary. "Explanations" of phenomena seemed to be nudging God further and further from the center of control and attention. These fears, as it turns out, were well founded, and the anxious forecast of troubled traditionalists was entirely correct. God receded into the background, and with Him went dogma, creed, faith, and the hegemony that Christianity enjoyed in Western thought.

This accounts for the fact that by the time the Constitutional Convention met in Philadelphia, the religious flavor was deist rather than Christian. The men who drew up the blueprint for America were certainly *religious* in that they saw themselves and society as existing and functioning in an ordered universe designed by a sovereign deity. But if any of them were Christian, that point of view did not find expression in the national blueprint. It was a secular political entity that they fashioned.

Here the root of the American civic and religious ambiguity is to be found. Perhaps in their own minds, and certainly in the minds of the generations that followed them, there was anticipated no very lively threat from radically different viewpoints. They concentrated on the task of insuring an ordered, tranquil, prosperous society that would safeguard the lives, interests, and consciences of its citizens. Perhaps the whole enterprise was thought to proceed along God-fearing lines, at least in the sense that society as a whole would accept the general Western moral frame. Public child-sacrifice, for instance, or the abandonment of the idea of the family unit, were not options, and hence are not provided for or against in the Constitution. What *is* provided for is liberty to express and practice one's own ideas insofar as these do not actually threaten or assail the "general welfare."

That general welfare, of course, is itself Western, rationalistic, perhaps deistic in flavor, in that it identifies welfare with the absence of bloodshed, violence, and coercion, and a certain amount of prosperity, or at least freedom from starvation and exposure. This notion of welfare is far from axiomatic or universal, as any witch doctor or priest

55

of Moloch, or any Stalinist secret agent or Marcusian theoretician would insist. Each of them would say, as he slit your throat or tightened the screws, "Yes, but I (officialdom) know *better* than you do what the general welfare is. We *need* your blood for this rain dance; we *need* your child for this festival slaughter; we need that information for the state."

These horrors shock the imagination of Americans exactly because they think and feel inside a rationalistic, egalitarian frame that pictures man in a different light. It is neither a rigorously religious pattern, which allows for an inquisition, nor an elitist one, which permits the imposition of the will of an enlightened minority upon the churlish masses. The philosophical assumptions of the men in Philadelphia in 1789 were rationalistic and egalitarian, then, rather than officially Christian.

The nation they brought into being contained a fairly homogeneous population, both ethnically (Northern and Western European) and philosophically (nominally Christian). There were, of course, some Africans, but they did not count, and there were occasionally atheists and agnostics and a few Jews. But the general popular assumption was vaguely Christian. Sunday, church, the Ten Commandments, Christmas, Easter, "O God Our Help"—these were part of the national sensibility. Officially the nation was deistic or, at the most, mildly theistic, as revealed in such mottoes and phrases as "In God we trust" and "those inalienable rights to which the laws of nature and nature's God testify." However, in the warp and woof of common life, most Americans were Christian, and they had the luxury of assuming that nobody was going to raise a tempest over whatever public hospitality there was toward that viewpoint.

THE ATTACK UPON CHRISTIAN AMERICA

In the century or so following the revolution, the national ingredients changed radically as millions of "other" people arrived—among them Irish, Italians, Poles, and Jews. But the public imagery, and therefore the officially acknowledged sensibility, did not change accordingly. In the '30s, '40s, and '50s even, one would still notice in public iconography blond, blue-eyed Aryans shopping on Main Street, going to church, and saluting the flag. Insofar as other people appeared, they were *adjuncts* to the official imagery: Mammy with the polka-dot bandana, or little Solomon Levy, the shopkeeper, peering over his eyeglasses. They served the real citizens but were not part of the Christian, vaguely Saxon, substance of the nation.

In those days the Bible was read and the Lord's Prayer said, along with the flag salute, in the morning at school. Hymns such as "Fairest Lord Jesus," "Holy, Holy, Holy" (with its blessed *Trinity*), and "Come Thou Almighty King" (with its incarnate Word) were sung during school assemblies. The Christmas holidays were *Christmas* holidays, not winter holidays. In December, angels, mangers, and wise men—as well as Santa Clauses and holly leaves—decorated the schoolrooms. There were invocations at public events, usually from Protestant ministers, and it was not unusual to hear America referred to as a Christian country. There was, on the other hand, a corollary to all this, a religious inclination to see "Americanism" as a sort of political apotheosis of Christianity. America was not just vaguely considered Christian; believers actually looked upon the American way of life as a basically Christian one, and hence regarded any threat to that way as a menace to Christianity itself. [3]

There is, of course, a very real sense in which such a threat does imperil Christianity, or—an important distinction—the church's life in society, since the American way of life *has* been hospitable to the church. Christianity in all of its odd, even bizarre, forms, has been allowed to flourish. From the quasi-official Protestant denominations, to the Roman Catholic Church, to the evangelical and fundamentalist movements, to the ethnic varieties of Christianity, such as the Serbian Church or the Abyssinian, to the sects, religion has been officially and unofficially encouraged in America. The possibility of a major change can provoke concern as to whether things will be as congenial under a new order. When the threat is not just religiously neutral, or merely political—for example, replace Congress with a parliament, let the South secede, or give fifteen-year-olds the vote—the grounds for anxiety are understandable. Christians, who have enjoyed a favorable position for over three centuries in a situation that posed no serious threat either to their creed or way of life, may be pardoned for a telltale quaver in the voice as they ask, "Where is it all leading?" They realize that the change occurring in our society will entirely revamp the relationship between public life and sensibility on one hand and Christianity on the other.

Moreover, if anyone had thought through the nature of American society with its particular economics and its individualistic, independent-spirited, competitive values, he would have had a difficult time aligning it with the Christian view of man, or deriving it directly from the biblical perspective. This is not to say that some other political order is derivable from Scripture, or even from scriptural principles. Indeed, *all* blueprints for society—feudal, communistic, republican, anarchic—invariably claim some ancient or divine warrant, and it is no new thing to line Christianity up with the prevailing order. It was done far more effectively in the Middle Ages than our most lusty Fourth of July hymnody ever dreamed of doing.

Every political order exhibits something of the City of God, and also contains as well within itself some massive breakdown. That is, the very attempt at "society"—men living and working, not merely in juxtaposition, but in harmony—is an image of that city. The awareness of mutuality—that one's life depends on the work of others—and

58

exchange—the product of one's labor must be exchanged for that of another so both may survive—is also an image of that city. On the other hand, no political scheme has ever functioned the way its prophets and zealots claimed that it would, and the politics of any nation or empire exhibit the remorseless record of how each attempt results in a swamp of intrigue, machination, and cynicism—in a denial, in other words, of the City of God.

The vastness of human society and the selfishness of men inexorably compel people to organize themselves into a system of guarantees in order to prevent chaos. No one— whether it be a Genghis Khan, Thomas Jefferson, Charlemagne, Mao Tse-tung—wants chaos. Each of these men had an idea as to the best way to arrive at those guarantees, and each engaged in the enterprise of securing and perpetuating them.

The need to deal with the possibility of chaos has restricted Christians in applying divinely enjoined principles of personal behavior to society. The church at large has never seriously pursued any of the utopian efforts to put into practice the words of Christ: "Turn the other cheek," "Give him thy cloak also," or "Forgive him seventy times seven," in the political order. How can a *society* turn the other cheek? Is it possible for a nation to give away its cloak? How does public jurisprudence forgive the rapist? Nettlesome questions attend this line of inquiry, and no Brook Farm or Utopia, much less any historical state, has ever had any long-range success in building a political order in the light of these injunctions.

If one is to avoid a cynically impartial view of societies which would lead to the judgment that Ivan the Terrible cannot be distinguished morally from Woodrow Wilson, he *will* take issue with various political ideologies. This disagreement, of necessity, will proceed from his ethical, anthropological, and metaphysical presuppositions, and so the Christian may justifiably say, "Yes, but the American

59

way *is* better than the Mongolian." The Christian has a view of man—he is evil and must be restrained, therefore anarchy is unacceptable; or he has a free will and society is obligated to provide a maximum of choices for him, therefore neither feudalism nor Marcusian elitism is acceptable. Depending upon his idea of man, the Christian will formulate a political theory.

Few have questioned very loudly the merger between American politics and the Christian religion. It is curious that evangelists and earnest preachers did, in fact, assail the whole business—"America is a Vanity Fair! Her people are turned loose to dissolute living, her institutions encourage greed, and her national values are grossly materialistic!" But no one thought of pushing this line of thought to the point where it might spawn serious political disaffection, much less revolution. The people who clucked at the excesses of Vanity Fair were the beneficiaries of the system, so the task of tearing down the booths was not undertaken. 4

But then it *was* undertaken, and the terrifying aspect was that the enemy was not a horde of alien Tartars but an inside crowd. It was a two-pronged attack, and was "American" in the sense that no foreign tanks appeared in the streets. The first sally was made in the name of American democracy by secular forces who saw the American-religious continuum as a confusion and contradiction of the country's political ideas. Their weapons at first were legal—the courts and the Constitution. The second thrust was made in the name of Christianity itself by passionately devout forces who saw the American civic religion as a mockery and a contradiction of Christian dogma. They adopted the weapons that their allies in the first group had by this time taken up—civil disobedience, rallies, protests, and violence.

The origins of this movement may be found in ideas which matured in the nineteenth century—the political ideology of Marx, the new discriptions of man found in Darwin and Freud, and the epistemological and ethical doctrines of Hegel and Schleiermacher. In this sense, of course, the movement *was* alien in that the ideas came from Europe. But then, democracy, rationalism, and even Christianity were in the same sense alien ideas.

The nineteenth century saw the growth of nations that not only challenged the traditional Christian view of the world and human existence but also became the new norms of society. Hence, the generations that were born and educated in the late nineteenth and the twentieth centuries were nurtured on a set of notions about man that was at an opposite pole from the views of Christian traditionalists.[5] The Creator-creation relationship was abandoned and, with it, all ideas of revelation and of ultimate authority in matters of truth and morals. Man was alone, but progressing, and the record of human civilization, pitted though it is, may be read as an upward path. Man has the tools to subdue his environment, build a better life, and conquer the psychological, demographic, technical, and ecological problems that beset his society. These hopes were damaged by the two world wars and the difficulty of finding any philosophic grounds for affirmation in the new, postreligious era. But optimism is a phoenix, and from the ashes of despair the widespread notion has arisen that, given a good, long, concerted pull, the Vietnams and smokestacks and segregated classrooms that blight American society can be overcome. Affirmation, ebullience, and celebration have replaced paralysis, *Angst*, and blackness as suitable frames of mind for authentically modern people. Once more the golden age beckons America.

It is to be an age of freedom ("Now!") and brotherhood ("Smile on your brother"), and peace ("All we're saying is . . ."). It is to be an age of kaleidoscopic spontaneity (of a Greening, we are told), and hence of rapidly changing vogues (Batman last year, Jesus Christ Superstar this year, perhaps

Attila the next). Society will one fine day emerge, having learned all the lessons that our fathers so signally failed for so many aeons to learn, and having conquered all the problems that have appeared for so long to be intractable. Somewhere along the line, an immaculate conception appears to have generated a mutation on the human species that is innocent of the cupidity that tarnished the older species and its efforts. This mutant species will populate the new earth.

But, of course, to bring this about you have to mount the barricades and assault the foundations of the old (bad) order. The institutions that perpetuate discrimination and tyranny and the traditions that undergird those institutions, must be destroyed. The religious edifice that hallows those institutions and traditions and that has played the whore with established power for so many centuries of European and American history must also come down.

Hence, a generation that cries passionately for destruction and change nurses a set of hopes for a different and better order. Supporting those cries and nourishing those hopes is a colorful public imagery of revolution, celebration, liberty, spontaneity, camaraderie, and innocence. The new Green has sprouted; the lichens and fungus will soon claim whatever ruins remain of the old citadel. Thus, this widespread feeling commands a great deal of national attention.

Accompanying this shift in national sensibility has been a less spectacular but equally radical grinding of the national legal machinery in response to protests that America stop its duplicity. On the one hand, the establishment of religion is prohibited, goes the protest, but in effect Christianity is established nevertheless. Freedom of religion is guaranteed to all but limited for those millions of citizens who do not accept the Hebrew and Christian Scriptures as normative. Legality is entirely on the protesters' side and so "Christian" America has had to engage in the methodical disestablishment of religion. It is a course of events unforeseen by the fathers of the eighteenth century, but one for which they had unconsciously but meticulously provided.

WITHER NOW, EVANGELICALS?

American evangelical Christians must come to terms with these changes. First, they must accept the simple fact that the times, they have a-changed.6 For good or ill, God, Mother, and apple pie are not the images to which public sensibility attaches itself now. Apple pie may come round again, Mother will presumably be here in some form or another as long as anyone lives; but God, barring a new Constitutional Convention dominated by religious people—a wildly improbable event—is out. America is neither de jure nor de facto Christian. Second, Christians must decide whether to say *"D'accord"* or *"Alas"* to this.

On the *alas* side of the ledger would be the memory of America's first settlers, their reasons for coming here, and their visions of what the new world might become. There would also be the recollection of the tradition of cordiality between American society and Christianity, and the biblical influences that helped to form the national consciousness. One might also point to the position of the church in the enormously prosperous society, from which it was able to launch programs of world evangelism. 7 And, setting the past aside, there is also the feeling that insofar as nations cut their connections with heaven, they set themselves adrift in currents that run toward shoals. Finally, there would be some anxiety as to the particular shape that the national imagination, and therefore national institutions and morals, will take when the new order matures.

On the *d'accord* side of the ledger is the realization that its new situation in society is by no means a novel one for the church. Christianity did not begin under such hospitable circumstances as it has enjoyed in America, but yet the early church was vigorous and dynamic. The church's power and prosperity gained through cooperation with the political establishment have perhaps deprived it of the spiritual power that primitive Christianity enjoyed. Christians have often wondered whether this was a "normal" state of affairs for the church or whether its true glory lay elsewhere. The popes found out soon enough that the relationship between the vicariate of Christ and the princes of this world was an ambiguous one at best. Further, there is little in the New Testament that would lead the church to expect any official, or even special, place in society. The church in America has become accustomed to a luxurious existence, but it should not be regarded as a normal course of things for the body of Christ. It is now necessary for American Christians to begin living as a minority presence in a society which is officially nonreligious. It is possible at long last to taste the fare that has been the lot of the church in other centuries and in other cultures, and that is surely the "normal" state of affairs anticipated in the New Testament.[8]

Questions arise, to be sure, about America. What ideology will pervade her national consciousness now, determining her sensibility and her morals? And what imagery will rise from that ideology? What shall we put in place of God, Mother, and apple pie? What commonalty of tradition and imagination will undergird our enterprises? Are we to understand the imagery of the late 1960s and early '70s as a bellwether of the new America?

Those are questions for Christians to answer insofar as they are Americans. But perhaps it is possible to see the divorce of America and civic religion as lifting a burden—the weight of officialdom—from the shoulders of Christianity. Was it a burden the Christian faith was ever expected to carry?

4

Women and Evangelical Christianity

THE ROAD TO LIBERATION

"Christianity has done more to liberate women than any other force in history." That is the boast which Christians like to make whenever the question of women's rights comes up, but it is a difficult claim to substantiate.

Jesus certainly treated the women around Him in a revolutionary way, but His disciples were often shocked and dismayed by His actions. Women took an active part in the early church, but soon church councils were denying them the right to any official duties. In the Middle Ages women held great power as abbesses who headed large double monasteries housing men and women—until the twelfth century when convents became separate, cloistered institutions. At the Reformation, Luther urged women to come out of the convents, but he soon relegated them to kitchen and nursery. The Anabaptist tradition which gave birth to many of today's evangelical churches was spread across the American frontier by women preachers and missionaries who risked their lives for the gospel. But as the evangelical church became a respectable institution in middle-class suburbia, women were no longer seen in many pulpits. In fact, they were often banned or at least commonly excluded from church governing boards.

Generally women have not rebelled against their lot, but have served God in whatever limited manner they were allowed. Just as slavery was allowed to continue and even grow worse throughout the 1,800 years of the Christian era, so women's rights were not a particularly burning issue until the nineteenth century. Some Christian men and women finally began to see that the buying and selling of another human being, whatever the color of his skin, was against God's Word. The American feminist movement was born when American abolitionists sent a delegation to the 1840 World Anti-Slavery Convention in London, only to have eight women delegates barred from the proceedings because of their sex.

Within the abolitionist movement women began to realize that they were as much in bondage as the slaves. Many Bible-believing Christians denounced both freedom for slaves and rights for women on the basis of the same scriptural passages. Religious arguments for the perpetuation of slavery were illustrated by the supposedly parallel duty of the wife to be forever in subjection to her husband. Women who lectured on behalf of abolition were denounced from pulpits as being unfeminine and unchristian in their behavior.

It soon became evident that not only did these women have to present biblical arguments in support of freedom for slaves, but they also had to come to a new theological understanding of their role as Christian women. Most of them took the Bible seriously and pondered its teachings. It is ironic that most Christians have been convinced by their arguments that God did not create any person for slavery to another, but few Christians, liberal or conservative, even remember their biblical defense of the thesis that God also did not create one sex for subordination to the other.

The courageous women of the last century continued to preach the truth of equality of all human beings despite opposition from fellow Christians. They persevered through the Civil War and when it came to an end they graciously stepped back, as their male colleagues suggested, and watched the Fifteenth Amendment give the vote only to black men. Weary of the long struggle, women eventually narrowed their vision from full equality in all realms of life simply to a plea for the right to vote. Although biblical expositors now turned full effort to proving that God did not approve of women helping to "rule" in a democracy and the majority of evangelical ministers fought them all the way, women won the right to vote in 1920.[1] As Susan Anthony said, "The ballot is not even half the loaf; it is only a crust—a crumb!" Yet when the Nineteenth Amendment passed the House of Representatives, the gallery erupted with fervent strains of "Praise God from Whom All Blessings Flow."

For a time in the 1920s and 1930s, women were relatively free to follow a career. Many devoted Christian women began long and fruitful ministries on the foreign mission field or as professors in Bible schools and Christian colleges. Other women became frontier evangelists and supply preachers, holding many a struggling evangelical church together. These women were accepted and honored.

But with World War II came a change in attitude. After the war, women were told to go back to the home and motherhood. Single women were no longer viewed as servants of God but as sexual neurotics who couldn't make good at the only thing a woman was meant for—making some man happy. Even in the churches women were told to "move to the back of the bus," and this suggestion was fortified by scriptural proof texts. Today most evangelical churchmen express surprise when asked about women ministers in their denominations. "We used to have them when I was a boy," they admit, "but God doesn't seem to be calling women to the ministry anymore."

In the 1950s the mass media glorified housewifery and

motherhood until every little girl's dream was to have a houseful of the latest appliances and four kids. But all was not well in suburbia. Betty Friedan, in her 1963 book *The Feminine Mystique*, called it the "problem that has no name." Women began to wonder if there was more to life than being Fred's daughter, Jim's wife, and Bobby's mother. They began to ask if shiny linoleum and sweet-smelling sheets justified their existence. After reading Friedan's book, they decided there was more to life and they were going to find it. Contemporary women's liberation was born.

An impetus to the movement came unexpectedly as part of a joke. An elderly Virginia congressman amended Title VII of the Civil Rights Act with the word "sex," thinking that prohibiting discrimination in employment on the basis of race *and* sex was sure to doom the bill. He was wrong. Subsequent enforcement by the Equal Employment Opportunity Commission has found that women are as discriminated against in employment as are blacks.

Few Evangelicals would argue that women should not receive equal pay for equal work—though some might have doubts that a married woman should work outside the home. The fact is that 43 percent of all women in America today are working—32 million of them—and working on the very same jobs women on the average receive 58¢ for every $1 paid to men. 2 They are also discriminated against in such matters as insurance benefits, overtime work, promotions, and many others.

On the other hand, there are many areas of women's liberation with which Evangelicals take more exception. Seeing and hearing only the radicals portrayed by the mass media, many Christians dismiss Women's Lib as a group of "crazies" who want to dispense with certain articles of clothing, the legalities of marriage, and the "bother" of children. It is true that many of the women in the national movement are graduates of the civil rights struggle and the New Left. Their radical rhetoric offends many, confuses even more, and allows people to ignore the real issues too easily. As with any movement, we as Christians must first ask, "What are these people really saying?" and then, "How does this square with my faith?"

WHAT IS WOMEN'S LIBERATION?

So what is Women's Liberation all about? Beneath all the rhetoric and controversy, women simply want to be recognized as *persons*. The feminist movement grew out of the black civil rights crusade because the "nigger mentality" is the same — in both groups whatever one does, one ends up as a thirty-five-year-old busboy or housewife. Blacks have been stereotyped as inferior in intelligence, emotional, childlike, irresponsible. The "weaker sex" has been stereotyped as "dumb broads," "silly girls," naive, emotive, passive, and pliable. "All" blacks have rhythm; "all" women have the maternal instinct.

Christians are quick to deplore the Playboy philosophy which views woman as mindless sex objects, yet these same Christians see women only as another type of sex object — mother. For example, Billy Graham has declared: "Wife, mother, homemaker — this is the appointed destiny of real womanhood." The president of a leading evangelical seminary declared in a religious magazine for university students: "She finds her true womanhood in this male-female relationship, recognizing her role in relationship to her husband." An authority on marriage in a chapter concerning women wrote: "The plan of God is marriage. Singleness for religious service is a cultural tradition and not the plan of God." A radio evangelist described "the original function for which woman was created" as "to be a helping partner suited to the man. To achieve this, she of necessity will subordinate her interests to his." [3]

Secular feminists are quite right in charging that a woman is never allowed to be a person in her own right in the way that a man is. No one would think of telling a man that his

69

one vocation in life was husband, father, or homemaker. A man is seen as a person with unique, individual talents given him by God. And he is judged on his use of those talents in preaching the gospel, tilling the soil, operating a lathe, or compiling a stock portfolio. A woman is seen as a body containing a womb. She is judged on how attractive that body is to men and how she succeeds in her predetermined role of wife and mother. Those who never manage to become wives or to bear children are stigmatized by the church.

What women really want is a *choice*. When Dr. Benjamin Spock declared, "Women were made to be concerned first and foremost with child care, husband care, and home care," one feminist replied, "Dr. Spock wasn't born a pediatrician. He chose to become one." One might ask Billy Graham if he wishes to contradict the Word of God which declares that the Spirit "apportions to each one individually as he wills," all of God's gifts without restriction as to sex."[4] Would he deny God the right and possibility to call a woman to be a judge of Israel, a prophetess, a deacon, a Bible expositor — as women were in the Bible?

Some secular feminists appear to be "man-hating" because at times their resentment and rage at their oppression and frustration boil over, just as the feelings of the blacks did in the riots of the 1960s. Christian women sometimes feel the same frustration, but the lid of repression is clamped down on them by the appeal to Scripture. When women suggest that they should be allowed to hold church office or be ordained or teach an adult Sunday school class, churchmen piously transfer the blame to God (following, no doubt, the example of Adam in Gen. 3:12). To those who ask if women's position as purportedly outlined in the Bible is a bit unfair, one pastor replied, "No, it is not unfair. It is simply the way God made things."

Women who accept as true the teaching that the Bible says women are inferior often just give up the Christian faith altogether and quit the church—this is particularly true on university campuses. Others suffer stunted lives trying to reconcile what they know of a loving God who seems to have called them to full humanity and certain Christian males who keep trying to cut them down to the size of a pigeonhole.

Evangelical beliefs about (prejudices toward?) women have been codified in three or four snippets of Scripture—seldom whole verses and never complete thoughts. Woman is "a help meet," "the weaker vessel"; she is to "keep silence in the church" and "be in subjection to her husband." Secular feminists, hearing nothing else from Bible-believing Christians, label the Bible a myth and declare that it certainly is not "Good News."

WHAT DOES THE BIBLE SAY?

We as Evangelicals say we are committed to the written Word of God in its entirety. The Bible has much to say about women, and it is about time we took an extensive look at it—through glasses untinted by the prior assumption that women are inferior, or secondary, only "relatives of people."

So what does the Bible have to say?[5] It affirms that "in the beginning" "God created man in his own image, in the image of God created he him; male and female created he them" (Gen. 1:27), and God said to *both* of them, "Be fruitful, and multiply, and replenish the earth, and subdue it: and have dominion" (1:28). God created both sexes as an earthly mirror of His own image, and He charged them both with the care of His world. There is no indication here that woman is secondary or under the rule of man.

Conservatives have downgraded woman's place to such an extent in their interpretations of Genesis 2 that many liberals are encouraged to use the documentary hypothesis and discount chapter 2 as an inferior myth. But a proper interpretation of the chapter makes this unnecessary. Genesis

2 does not contradict but complements the teaching of Genesis 1:27-28. Man in surveying all the animals finds none which share his nature, that is able to be his coregent over the earth. So God makes for man a partner.

The misinterpretation here stems from our continued use of the King James Version's "an help meet for him" (2:18) long after we have forgotten what the archaic words really mean. The word for "help" is used twenty-one times throughout the Old Testament and never of an inferior or subordinate. Its most customary use is in such verses as Psalm 33:2: "Our soul waiteth for the Lord: he is our *help* and our shield." "Meet" simply means "suitable" in English; the Hebrew word is the same as that used in Psalm 23:5, "Thou preparest a table *before* me." Thus woman was not created as a "helpmate," a servant, or a subordinate, but as an equal, capable of sharing all man's intellectual, social, emotional, and physical aspects, a "mirror" image with which he could find true communion. Adam's joy and recognition of this equality is seen in his exclamation, "This is now bone of my bones, and flesh of my flesh" (Gen. 2:23). Man and woman were created for fellowship with each other and with God; they were also charged equally with the task of ruling the earth as God's vice-regents.

But they fell—out of right relationship with God and with each other. Although many have tried to place all of the blame for that calamity on woman, Genesis 3:6-7 reports that they *both* were together, they *both* ate, and then "the eyes of them *both* were opened, and they knew that they were naked." Despite the effort of each of them to escape the blame, God declared that the results of their disobedience would fall equally on all involved. He charged neither Eve nor Adam with ultimate responsibility. God did not speak of His choice in the matter but of the consequences of their sin, and therefore His words are not prescription but prophecy—not what should be but what would be.

72

The serpent would be at enmity with the woman, whose seed would eventually crush him. Even though woman might look forward to the birth of the Messiah, her childbearing would be in pain. Though she longed to have that communion of partnership with her husband that they had enjoyed in the garden, he would seek to overpower and dominate her. The man would find his life filled with toil and sorrow, sweat and pain. All would be subject to death. The fall destroyed all human relationships—with the earth, with the animal kingdom, with each other, and with God. As one theologian put it so poignantly, "Sin renders men lonely."

However, this was not the end, but only the beginning. Immediately God put into effect His plan of salvation which would restore the fallen world to the fullness of communion with Him—and ultimately with each other. And so in the fullness of time "God sent forth his Son, made of a woman, made under the law, to redeem them that were under the law" (Gal. 4:4-5).

Jesus' life provides an example of how God expects women to be treated. In a day when women were often sequestered and secluded behind harem walls and marriage veils, when righteous men closed their eyes and stopped their ears rather than see or hear a woman, when a woman's word was not accepted as valid testimony, when women were periodically "unclean" and banned from all human contact, Jesus came to set men *and* women free. He taught both men and women— though most rabbis considered women incapable of learning God's truth. He listened to women and allowed them to travel with Him. He touched and healed them. He did not condemn them, and even forgave the sins of one woman whom others wished to stone. He encouraged them to come out of the kitchen and sit at His feet with the disciples. He shared with them some of the greatest and deepest theological truths about God, and He commanded them, along with His male followers, to spread this truth to the ends of the earth. Women were first to know of His birth and last to linger at His cross. Though the disciples refused to believe them, women were also first to see Him resurrected. 6

Women were present on the day of Pentecost, and the Holy Spirit descended on them as well as on men. Peter in his sermon noted that Joel had prophesied that at the Messiah's coming both men and women would prophesy. And many women did in the early church. They opened their homes for meetings of the believers. They traveled beside the early apostles and on behalf of the church. They taught others what they had learned from Christ. 7

The gospel of Christ turned the world of the first century upside down. Jesus came to take away the sins in the hearts of humans, but as He did so they began to modify their relationships with others. Perhaps the greatest formulation of what such love can do is the declaration of Galatians 3:27-28: "For as many of you as have been baptized into Christ have put on Christ. There is neither Jew nor Greek, there is neither bond nor free, there is neither male nor female: for ye are all one in Christ Jesus." Many in that day and in this have sought to spiritualize these words, to deny their meaning and immediate consequences. In the context of Galatians, Paul is talking bluntly to those who said that they had "put on Christ" and yet felt as Jews that they could separate themselves from Gentile Christians who would not adopt Jewish rules and customs. Paul did not agree that it was enough to affirm Christian unity verbally in the assembly and then segregate for dinner. He demanded immediate concrete implementation of the consequences of this unity in the life of the church.

It is often charged that Paul condoned the institution of slavery, yet here he declares that there is no difference between slave and free men. And when he returned Onesimus to his master Philemon, he requested that he be considered "not now as a servant, but above a servant, a brother beloved, specially to me, but how much more unto thee, both in the flesh, and in the Lord" (v. 16). Could one treat another as his physical and spiritual brother and yet dominate and demean him? Just as Christians can now see that New Testament teaching planted the seeds which bore fruit 1,800 years later in the abolition of slavery, so it is time to recognize that biblical teaching can also free woman from the subjection into which a sinful world has forced her.

But what about other New Testament passages which refer to woman's place? In two areas, marriage and worship, traditional biblical interpretation makes woman eternally subordinate to man, or at least married women to their husbands. Perhaps the most quoted passage on marriage is found in Ephesians 5. Unfortunately most commentators begin with verse 22 ("Wives, submit yourselves unto your own husbands") rather than at verse 21 ("submitting yourselves one to another in the fear of God"), where the thought logically begins. Throughout the passage Paul is describing the mutual, self-giving, *agape* love and unity that should characterize Christ's church. Wives should love and work with their husbands as the church does with Christ; husbands should love and sacrifice themselves for their wives as Christ gave His life for the church. Paul is not setting up a hierarchical relationship here or encouraging men to think of themselves as playing God to their wives. Rather, he is encouraging all Christians to conform to Christ. Wherever the New Testament speaks of the marriage relationship (Col. 3:18-19; 1 Co. 11:11-12; 1 Pe. 3:1, 7), both husband and wife are addressed and both are admonished to love and submit to one another. The relationship is always seen as reciprocal.

Young couples today who seek a companionate, partnership marriage should not feel that they are disobeying God's Word by not forcing the wife to submit or the husband to carry the entire load of decisions. God did not intend marriage as an authoritarian hierarchy, but a loving partnership of equals. Often the argument is raised that "every unit has to have a leader: a coach for a team, a sergeant for a squad, a conductor for a band," as an evangelical magazine for teenagers once put it. And, of course, men have appointed themselves the leaders. Somehow a Christian view of marriage has come to mean that "the two become one" and that "one" is the husband. But a business partnership has two equal directors. The American government has authority invested in three branches. Jesus did not institute a hierarchy among His disciples but gave His power to all who believed. 8

The other question is whether or not women should keep silence in church as they are supposedly commanded in 1 Corinthians 14:34 and 1 Timothy 2:11. Both of these, along with 1 Corinthians 11:1-15, are extremely difficult passages to interpret. Involved are arguments concerning Genesis that seem to rely more heavily on Jewish tradition than the Old Testament. They also seem to contradict the practice of the church as recorded in Acts and other epistles. Particularly in 1 Corinthians, Paul seems to be primarily concerned with custom, with maintaining church decorum, with having things done decently and in order (14:10).

Various interpretations of these passages have been put forward. Perhaps the women in some churches were uneducated and previously secluded from public life to the extent that they were unready to handle the freedom which the early church did offer them. Perhaps their exuberant behavior in church meetings was causing dissension within the congregation. After all, in the same section of 1 Corinthians, Paul tries to put a damper on those who monopolized the meetings by speaking in tongues. Another suggestion is that certain women who opened their homes to Christian assemblies might have felt that this entitled them, whether or not they had gifts of teaching and leadership, to dominate the meetings.

Perhaps the most helpful is the solution worked out by Russell Prohl in *Woman in the Church*. He found evidence throughout the New Testament that services were divided between a preliminary service at which inquirers were present to hear what the gospel was all about and a closed meeting held afterward in which only baptized Christians celebrated holy communion. Those passages commanding women to be silent appear to deal with the open meeting, during which the church was trying to impress and convince nonbelievers. Women being in a low position in that society, unbelievers might have been shocked and turned away by women teaching. However, in the service of holy communion (1 Co. 11:20-34), women were permitted to preach and prophesy (1 Co. 11:5). Paul's primary concern there was that women should retain the symbol of their marriage, lest even believers be misled into thinking that Christianity was destroying the family.

One might ask whether in the present day, nonbelievers would be shocked and offended by a woman speaking in public. With women in places of business, educational, and political leadership, it is much more of an affront to non-Christians to learn that women are denied equality of opportunity in the church. As the *New York Times* once commented, "Churches are one of the few important institutions that still elevate discrimination against women to the level of principle." And one might also ask in this day when no one except the minister usually speaks in most churches, just how much of a "witness" silence is.

CHRISTIAN WOMEN'S LIBERATION

Evangelicals declare that Christ has freed us from the domination of sin. We claim that His teaching and the leading of the Holy Spirit have enabled man to alleviate sickness and disease, to prolong life, and to invent machines and agricultural techniques that make food production a less rigorous task. Man has not only been redeemed, but also the force of his punishment has been lessened. Woman's soul has also been saved by Christ's sacrifice—yet men of the last century argued that to give her anesthetics in childbirth would violate God's direction; to give her the franchise would deny God's intention. Can Christ redeem us from the sinful tendency to dominate others? Can we learn to live in the unity and love which biblical writers continually claim should mark Christ's church? Can we truly be one in the Spirit, one in the Lord, as long as women are labeled "different" and "subordinate?"

What would true Christian women's liberation mean? First of all, women would be freed to grow into the maturity for which God destined them. A study of the New Testament reveals that *every* Christian is expected to grow in likeness to Christ, to mature in his faith, to go on to the "deeper life." Liberation for women would mean that they were no longer required to remain in or least fake a resemblance of childishness or adolescence. They would be free to develop to the fullest extent the talents or capabilities with which God has endowed them—and to foster these attitudes in their female children. Women would become fully responsible to God for themselves—and thus they would gain self-respect. Women would not become "men" but would become fully themselves, unique individuals made in God's image and in the process of being conformed to His Son.

Second, family life would be strengthened rather than destroyed, as some fear. There is evidence that homosexuality is caused *not* by blurring of the sex roles, but by a reaction against the rigidity of the traditional stereotypes. Studies have also shown that egalitarian, partnership marriages are stronger and more rewarding for both members than are traditional, patriarchal marriages. And we have seen in Genesis and Ephesians that this is the way God intended marriage and the family. When all members are accepted as persons, equal partners in the adventure of living in relationship to each other and to God, then each has a very solid basis from which to develop his or her life. No one—husband, wife or child—is forced to submerge his interests or personality to another, but each is supported and encouraged to develop full Christian maturity.

Finally, the church would be strengthened by the full participation of all of its members, not just half of them. The church would be freed to utilize rather than repress the gifts of administration, leadership, teaching, and preaching which the Spirit has given to women. And men in the church would be offered an opportunity to manifest such "fruits of the Spirit" as meekness and love without feeling that they had sacrificed their masculinity.

There will be resistance to liberation—both by men and women. For men to give up their positions of power and domination will be difficult, despite the heart attacks and ulcers which the pressures of total responsibility bring. For women to shed their irresponsibility and shoulder their share of the burdens will not be easy, and many will long to revert to easier times when men made all the decisions. But God created *all* of us in His image, and Christ calls *all* of us to His service.

5

Evangelical Christianity and the Radical Left

THE SHIFT TO THE LEFT

From the perspective of the 1970s, it is almost impossible to remember that America entered the decade of the 1960s with such hope and confidence in the innate strength of its society and governmental institutions that the Eisenhower Administration took the unprecedented step of establishing a commission for the purpose of defining future goals for the nation—as if all the present needs and aspirations of the American people had been met! [1] In 1962 the noted political scientist Clinton Rossiter confidently predicted a shift to the right in American politics. In his volume entitled *Conservatism in America* he stated:

> It scarcely seems the part of bravery to foresee no sudden check or reversal in the glacial shift of the American intellect toward the Center and beyond toward the Right. Trustworthy observers have pointed to several developments that are making it easier for ordinary men to live as conservatives and thus for extraordinary men to think as conservatives. [2]

Only two years later, Senator Barry Goldwater—whose best-selling volume, *The Conscience of a Conservative*, helped make him a national political figure—won the 1964 Republican nomination for President of the United States. 3

Yet, while the establishment was confident that American society was entering a period of quiet building and mending, there were already signs that the country in fact was approaching a time for scattering stones and tearing down. In 1962 Michael Harrington's book *The Other America* brought to the nation's attention that significant numbers of Americans lived in poverty, passed by and unnoticed by the silent majority of the technocratic society. 4 In 1963 Martin Luther King began the much-publicized protest demonstrations in Birmingham, Alabama, against discrimination, and the march on Washington in quest of a new civil rights law. In the fall of 1964 the "Free Speech Movement" broke out on the Berkeley campus of the University of California—and millions of American TV viewers were stunned to hear student leaders shouting four-letter obscenities at their professors and administrators. In 1965 the Johnson Administration escalated American military involvement in the Vietnam War on the pretext that United States naval vessels had been attacked without provocation on the high seas by North Vietnamese troops. And by 1966 such groups as the Students for a Democratic Society (SDS) and the Student Nonviolent Coordinating Committee (SNCC)—originally gradualist and democratic in their approach to social and political problems—were advocating violence as the only means of redirecting and reordering the priorities of American society.

Thus a decade which began in quietness and self-confidence ended in violence and despair. Black uprisings occurred in the nation's largest cities. Students closed down some of the most prestigious educational institutions. Political leaders fell to the assassin's bullet. The national political conventions were forced to meet behind barbed wire fences, protected by thousands of National Guard troops. Thousands of young and old joined together to march on the Pentagon to protest the Vietnam War. Coalitions of students, blacks, and the poor attempted to move the American political system radically to the left, using violence when they thought it necessary to their cause. Within the decade, political life had become so radically polarized that it was commonplace to hear political analysts speak of the crisis of confidence in American society and government.

As the radicals on the left mounted their attacks on the American system, political observers disagreed as to both its meaning and its importance. Was the radical left being blown out of all proportion by the news media? Was it calling America back to its stated ideals of liberty and equality for all, or was it nothing more than the impassioned and undisciplined outbursts of Bohemian students, socialist intellectuals, and militant blacks? Some were convinced that the radical left was secretly being financed and organized by Communist groups. Others maintained that the movement represented a dramatic reawakening of the national conscience to the issues of war, race, and poverty. To some, the radical left represented the rejection of traditional Western standards of civility—it was associated with the rising drug culture, a communal life-style, and acid rock. Yet others saw in the far left a rising idealism which in its refusal to compromise with the materialism, militarism, and racism of American culture was nothing less than the beginning of a new historical consciousness which would eventually bring about "the greening of America."

But for all of the talk and concern over the radical left in the 1960s, it seems to have dissipated just as quickly and mysteriously as it appeared. By 1972 the radical left had become passe in most academic and political circles. Civic discussion groups and polite cocktail party conversation substituted Jesus Christ Superstar for Abbie Hoffman, the wage-price freeze for the Vietnam War. On the campuses, black arm bands were replaced by little yellow buttons with smiling faces serving to remind everyone that "happy days are here again."

While there has been an apparent return to normalcy in American politics, the suspicion still lurks that it is much too early to become sanguine about the future of American politics—the sounds of silence may indeed be ominous. Nonetheless, the present calm in American politics affords an opportunity to confront several lingering questions regarding the meaning and importance of the radical left. What were its origins? What were its goals? How can Christians minister to the needs of the people associated with this movement? And perhaps most important of all, what can Christians learn from the radical left?

THE RADICAL LEFT: NEW OR OLD?

Two of the questions most often asked about the rise of the radical left are (1) What are its origins? and (2) In what ways is it distinguishable from the "old left?" Most scholars agree that both the intellectual and institutional roots of the new left can be traced rather directly to mainline liberalism, that is, the old left. And most also believe that distinct differences have arisen between the two. Thus, to answer these questions it is necessary first of all to deal briefly with the characteristic features of mainline political liberalism.

THE OLD LEFT

Political liberalism had its origins in the seventeenth and eighteenth centuries. In some respects, it can be regarded as a political counterpart to the Reformation. Just as the Protestant Reformers opposed the institutional authority of the Roman Catholic Church and asserted the priesthood of the individual believer, so the political liberals argued against the arbitrary powers of the state, contending that it should have no governing powers other than those specifically contracted to it by individuals. Political liberalism was concerned with the problem of maximizing the freedom of all individuals who, the liberals asserted, had inalienable rights to life, liberty, and the enjoyment of their personal property. The American Revolution in 1776 was justified on the basis of these very concepts.

Most of the political liberals believed that man's nature was basically rational and good. If the arbitrary use of state power could be eliminated, individuals would use their freedom to live rationally and virtuously. For this reason, they generally argued that the government which governs best is that which governs least—for such a government would allow individuals to maximize their individual freedoms, and hence to maximize their capacity for a rational and virtuous life.

In the nineteenth and twentieth centuries, however, the thinking of political liberals changed concerning the proper role of government and the problem of maximizing human freedom. The growth of huge urban centers and a highly industrialized economy created a society in which individuals became increasingly interdependent. And while a person might enjoy a great deal of political freedom, it was apparent that technology was rapidly diminishing the number of individuals who could ever attain economic and social self-sufficiency in such a society. The industrial revolution had transformed a society of independent and self-sufficient artisans, farmers, and laborers into one of increasingly interdependent and intertwined businesses and corporations. If the economic and social freedoms of individuals were to be protected, argued the new political liberals, the conduct of these large corporate enterprises must to some degree be limited and directed by the state. Thus, the later liberalism took a much more positive attitude toward the role of the state than did the liberalism of the seventeenth and eighteenth centuries. [5]

The modern liberals often disagreed as to what extent state intervention was necessary to protect the social and economic welfare of individuals. Some maintained that a minimal amount of regulation of large corporate organizations was adequate. Others argued along more socialistic lines, believing the state should seek outright ownership and management of major corporate entities or should assume the obligation of guaranteeing national standards of economic and social well-being for its people—in other words, a welfare state.

Although modern liberals believed in an expanded role for the state, they did not reject concepts of limited government or individual human rights. To the contrary, they argued that by expanding the role of the government into social and economic spheres, limited government and human rights were strengthened against the threats of radical revolutionaries who questioned the ability of democratic institutions to respond to the rising political, economic, and social aspirations of the working classes. This is illustrated dramatically by Franklin Roosevelt's famous "Four Freedoms" speech which linked such social and economic freedoms as freedom from fear and hunger with the more traditional political ones of religion and expression.

It is important that the modern liberals and democratic socialists described above be distinguished from the revolutionary socialists such as Karl Marx. The revolutionary socialists—which are generally designated as Communists today—contend that violent overthrow of established authority is the only means of achieving desired social, economic, and political reforms. Thus, the distinction between the democratic left and the nondemocratic left is a crucial one.

Although early and later liberalism disagreed regarding the proper extent of state intervention in the social order, they continued to agree on several fundamental points. First, they both believed in maximizing human freedom. The emphasis in all liberal political movements has been on freedom as opposed to order, liberty as opposed to authority. Second, both early and later liberalism tended to believe that the nature of man was basically good.

86

When men did bad things, it was because they had been affected negatively by a bad environment. To make men good, all that was necessary was to remove the inequities and artificial restraints which interfered with man's natural tendency to goodness.

These basic tenets of liberalism are important to remember at this point for two reasons. First, as will be demonstrated shortly, the new left movement of the 1960s had its roots in this intellectual tradition. While the new left often seemed utopian and anarchical to outside observers, it was in fact based solidly on the presuppositions of the old left. Second, it is important to stress that political liberalism as an ideology has several serious shortcomings from the perspective of the Christian faith.

First, Christians must reject the liberal concept of freedom as nothing more than the absence of restraint. Freedom, for the Christian, involves the spiritual dimension of man's being as well as his relationship to the state and society. Thus, it involves the acceptance of legitimate authority as well as the rejection of illegitimate claims to authority. The Christian insists that freedom is not just an abstract possession, but rather, it must have some purpose. He asks not only if a man is free, but for what he wishes to use his freedom.

Second, the Christian rejects the liberal concept that the human condition is fundamentally a product of the environment. Liberals have tended to believe that improvement in the political community in which men live will result in the substantial modification of the conduct of individuals within that community. While not rejecting the obvious truth that human behavior is in part conditioned by the environment, Christians recognize that the root cause of evil in society rests with man's rejection of God. Therefore, the primary social problem for the Christian is not how social institutions can be modified to change human behavior, but rather how individuals themselves can be changed by God, and how changed individuals can effect change in the larger social order.

These two basic weaknesses in the liberal ideology help in understanding not only the origins of the new left, but its increasing radicalization as well. The new left began by asking why the old left had failed. The answer—at least initially—was that the principles of the old left had not been applied with enough vigor and çonsistency. But as the institutions of political liberalism proved increasingly unable to solve the problems which the new left sought to attack, it began to turn away from the old left ideology and to create a counterculture with a new set of values all its own.

THE NEW LEFT

The goal of the old left was the gradualist reform of the social, economic, and governmental institutions of society through democratic means aimed at insuring that all Americans would share justly in the wealth of a highly industrialized society. It sought further to manage the economy to protect individuals from the vagaries of economic depression. And it was concerned—although to a much lesser extent—with securing full human rights for minority groups within society.

The new left, however, was upset with the complacency of what it contended had become "establishment liberalism." This was particularly true of college and university students across the country who had become involved in the civil rights struggle. Student political activism, which has played such a key role in the new left, is nothing new in American history. [6] In 1823, for example, half of the Harvard senior class was expelled for becoming involved in disruptive activity. Between 1886 and 1930 the Student Christian Volunteer Movement was an active force on scores of American campuses—generating interest in causes as diverse as foreign missions, educational reform, and women's liberation. It was in the 1930s, however, that the first signs of organized *radical* student political activity began to appear on American campuses. Groups such as the Student League for Industrial Democracy and the Intercollegiate Disarmament Council supported socialist causes on many campuses.

However, the student activism of the new left was qualitatively different from previous experiences. First, by the 1960s the numbers of college and university students in the United States had grown phenomenally. Students outnumbered farmers, for example, and recognized that if they organized as a visible political pressure group they could as students directly affect American politics in much the same way as farmers influence politics through the American Farm Bureau Federation or the National Farmers Union.

Second, as the absolute size of the student population grew, it increasingly took on its own identity as an independent force in American politics and dissociated itself from the sponsoring organizations in the adult community. For example, until 1966 the Students for a Democratic Society was tied to the League for Industrial Democracy and received substantial financial support not only from the league but from national labor unions such as the United Auto Workers. But as the collegiate groups declared independence from their adult sponsors, they were freed of many of the restraints which had applied to earlier attempts at youthful political activism.

Third, student political involvement prior to the 1960s had generally been educationally oriented. Traditionally, such groups concerned themselves with sponsoring campus forums and lectures. In the new decade, however, they turned to direct political action. It is as a part of the history of student attempts at political activism—and the continuing failures which the young encountered—that the growth of the new left can best be described.

In 1954 the Supreme Court rendered its decision declaring segregation in public education to be in violation of the law of the land. In the next few years students organized to pro-test noncompliance with the Supreme Court decision in the Southern states. At this point the students were rather ob-viously operating within the system to make it work—not against the system in an effort to destroy it. The Student Nonviolent Coordinating Committee (SNCC) was established to help fund and coordinate student activism in the civil rights struggle, and among other things SNCC sought to have the Justice Department provide protection for students who were involved in civil rights activities in the South. However, the federal government refused to provide protection for the young people, despite the fact that in many cases they were victims of mistreatment by local law enforcement officials in the South. Hence, a crisis of confidence developed between the students actively involved in the civil rights struggle and the government which refused to use its powers to insure enforcement of the law.

In the summer of 1964 several hundred college and uni-versity students participated in a SNCC-sponsored voter-registration drive in the Mississippi Delta, a region where blacks substantially outnumber whites. When they returned to their campuses in the fall, they told of being beaten by local whites and of having seen abysmally shocking poverty. They elicited sympathy among fellow students and tried to raise money to continue the project on a permanent basis. Several campuses sought to restrict these fund-raising activities by the students. Attempts at such restriction often resulted in open confrontation between students and campus administrators, and the students insisted that their rights to free speech and political association were being violated. The most dramatic instance of this emergence of the Free Speech Movement occurred at Berkeley. The result was that the students, who were already beginning to doubt the integrity of the government's commitment to the civil rights struggle, now began to question the educational estab-lishment as well. Mario Savio at Berkeley led the FSM students into dramatic confrontations with campus authorities which received extensive television coverage. The most significant action was a campus sit-in which resulted in the arrest of over eight hundred students.

As this was occurring, American military involvement in Vietnam was escalating. In the summer of 1964 President Lyndon B. Johnson secured the passage of the "Gulf of Tonkin Resolution," and by the end of the year there were over 23,000 American military personnel assigned to the Vietnam War. The students were the first to see the futility and morally questionable character of the conflict in Indochina; and as the number of troops in Vietnam climbed to over half a million, the students helped to spark a national debate on American policies there. In 1965 the first "March on Washington" in connection with the war drew 20,000 demonstrators, most of whom were students. In 1967 the "March on the Pentagon" attracted at least 55,000 persons, and brief clashes between police and demonstrators took place.

As students became increasingly disillusioned with the political system and with their academic communities, the New Left began to develop into a counterculture, as exemplified by the "hippie" and "yippie" movements. The use of drugs, the growth of long hair, and the development of the underground press became the characteristics of the youth revolt. Before long, the student movement divided between more moderate students (who could best be described as old left liberals) and those who began to develop a new rationale for political action. The assassinations of Martin Luther King, Jr., and Robert Kennedy in 1968—both heroes of the young—together with the brutalities of the Chicago police at the 1968 Democratic National Convention caused increasing strain within the student movement. It then began to fragment over the issues. This splintering of the new left soon led to its dissipation, and

91

since 1969 there has been a steady decrease in the visibility and vocalness of the radical movement.

In discussing the new left, it is extremely difficult to delineate its "characteristic features." The new left is more of a movement than an ideology. It was more a reaction to a series of historical events experienced by the student community in the 1960s than the product of any fixed ideology. Initially, the momentum of the new left was inspired by the ideological rhetoric of the old left; but as the students involved in the new left became disillusioned with establishment liberalism in the government and the academic community, they began to react strongly to crises as they encountered them. The popular press has tended to label the new left with terms such as *revolutionary, romantic, idealistic, utopian,* and *anarchic*, but these generalizations fail to withstand the scrutiny of empirical study. [7]

One of the most important documents to emerge from the literature of the new left which delineates an ideology for the movement is "The Port Huron Statement" issued by the SDS in 1962. [8] This document summarizes the objectives of the new left activists and the goals to which they are committed. Attacking the persistence of racism within the country and the military arms race between nations, the document indicts the educational establishment for its institutional complicity in perpetuating these problems:

> Making values explicit—an initial task in establishing alternatives—is an activity that has been devalued and corrupted. . . . Our professors and administrators sacrifice controversy to public relations; their curriculums change more slowly than the living events of the world; their skills and silence are purchased by investors in the arms race; passion is called unscholastic. [9]

The Port Huron Statement decries not only the institutional failures of American society, but points to the need for a renewed sense of community in a highly technocratic and bureaucratized world. It expresses the longing for a society in which people will participate more directly in making decisions affecting their lives ("participatory democracy") and one in which personal values will regain their rightful place against the culture of technology.

Ironically, as the new left became increasingly radical, it became less political, for students gradually began to lose faith in the political process itself. Charles Reich's best-selling book *The Greening of America* captures the spirit of the new left in the late 1960s when he writes:

> There is a revolution coming. It will not be like revolutions of the past. It will originate with the individual and with culture, and it will change the political structure only as its final act. It will not require violence to succeed, and it cannot be successfully resisted by violence. It is now spreading with amazing rapidity, and already our laws, institutions, and social structure are changing in consequence. It promises a higher reason, a more human community, and a new and liberated individual. Its ultimate creation will be a new and enduring wholeness and beauty—a renewed relationship of man to himself, to other men, to society, to nature, and to the land. 10

Thus, while the new left began in the liberal tradition of seeking to change men by changing their institutions, it moved during its brief lifetime to a position which in some ways is like a basically Christian approach to social problems; that is, one first concentrates on transforming individuals, and then institutions will change as a consequence. However, Reich's statement omits a crucial factor— man's need to renew his relationship with God as the means by which all other relationships can be transformed. Instead of turning to God, the new left turned to drugs and mystery religions. When these failed, many of the disillusioned new left radicals sought refuge in the Jesus movement! 11

Positive Contributions of the New Left

Because the new left has been associated so closely with the drug counterculture, and its leaders have at times advocated revolutionary tactics, most Americans were more concerned with how the new left could best be controlled and dissipated rather than with its message to society. Now that the threat of the new left has subsided, it is possible to make a more objective evaluation of the movement.

First, the new left has quickened the conscience of America in regard to social injustices such as poverty, racism, and militarism. The left's expression of moral outrage about these issues can be compared to the prophetic utterances of Amos and Hosea who condemned the calloused conscience of ancient Israel in the face of problems not unlike our own. Most Americans had grown accustomed to military spending levels which absorbed roughly half of the budget expenditures of the national government. Most people were oblivious to the pervasiveness of poverty within the richest nation in the history of mankind. They had learned to live with the evil of racism, believing that property rights should be held higher than human rights, and that relations between the races could not be improved by legislative fiat.

All too often, Americans rationalized the injustices in their own society by making comparisons with other countries where such problems were even more glaring, as if that were enough to excuse the perpetuation of injustice in their own land. The new left unconsciously reminded American Christians of the biblical concept that to whom much is given, much will be required.

Second, as the new left encountered opposition to its indictments of American society, it pointed out that the evils of society were much more deeply rooted than many citizens had believed. After all, it was not the revolutionaries of the left who assassinated social reformers such as Robert

Kennedy or Martin Luther King. These violent actions served to highlight the depths of the antagonisms which were eating at the soul of the American republic. The new left taught that although social reform was sorely needed to attack the institutional injustices, an even more important goal was the transformation of individual beliefs and behavior which passively accepted the existence of social evil.

Third, the new left brought to light the fact that the growth of technology in the modern world tends to mitigate sensitivities to human values. Students who saw themselves as nothing more than IBM numbers on a computer print-out sheet could sympathize with the plight of blacks and poor people who had also been reduced to statistical tables. They objected to cataloging the suffering caused by the war in Indochina in the simple form of kill ratios and body counts, and attacked the monotony of work in a technological society where human values were sacrificed to a higher GNP. The new left recognized that the dignity of men as individuals created in the image of God was being buried under layers of bureaucratic structures by government, industry, and the "great" universities. Realizing that these trends could become just as totalitarian in their impact on people as the older totalitarianisms of fascism and communism, it called for a reordering of priorities in which technology would serve the human spirit and not the other way around.

Fourth, and perhaps most important, the new left helped to reawaken the social conscience of institutional Christianity in America. For too long the church had remained silent in the face of social injustice, and through its silence it had forfeited the right to speak to the present situation. This was, unfortunately, particularly true of the evangelical and conservative churches which viewed their mission solely in terms of preserving the dogmatic orthodoxy of the Christian faith and thus remained oblivious to their obligation to attack social injustice in the name of the just God. The new left quickly recognized the irrelevance of faith without

95

works, and because of the failure of the churches the movement approached social problems in a secular manner. A Roman Catholic theologian notes with regret that

> the quest for human values in our society . . . has been radically secularized. It has moved outside the churches. If one wishes to be radically religious in our society—that is to say, radically committed to a vision of human brotherhood, personal integrity, openness to the future, justice, and peace— one will not, commonly, seek an ecclesiastical outlet for one's energies. One will, instead, find community under secular auspices, create one's own symbols for community and integrity, and work through secular agencies for social and political reforms.[12]

In view of this situation, leaders of evangelical Protestantism have begun challenging the church to face up to its responsibilities in the social arena. Sherwood Wirt, editor of *Decision* magazine, and Carl F. H. Henry, former editor of *Christianity Today*, have both recently published books urging the evangelical community to recognize the need for and the validity of witness in the social sector.[13] At the 1969 United States Congress on Evangelism, evangelist Leighton Ford called for Evangelicals to repent of their sins of social insensitivity and lack of concern with the great social questions of the day, while Senator Mark Hatfield of Oregon in a 1970 commencement address at Fuller Theological Seminary delivered a ringing call for social concern and activism on the part of evangelical Christians.[14] Both leaders were warmly received by their audiences. In His providential ordering of history, it appears that God is using the past failures of the Christian community to create the opportunity for repentance and renewal.

WEAKNESSES OF THE NEW LEFT
Having pointed out the validity and importance of the new left's critique of contemporary American society—and

what should be learned from it—it is equally important to touch on some of the weaknesses of the new left. First, the pride and self-righteousness evident in much of the rhetoric and behavior of the new left is open to serious criticism. Having pointed to the failures and institutional hypocrisies of American society, the new left has often been blind to its own moral bankruptcy. While the movement has given many valuable insights into the moral failures of modern technological culture, it lacks any authoritative basis upon which to create a renewed sense of morality or social justice. All too often, the new left merely proposes that individuals be allowed to "do their own thing" when it comes to such personal behavior as the use of drugs or extramarital sexual activities, but not when it involves social concerns such as business or government. The new left divides personal and corporate morality artificially, but oddly enough it reverses the direction in which this bifurcation generally takes place in American culture.

Second, the new left has done a better job of criticizing American society than it has in proposing viable alternatives. While its indictments of the status quo may indeed be accurate, these are not very useful unless they are coupled with specific and concrete policies which can transform these criticisms from mere abstractions into realistic opportunities for change. The new left has a great deal of vision, but not much of a program for implementing it. The Port Huron Statement of the SDS virtually confesses this when it states in closing: "If we appear to seek the unattainable, as it has been said, then let it be known that we do so to avoid the unimaginable." 15

Third, the new left suffers from the basic weaknesses of the old left discussed earlier in this essay. It basically accepts the liberal belief in the innate goodness of man. If only the social environment can be changed, argues the liberal, the basic human problems can be solved. This is clearly contrary to the Christian affirmation that man is a

97

fallen being and that God alone can transform men and re-suit them to the purposes for which they were created. In fact, much of the frustration and radicalization experienced by the new left results from its belief that men are basically good and rational. For if such is the case, how could the new left explain the inability of modern man to solve his great social problems other than to accuse the system itself as being the great corrupter?

Daniel P. Moynihan, addressing the 1969 graduating class at Notre Dame University, summarized the key weakness of the new left when he declared:

> The principal issues of the moment are not political. They are seen as such: that is the essential clue to their nature. But the crisis of the time is not political, it is in essence religious. It is a religious crisis of large numbers of intensely moral, even Godly, people who no longer hope for God. Hence, the quest for divinity assumes a secular form, but with an intensity of conviction that is genuinely new to our politics. [16]

The new left has come and now is on the way out. Hope-fully, however, it will leave its mark not only on the political institutions of American society, but on the churches as well. For only the gospel of Jesus Christ can fill the spiritual void that the secular saints of the new left uncovered in American society. When the Master returns, may He find evangelical Christians working as faithful stewards to carry out the divine mission to call people to repentance and to seek justice for all men.

6

Evangelical Christianity and the Radical Right

EVANGELICALS STAND ACCUSED

The assertion is frequently made that conservative or evangelical Christianity and the far right are closely related and that the one stands cheek by jowl with the other. Theologian Daniel B. Stevick contends that fundamentalists and Evangelicals "are overwhelmingly rightist politically and conservative socially and economically." The Midwest and the South, the two largest strongholds of political and social reaction, are also the "Bible belt." In similar manner a noted historian of American Christianity, William G. McLoughlin charges Evangelicals with being "the spiritual hardcore of the radical right," while a writer in *Ramparts* states that American fundamentalism "has always been associated with the forces of political reaction, with the blathering God-on-our-side cross and flag confusers."[1] To be sure, these accusations come from individuals not in sympathy with the evangelical position, but are they necessarily inaccurate?

A number of empirical studies during the past decade seem to support the assumption that conservative religion and politics are linked. Benton Johnson's 1960 sampling of Protestant laymen and 1962 survey of clergymen in Oregon demonstrated that those of "conservative" theological persuasion were far more likely to vote Republican than those indicating "neo-orthodox" or "liberal" views. In the same vein, Jeffrey Hadden revealed in *The Gathering Storm in the Churches* that theological "fundamentalists" and "conservatives" in the six major denominations he surveyed had in 1964 voted for Barry Goldwater from four to eleven times more than "neoorthodox" and "liberals" had done. Leland Harder's recent study of voting behavior among northern Indiana Mennonites showed that the individuals who scored high in orthodoxy (doctrinal commitment) were more inclined to have voted for Goldwater than those scoring low. Sociologists Mark Chesler and Richard Schmuck interviewed approximately sixty-five Midwestern "superpatriots" (characterized by patriotic and nationalistic conservatism, vigorous anti-Communism, and a clear commitment to action) and found that three-quarters of them were "religiously fundamentalistic and pietistically moralistic." The survey of United Methodist attitudes on extremism by Ezra Jones taken in 1969-1970 brought out that people in the theologically more conservative areas of the United States (the South) leaned quite significantly toward right-wing views. [2]

In is noteworthy that no studies have shown a similar relationship bewteen the evangelical faith and the left in the United States. Almost all "Christian" organizations which advocate such causes as internationalism, world peace, or socialism are dominated by theological liberals, and, with the exception of representatives from the historic peace churches (Mennonite, Friends, and Brethren), the participation of Evangelicals in these movements is quite limited. Thus, the attraction of the right to conservative Christians is considerably greater than the left, and the danger of political, economic, and social compromises that might undermine the effectiveness of the faith lies more on the right than the left.

THE FAR RIGHT

One who seeks to analyze the right is confronted with an almost insuperable obstacle, namely, that of definition. Conservatism is not a neatly packaged set of views and attitudes but a continuum stretching from the reasonable and respectable positions of an Edmund Burke, John Adams, or Russell Kirk to the excesses of the National Socialist White People's Party or the Minutemen. Most spokesmen for the right in the United States, regardless of their place on the continuum, stress the importance of limited government, decentralized federalism (states' rights), individual responsibility for the maintenance of liberty, traditional religion and morality, natural inequalities among men, opposition to socialism and communism, and unregulated or free-enterprise capitalism. They are emotionally committed to American nationalism, and they look favorably upon the military. To summarize, modern rightism is a curious and contradictory integration of almost anarchistic individualism with a high level of approval of the two primary authoritarian institutions of American society: the police (law and order) and the military. [3]

A useful scheme for discriminating among various groups which lie to the right of the center is to divide the continuum into three major segments. [4] *Moderate conservative* includes such groups as the Americans for Constitutional Action, Intercollegiate Studies Institute, and Young Americans for Freedom, along with *Human Events* and the *National Review*. They attribute those foreign and domestic policies which they disapprove of to the inherent stupidity of the liberal establishment, and they are willing to work through accepted political and judicial procedures to achieve their ends. The category *radical right* takes in such organizations as the John Birch Society, Christian Crusade, Twentieth

101

Century Reformation Hour, Dan Smoot Report, Manion Forum, Life Line Foundation, Liberty Lobby, and Conservative Society of America, to name only a few. They emphasize the existence of an all-pervasive Communist conspiracy, oppose most of the actions taken by the federal government since 1933, and offer few viable alternatives to the policies they dislike. The most extreme segment, the *hate right*, which includes the Minutemen, American Nazi Party, Ku Klux Klan, White Citizens' Councils, and various anti-Semites like the late Conde McGinley (*Common Sense*) and Gerald L. K. Smith (*Christian Nationalist Crusade*), combines racial bigotry with a paranoid belief in the all-consuming, domestic Communist conspiracy. These rightists offer no alternatives and are prepared to go outside the established political and judicial channels to settle their differences.

Because of its substantial basis of popular support and inherent hostility to the institutions of liberal democracy, the *radical right* poses the greatest threat to the American political system. What are its characteristic views? The internal conspiracy thesis is the cardinal doctrine of the radical right. Traitors have infiltrated into places of power and influence in American society—the government, schools, churches, and mass media. Although their number is small, they exploit others by the use of tactics so subtle and insidious that most loyal Americans are unaware of their activities and are led unsuspectingly along the path to Communism, especially when they are taken in by promises of government benefits. As the former vice-president of the Christian Anti-Communism Crusade declared, "One dedicated Communist at a strategic position at a crucial moment could literally have the population at his mercy. The number is almost insignificant." [5]

The conspirators cannot be dealt with through the political process. One must fight fire with fire, in other words, an anticonspiracy conspiracy. The Communist-infiltrated institutions of society must be counter-infiltrated, and the traitors exposed and rooted out. If necessary, traditional constitutional processes and civil liberties may be put aside to oust the domestic Reds. Also, the Communist-inspired government programs must be cancelled, including mental health, sex education, public housing, school desegregation, medicare, public assistance (welfare), and of course, foreign aid.

The radical rightist reduces complexity to simplicity. The nation's social turmoil is due to the actions of conspirators, not inequities in the social structure itself. Both the rise of the Soviet Union and China to world power and the colonial revolution resulted from an American refusal to assert her superior moral and military strength. In turn, America's problems will be solved if the government stands firmly behind law and order, stops meddling in the economy, and adopts an uncompromising posture toward international Communism. The far rightist lives in a rigid, two-value world where there are no grays, only black and white, bad and good, Communists and patriots. Such people often view the world in highly emotional and irrational terms, engage in stereotyping, and manifest deep feelings of hostility, especially toward those who appear to be their ideological foes. Also, the rightist wishes to transform the existing sociopolitical system into some imagined utopian state, although unlike the far leftist, he sees his utopia in the past rather than in the future. [6]

The far rightists utilize various tactics to gain their ends. For one thing, they form tightly knit groups which bring pressure to bear on governmental and community power structures. The latest (1965) edition of *The First National Directory of "Rightist" Groups, Publications and Some Individuals in the United States* lists 2,598 right-wing organizations. George Thayer estimates that 300,000 "hard core activists" belong to these associations, and they can count upon three to four million "part time to casual supporters" to assist them in their work. 7 Although small in relation to the total national population, these numbers are much larger than are found on the left. It should be emphasized that various rightist organizations often support worthy causes and thereby draw in many well-meaning Christian people unawares.

Through concentrated efforts, rightists infiltrate and gain control of political party organizations, civic and service clubs, school boards, PTA's, and local churches. Some of their tactics include whispering campaigns and open accusations of disloyalty to foster distrust of community leaders, and the monopolization of call-in radio programs. Letter-writing campaigns, anonymous telephone calls, economic boycotts, and heckling at public meetings are also used. A frequent practice is the sponsoring of "seminars" and "schools," which have the advantage of drawing from every segment of the conservative continuum, since local chambers of commerce, industries, churches, and veterans and military organizations contribute money and audiences to these. In addition, rightists grind out mountains of propaganda in the form of books, pamphlets, magazines, newspapers, tape recordings, filmstrips, and motion pictures, and many of them have regular radio and television programs.

The far right even maintains front organizations, a practice which most people assume is exclusively a leftist practice. Undoubtedly the most deceptive of these is the Freedoms Foundation, created in 1949 by three prominent businessmen and located at Valley Forge, Pennsylvania. George Thayer's accusation that it is "as carefully camouflaged as any communist front of the past" is definitely correct. 8 It recruited Herbert Hoover and Dwight Eisenhower as honorary officers and President Richard Nixon currently serves as honorary chairman, while hundreds of prominent Americans have been willing to identify with it by accepting awards and allowing their names to appear on the foundation's letterhead.

The group sponsors essay contests by schoolchildren and the dissemination of "freedom" literature and radio spot announcements, and it has built a complex of libraries and structures in Valley Forge. However, the Freedoms Foundation's most significant function has been to give awards to "patriotic" individuals and organizations who distinguish themselves in selling the American way of life. Among the recipients of these have been: Thomas J. Anderson (Southern leader of the John Birch Society), the militaristic Institute for American Strategy, Senators Barry Goldwater and Thomas Dodd, Walter A. Judd, Ronald Reagan, and the Free Enterprise Bureau of the Coast Federal Savings and Loan Association in Los Angeles. The notorious far right National Education Program at Harding College (Searcy, Arkansas) and its leader, George S. Benson, allege to have received Freedoms Foundation awards every year since 1949. [9] Prizes have also gone to respectable institutions and national figures like *Life* magazine, the National Broadcasting Company, Admiral Arthur Radford, General Nathan Twining, Walt Disney, Raymond Burr, Bob Hope, and many others. Even Billy Graham's *Decision* magazine was given the foundation's highest honor, the George Washington Medal, for a 1968 editorial which extolled the freedom bestowed by America's Christian forefathers upon the nation and denounced youthful radicals whose revolutionary demands for social change threatened the destruction of its freedom. [10]

THE IDENTIFICATION OF RIGHTISM AND CHRISTIANITY

It is well known that most leaders of the radical right regard themselves as Christians and identify their causes with Christianity. A significant number of the far-right groups are avowedly Christian, for example, Carl McIntire's Twentieth Century Reformation Hour, Billy James Hargis'

Christian Crusade, Edgar Bundy's Church League of America, Howard Kershner's Christian Freedom Foundation, George Benson's National Education Program, Fred Schwartz' Christian Anti-Communism Crusade, and Steuart McBirnie's Voice of Americanism.[11] Some of these associations are well financed, for instance, both Christian Crusade and the Twentieth Century Reformation Hour had estimated incomes of $1,750,000 in 1970, but these figures fall far short of "secular" rightist groups like the John Birch Society and the American Security Council.[12]

Interestingly enough, Erling Jorstad demonstrates that in the 1950s the Christian rightist organizations were the fundamentalist opponents of liberal Protestantism and had, above all, stressed pure doctrine and total separation from any kind of apostasy. However, expounding the principles of patriotism and conservatism was too tempting for them to resist, and they gradually shifted their primary emphasis from the theological to the political and economic. By the early 1960s the question, "How did one stand on the internal conspiracy?" was now the overriding issue and total separation was soft-pedaled. These associations and leaders accordingly became the "church-related spokesmen for the entire far right cause."[13]

The fact that the Christian rightist organizations had been taken captive by the secular movement raises serious doubt about whether evangelical Christianity by its very nature really must be right wing in its political and social orientation. To be sure, there are seeming affinities between conservative Christianity and ultra-conservative politics. The rightist view of life as a struggle between absolute good and evil seems to harmonize with the Christian tendency to see moral issues in blacks and whites, and the willingness of Christians to defend their moral and theological positions against sin and evil can easily be translated into a crusade against "godless" Communism. The teaching that Satan is everywhere present subverting the purposes of God in the

106

world provides a basis for belief in a conspiratorial control apparatus of evil, namely, Communism. The Christian doctrine of individual accountability to God and personal salvation, morality and service goes along with the rightist understanding of individualism. Both Christians and rightists share a pessimistic view of human nature, reject the idea that progress toward a better society is inevitable, and accept the view that all men are morally and spiritually equal before God.

However, these affinities are only apparent and the real attraction of far rightism to evangelical Christianity is cultural, not theological. An evangelical subculture has developed and it is this, not the biblical faith, that has become linked with the far right. What distinguishes this subculture? An important factor is the *individualism* which lies at the foundation of modern Western civilization. The emphasis upon liberty and autonomy meant that no external force, whether God, church, or government, could abridge man's freedom. Thus, man was responsible not for his fellows but merely for himself. Salvation involved simply rescuing the individual soul from the realm of sin rather than preparing the whole man for service in the world in conjunction with his fellow believers, namely, the church. Since the stress was on personal piety and uprightness, little engagement with the structures of society was expected. [14]

A preoccupation with *piety* is another characteristic. The Christian is concerned with his inner life and often he encounters his fellowman only when endeavoring to win him to Christ. It is assumed that if all men are brought to Christ, social evils will disappear through divine intervention, and it is not necessary or even desirable to involve oneself in restructuring society to make it more equitable. If one wishes to improve society, he will work more diligently at converting the individual members that comprise it. Of course, this overlooks the obvious fact that regenerated Christians remain remarkably sinful and have little to offer in the way of guidance in ethical behavior. 15

Also prevalent in the subculture is a strong sense of *legalism*. The conservative Christian tends to adopt a Manichean outlook toward the "world." By drawing up a list of taboos which relates to one's recreational life, personal habits, cultural activities, and community involvement, the Christian voluntarily limits the experiences open to him. This often is carried to the extent that one denies himself many of the finest things of life in order to avoid "evil." However, the norms are usually such that they place the conservative Evangelical among the most respectable elements of the community. Stevick notes that "most of his prohibitions are in the general line of the cautious, circumspect, often smug 'worldly asceticism' which distinguishes the Anglo-Saxon bourgeois mind. He risks little by his peculiar habits. He carefully removes himself from the publicans and sinners, but he joins the Pharisees." 16

This results in a *self-righteous moralism*. The conservative sets up a normative system which corresponds to the bourgeois, success-oriented values of hard work, individual effort, and self-denial. Those who fall short of this are judged harshly, and morality becomes more a matter of hostile demand than positive affirmation. He advocates punitive and retaliatory methods of social control, views things in simple terms of good and evil, and regards moral principles as fixed, eternal, sacred objects. 17

A commonly found trait in the subculture is *anti-intellectualism*. This may be manifested in a rejection of art and literature that is not specifically "Christian" and a downgrading of education and mental endeavors in favor of the more "practical" forms of activity. Emphasis is placed upon intuition and spiritual experience, and those engaged in intellectual pursuits are frequently dismissed with such caustic remarks as "You can't get it all from books" and "A little learning is a dangerous thing." That this anti-intellectualism is primarily due to factors in the historical development of American Christianity has been ably demonstrated in a recent article by Patricia J. Harrison. The entire democratic milieu of the common people encouraged such attitudes, and Christians internalized this milieu. Revivalism simply tended to reinforce the suspicion of learning, while the Fundamentalist-Modernist controversy permanently fixed anti-intellectualism in the evangelical outlook. [18]

Finally, one of the most pronounced features of the subculture is a *closed-minded separatism*. By withdrawing into the evangelical ghetto, the Christian shuts himself away from the influence of secularization and is oblivious to the changes occurring in the world around him. Thus, he thinks and acts in terms of bygone values. All new data is measured against a system where the answers are already in, and he is unable to learn from his culture. This social isolation makes the conservative Christian a stranger in the larger society, distrustful of its inhabitants, intolerant of divergent views, and deeply insecure. It may even lead to mental illness. [19]

These traits are commonly found among adherents to the radical right, and this leads to the obvious conclusion that the connection between it and evangelical Christianity is primarily cultural in origin. Further, the American fundamentalist or evangelical subculture is in itself an aberration. Historians of American Christianity, most notably Timothy Smith and Bruce Shelley, have shown that in the nineteenth century there was a deep sense of social concern among Christians. [20] But various forces contributed to the erosion of this concern and the transformation of evangelical Christianity into a cultural backwater. The problems of industrialization and urbanization, the attack of new ideas like Darwinism and higher criticism, a revivalism that emphasized individual conversion and social quietism, dispensational premillennialism, controversies over biblical inspiration and inerrancy, religious nationalism, the impact of the Russian Revolution, and the predominance of wealthy businessmen in the churches who wished to preserve the socioeconomic status quo are all factors that produced a fundamentalist subculture. In the years after World War I orthodox Christians were largely cut off from the mainstream of American life, and theological conservatism came more and more to be identified with political, economic, and social conservatism.

THE RELATIONSHIP EXPLOITED

This provided the basis for the apparent affinity between the far right and evangelical Christianity that exists today, and which the extremists are exploiting. For instance, the Glendale, California, "news analyst," William Steuart McBirnie, in late 1971 distributed to his radio audience a pamphlet entitled *How to Protect Your Young Person from Becoming a Communist*. It is an excellent example of the use of emotive language to frighten devout Christians into combating the all-pervasive conspiracy. McBirnie asserts that since the Reds know that the United States must be taken, they make their ideology attractive to American young people. Christian parents must begin early in life to indoctrinate their children against this alien ideology by teaching patriotism and love of country. Communism is a grave danger, since 54 percent of the college students now prefer to surrender to the Soviet Union if that would avert a world war.

McBirnie recommends to parents the following methods for safeguarding young people from Communism:

1. Provide a firm religious foundation by giving them "solid training in *fundamental* Christianity. The social gospel is of no help because it is "willing and even eager to compromise with all forms of collectivism." The children must learn that "true Christianity and communism are irreconcilable," as godlessness and the destruction of religion is basic to Communist doctrine.

2. Make the young people aware of the "brutality of communists," since their school instructors and textbooks mislead them into believing it is just "another political system."

3. Use every opportunity to expose Communist deception and show that the Soviet regime is as warlike and aggressive as ever. Although the Russians claim world peace is their goal, they simply have not bothered to use their army to conquer other countries because each one "has been taken by subversion from within, master minded by Russian agents planted within the country."

4. Teach the youth to believe in the superiority of the American way of life and give them ammunition to answer Communist arguments against this. Have them learn how American freedom is vastly superior to the Communist version of freedom, which is merely repression and regimentation, and that the free-enterprise system with its prosperity is far better than the controlled economy of the Soviet Union. Because "skilled advocates of atheism and treason" go around college campuses delivering emotional, obscene harangues against morality and reason, and their ideas are "reinforced by the lectures of extreme left wing professors advocating treason," young people must be prepared to defend American and Christian values against the onslaught of these radicals seeking to win them as recruits for the revolutionary cause.

It is easy to dismiss this as the ranting of an irresponsible extremist on the fringes of evangelical Christianity, but the truth is that these ideas frequently filter through to the mainstream. Two examples should suffice to make this clear. A faculty member at a leading Bible institute, an educational institution that has not been associated with the far right, recently published an essay about preserving the nation's freedom. Comparing the current situation with that of the time of Nehemiah, he argued that the United States is plagued by adverse forces, namely, the Communists without and

111

"accommodators" within." Our deadliest enemies are not necessarily outside our borders, but within them—apathy toward moral disintegration, complacency in the face of increasing crime, indifference toward men who enter public office, corruption in high and low places, disloyalty to our country." The people of Cuba in 1958 said that loss of liberty could not happen there, and some Americans are saying the same thing now. However, only through self-discipline, vigilance, courage, and faith in God will it be possible to preserve American freedom.[21] This theologian's assessment of the nation's problems could hardly be distinguished from that of Billy James Hargis, Carl McIntire, or any other luminary of the Christian right.

In an article by the founder and general director of an interdenominational foreign mission society, a man highly regarded in evangelical circles, the question is raised: Who was the first Communist? The answer is Judas, who said that the anointing of Jesus by Mary at Bethany was waste and that the ointment should have been sold and given to the poor.

> Communism is the brain child of Satan. Judas was its first disciple. He betrayed and murdered Christ. Thousands of God's children have since been murdered by the followers of Judas. Thousands are dying as martyrs today by the hands of those who like Judas pretend to tolerate Christ, but in reality await their time to betray Him.
>
> The hammer and sickle of atheistic Communism rules one-third of the world. Its shadow moves swiftly across the remainder of Asia—and then—YOU ARE NEXT![22]

COMBATING CHRISTIAN RIGHTISM

Since Christian rightism is bound up with the parochial evangelical subculture, the believer concerned about the problem should first of all involve himself in the community at large. He must form friendships with people outside the ghetto of his church community and make an effort to understand their doctrines, presuppositions, and practices. As

112

the Evangelical discovers how the ghetto mentality has shaped his own outlook on political and social issues, he will naturally begin rethinking the rightist assumptions that he hitherto had regarded as inherently Christian. This may well be a traumatic experience because many of his evangelical brethren are quite hostile to those who question rightist tenets.

Journalism professor Dixon Gayer aptly remarked that the apostles of the far right have learned an important truth: "If you wrap yourself tightly in the flag, if you carry a Bible, and if you protest your opposition to Communism, you can advocate almost any cause with confidence, and those who disagree with your cause soon find themselves accused of standing against the church and the country and in favor of communism." [23] It will, therefore, not be easy to break out of the shell of the American Christian subculture, but it is the only way that one can become an effective witness for Jesus Christ in today's world.

Moreover, the Christian needs to recognize the social sources of rightism. Several studies have shown that socioeconomic status plays more of a determining role in political conservatism than religious beliefs. For instance, Raymond E. Wolfinger and associates found that the participants in an "Anti-Communism School" sponsored by the Christian Anti-Communism Crusade in Oakland, California, in 1962 were "predominantly an upper-status group" in occupation, family income, and education. They concluded that the crusade's appeal was "to the well educated and well-to-do."

Fred Grupp's 1965 survey of the John Birch Society discovered that the percentage of members drawn from high-status business and professional ranks, as well as those having family incomes over $10,000, were more than twice the national average for whites. Furthermore, two-thirds of those who indicated a Protestant church affiliation identified with "liberal" denominations.

James McEvoy's study of early Goldwater supporters revealed that a significantly smaller number were associated with "pietistic Protestant" and "neo-fundamentalist denominations" than the traditionally high-status "Reformation Protestant" churches. The trait of religious fundamentalism was not disproportionately present among the early Goldwater backers, but middle and upper middle-class social status was. [24]

Ralph Lord Roy's comment about the theological stance of many rightists is most appropriate. According to him, "Many important and affluent figures on the Far Right are exceedingly liberal theologically. Biblical literalism, for example, and such doctrines as the vicarious atonement of Christ play no part in their thinking." [25]

These findings reveal that the radical right has just as strong an appeal to the secular, indifferent type of Christian as to the devout, and they open to serious doubt the popular notion that religious and political conservatism are inherently related. However, since those of higher socioeconomic status generally occupy the most important posts in the churches and evangelical agencies and schools, they are in a position to make their influence felt. Thus, the organizations they control often adopt right-wing stances that reflect their patrons' socioeconomic class interests, and believers, aware of this fact, must be prepared to resist such unchristian subversion by the wealthy.

An excellent example of the insidious nature of the dominance of evangelical institutions by secular Christians is the manner in which some religiously oriented colleges seek to capitalize on rightist ideology. The record of Bob Jones University in this respect is well known, but a Church of Christ leader reported recently that at least three schools identified with his denomination also "found a hawkish, ultra-pro-American stance invaluable for fund-raising, recruitment, and community relations." A staff member at one institution openly admitted that generous gifts from conservative donors who were impressed with its right-wing position "have enabled us to build most of our plant."

Another college adopted an official policy statement which declared: "It is the duty of every citizen, under the sovereignty of God . . . to defend the nation against all its enemies." The same school in April, 1971, observed "Freedom Preservation Week" and brought in General William C. Westmoreland to dedicate a new building. After a speech by the general uncritically defending the army's record in Vietnam, the enthusiastic audience was treated to a performance by the college's a cappella chorus—a musical tribute to the country's fighting men, during which a spotlight illuminated a huge American flag suspended over the stage. [26]

The radical right also exploits and harms Christianity. Anti-Communist crusades and schools drain off resources which could be better used for the spreading of the gospel and helping the poor and needy. Innumerable well-meaning Christian people have been bilked out of money by right-wing evangelists with their impassioned appeals for funds. Further, extreme rightism tends to do the greatest damage at the grass-roots level. The national government can ignore the prophets of doom (for example, President Nixon's visit to China), but in a local congregation, service club, school board, or PTA a small band of radical rightists can exercise a great deal of negative influence.

Rightism serves as a false gospel which detracts from the real ministry of the church. Ted Ward correctly observes that the communication of Christianity as anti-Communism is a "confusing secondary message that weighs down the primary message of the gospel. . . . Could we be so busy communicating anti-Communism 'on behalf of Christ' that to the desperate farmer in India, the oppressed peasant in Greece, and the black man in the Union of South Africa we seem to have nothing to offer?" [27] To link the faith with the status quo means that a man may come to Christ without

115

experiencing a genuine life transformation. Latin American student leader Samuel Escobar comes right to the heart of the matter when he declares:

> Our gospel is false if it leads us to believe that after an encounter with Christ, after conversion, the property owner continues to do whatever he feels like doing with his property; the capitalist stops smoking or being an adulterer but goes on exploiting his workmen; the policeman distributes New Testaments to his prisoners but continues to apply physical or mental means of extracting their confessions. 28

The concerned Christian will do all he can to resist the right-wing extremists because their activities not only harm the ministry of the gospel but also their teachings are at cross purposes with biblical religion. Biblical Christianity stresses humanitarianism, selfless love, and an active concern for others. The far right, consciously or not, emphasizes selfish individualism and ignores economic and social justice. The Christian recognizes that freedom is not absolute; for one thing, Christ does not allow him the option of racial prejudice. The right-wing conservative seems to feel that the purpose of man's existence is to acquire wealth and property and to do as he pleases with it; the Christian knows that all things belong to God, and he has the obligation to practice good stewardship. The rightist glorifies the nation and its symbols and virtually deifies them; the Christian holds that allegiance to an earthly kingdom is qualified by that to a higher one. 29 The Evangelical must say that the practice of the right to baptize the status quo and place it above criticism is totally unacceptable. To link the faith with economic individualism, anti-Communism, or American nationalism is idolatry, plain and simple, and the Evangelical must acknowledge this without equivocation.

Finally, the Evangelical must confess that the Christian radical right has sold out to forces that wish to destroy

America. The extremists are closely tied to the military-industrial complex, and the danger is always present that direct action may someday be taken to squelch the advocates of peace, civil rights, and social justice in the United States. There is great potential for a fascist revolution in this country, and the hatred and suspicion unleashed by the radical right can only serve to abet this tendency.

Methodist theologian Franklin Littell contends that the United States may be moving into the preliminary stages of a church struggle much like that which tested Christians in Germany during the Third Reich. He argues that groups like the Church League of America are counterparts to the "German Christians" who collaborated with the Nazis and the "League of Progressive Catholics" who currently collaborate with the Communist regime in Poland. The radical right's function is to provide "cover" for the conspirators who plan to slay the "godless" and seize power. The covert forms which their violence now takes "herald the final conflict toward which they work, when violence and destruction may become overt and unrestrained." [30]

The devout Christian must have no part of the radical right. His faith does not obligate him to work hand-in-glove with rightists and, in truth, an alliance with them can only harm Christianity. Armed with the understanding that far rightism is a doctrine espoused above all by those who wish to preserve their own social and economic status and whose selfish interests take precedence over the basic principles of both American democracy and biblical Christianity, the dedicated Evangelical is prepared to take his stand. He knows the liberal accusation that his faith and rightist ideology are indissolubly linked is invalid, and he needs only to separate himself from those alien teachings that have become identified with conservative Christianity because of the development of an unbiblical subculture. [31]

Christians should discontinue giving money to rightists, refuse to support their meetings and publications, and expel

117

them from their churches. A resounding defeat of the Christian right would be a giant step toward elimination of the cancer of the radical right from the American body politic. Evangelicals must act *now* to purge their ranks of this barrier to the spread of the gospel. Tomorrow may be too late!

7

Christian Racism

UPDATING AN OLD STORY

"Some white Christians find it hard to worship with other races. They may close their churches to others." "Brothers in Christ stand equal in God's sight." "We sin if we say that we are more valuable than other Christians."

When statements like these appeared in the youth quarterly of a major denomination recently, distribution of the issue was halted and the offensive quotations were labeled as "subject to misinterpretation" and "potentially inflammatory." "The material promotes integration in churches, and this is not our job," said one spokesman for the denomination. [1]

There is reason to believe that such attitudes and behavior may be found in decreasing proportions within the Christian community. However, much remains to be done before the goal of eliminating Christian racism will have been achieved. It is still possible to read news reports of a Christian grammar school refusing to admit black children whose parents are members of the same denomination and to find the administrator of that school "too busy seeing that our children get a good Christian education to worry about these things." An excellent illustration of this is the controversy which arose over the Timothy Christian Schools in Cicero, Illinois. [2]

119

Frequently one hears of the dismissal of pastors who insist upon allowing black Christians to join the church. For example, in 1966 the Tatnall Square Baptist Church in Macon, Georgia, ousted its ministers because they favored racially integrated worship, and more recently the pastor and many members of the First Baptist Church of Birmingham resigned in protest against the decision of a segregationist majority to refuse admission to blacks. [3]

A recent nationwide survey of racial attitudes conducted by the University of Michigan's prestigious Institute for Social Research found that only 56 percent of the white Protestants interviewed favored interracial contact. A still smaller proportion were aware of racial discrimination toward blacks, and only half saw the need for improvement of conditions for blacks. Moreover, 56 percent of these white Protestants opposed civil rights legislation and 64 percent were unsympathetic toward black protest marches.[4] The following table summarizes the attitudes of whites who indicated a religious affiliation in the institute's survey:

Shows little awareness of discrimination against blacks.

Baptist	55%	Episcopal	36%
Methodist	52%	Catholic	40%
Lutheran	43%	Jewish	24%
Presbyterian	44%	No affiliation	23%

Problems of blacks are their own fault.

Baptist	70%	Episcopal	34%
Methodist	64%	Catholic	65%
Lutheran	65%	Jewish	41%
Presbyterian	67%	No affiliation	41%

Believes whites have right to maintain segregated neighborhoods.

Baptist	40%	Episcopal	15%
Methodist	36%	Catholic	32%
Lutheran	34%	Jewish	18%
Presbyterian	33%	No affiliation	15%

Would mind having black of same status move next door.

Baptist	40%	Episcopal	43%
Methodist	54%	Catholic	51%
Lutheran	48%	Jewish	32%
Presbyterian	57%	No affiliation	22%

Has no black friend living in the same city.

Baptist	41%	Episcopal	34%
Methodist	27%	Catholic	37%
Lutheran	45%	Jewish	44%
Presbyterian	43%	No affiliation	28%

Has no regular friendly contact with blacks.

Baptist	37%	Episcopal	31%
Methodist	25%	Catholic	33%
Lutheran	42%	Jewish	37%
Presbyterian	40%	No affiliation	25%

Prefers white friend of different status to black friend of same status.

Baptist	63%	Episcopal	60%
Methodist	62%	Catholic	66%
Lutheran	64%	Jewish	57%
Presbyterian	40%	No affiliation	40%

Prefers children to have only white friends.

Baptist	43%	Episcopal	25%
Methodist	38%	Catholic	37%
Lutheran	36%	Jewish	28%
Presbyterian	40%	No affiliation	16%

Believes blacks are "pushing too fast".

Baptist	74%	Episcopal	69%
Methodist	70%	Catholic	71%
Lutheran	70%	Jewish	58%
Presbyterian	71%	No affiliation	42%

Believes protest marches by blacks are not justified.

Baptist	41%	Episcopal	22%
Methodist	38%	Catholic	33%
Lutheran	29%	Jewish	14%
Presbyterian	25%	No affiliation	18%

Opposes Civil Rights legislation.

Baptist	25%	Episcopal	30%
Methodist	34%	Catholic	28%
Lutheran	30%	Jewish	11%
Presbyterian	19%	No affiliation	16%

Sees "get tough" policy as best solution to urban riots.

Baptist	52%	Episcopal	42%
Methodist	50%	Catholic	53%
Lutheran	55%	Jewish	36%
Presbyterian	53%	No affiliation	36%

Average for the 12 items listed above.

Baptist	50%	Episcopal	37%
Methodist	46%	Catholic	46%
Lutheran	47%	Jewish	33%
Presbyterian	44%	No affiliation	27%

Statistics such as these dramatically testify to the racism found among Christians today. What has happened to the message of "love and brotherhood" in a church where half the members resent a black moving next door while less than one-fourth of those who claim no religious affiliation express such resentment? Do the words of "Jesus Loves the Little Children" ring true in the ears of children whose parents prefer that they have only white playmates? Or shall we assume that those church members who express this preference do not know the words of the chorus?

If one follows the daily activities of the white church member, he will find that his behavior with respect to other races hardly differs from that of the larger white population. Surveys of racially changing areas show that the composition and ownership of churches follow a pattern similar to that of residential dwellings. It is both interesting and enlightening to hear Christians pray for God's help in carrying out a transaction involving the sale of church property as they join the flight before blacks in quest of living space.

It is certainly logical that white Christians would want to leave racially changing areas *if* property values fall as blacks move in and *if* Christians are motivated by economic interests. But there is reason to believe that the former *need not* and the latter *should not* be true. Christians should not be criticized for expressing the attitudes reported in the Institute for Social Research survey *if* principles of socialization account for human behavior. But Christians are supposed to be "new creatures" in Christ. They are not to live in conformity to the world, but rather, through the life-giving power of the Holy Spirit, they are expected to rise above the confining influence of their environment and culture (2 Co. 5:17; Ro. 12:1-2). As Billy Graham eloquently affirms: "Christ has taught the dignity of man and the possibility of the brotherhood of man in Himself. Whenever there is discrimination, Christ is at work with His sword cutting out hatred and intolerance. The Bible says plainly that God is no respecter of persons. This cuts across the theory of racial supremacy and makes all men equal in the sight of God." [5]

American blacks are profoundly aware that their white Christian brethren have little concern about their spiritual welfare. Just to cite an example of how deep-seated this consciousness is, a recent Harris Poll quoted in *Christianity Today* revealed that only 16 percent of American blacks felt white churches "really cared" about achieving racial equality. Trailing closely behind were realtors whom 14 percent of the blacks surveyed believed "really care." What a blazing indictment of white Christian racism! [6]

UNDERSTANDING THOSE THINGS WHICH PASSETH UNDERSTANDING

Perhaps we ought not be surprised to find this strange wedding of Christianity and racism because, after all, racism has had some rather definite practical advantages. America is itself a testimony of the benefits of such practices. It was through the institution of slavery that the agricultural foundation of the nation was laid and through a minimally modified system that the industrial superstructure was erected. The modern corporate giants would have been difficult to create under a system of racial and ethnic equality. To these economic advantages may be added the psychological satisfaction and sexual exploitation which are the concomitants of racism.

Given this situation, the existence of an alliance between Christianity and racism is not difficult to understand. If Christianity is the semiofficial religion in the land, and the Bible is the chief source of authority for Christians, they will naturally try to remove any cognitive dissonance or moral dilemma by reconciling that which is advantageous with that which is right. The classic example of such attempts is the late nineteenth-century work of Charles Carroll that sought to demonstrate empirically that "the Bible stands as an impregnable bulwark against the belief that all men, regardless of color, are blood brothers." [7]

Those who study the social origins of knowledge realize that the arts and sciences of any given period reflect the social conditions of that time. Theologians are not immune to the infectious trends that affect their contemporaries. It required little creativity, insight, or imagination to develop a theological justification for the social plight of blacks. The "Curse of Ham" (or Canaan) mentioned in Genesis 9 conveniently served to show that *God* had predestined the Middle Passage, the slave auction, the urban slums, and the current oppression and exploitation of black Americans. [8]

White Christians, in sheeplike fashion, accepted the racist interpretation without question. Indeed, it became fashionable, erudite, and sophisticated to be able to see the fulfilling of prophecy in the oppression of human beings. Theologians, ministers, and laymen alike, perhaps in the interest of injecting divine meaning into human affairs, seized upon passages like Acts 17:26 (God "hath made of one blood all nations of men for to dwell on the face of the earth, and hath determined the times before appointed, and the bounds of their habitation") as explanations for existing social arrangements. The notion that God demands a separation of nations and races fitted well into the current scheme of things. Simultaneously it provided satisfaction for economic social, psychological, and theological attitudes.

Scriptural material can be utilized in other ways to bolster racist thinking. It would be highly profitable to identify these methods so that Christians can be made aware of how a racist culture has shaped their own religious thinking. It virtually passes all understanding how Bible teachings so often are warped and twisted to fit into the racist mold. What are some of these? 9

ETHNOCENTRISM

It is clear that the biblical writers were conscious of ethnic differences. Ethnic identity replaces the use of surnames in the Bible as well as in ancient secular writings. "The Hittite," "the Egyptian" and "the Syrian" were terms that identified Uriah, Hagar, and Laban just as Graham, Agnew, and Hope identify Billy, Spiro, and Bob. However, when ethnic origin rather than family origin is the basis of identification, the probability of inaccurate association and stereotyping is increased.

Reading the Bible does more than simply create a consciousness of national origin. One becomes aware of a differential and unequal treatment of ethnic groups—and these distinctions are approved by God. Descendants of Abraham through Isaac and Jacob were accorded a special place in the plan of God. On the other hand, Abraham's heirs through Ishmael and those of Isaac through Esau, although not as highly regarded as those in the direct line, were favorably mentioned more often than those outside of the Abrahamic clan. The distribution of rights and privileges followed

125

these lines in an ethnocentric fashion. Moabites and Ammonites were forbidden to come into the congregation of Israel (Deu. 23:3), and the daughter of a Levite who married a stranger was not allowed to eat the offerings allocated to the Levites (Lev. 22:12).

SEPARATISM

Both the Old and New Testaments make clear distinctions between the people of God and "outsiders." It is usually indicated that their behavioral practices are different, and that those of God's people are better. Limitations are placed upon contact with those who are not part of the nation or church. Emphasis on the notions of separatism, sanctification, and superiority carries potential for a psychology of racism. The phrase "be ye not unequally yoked" (2 Co. 6:14) has frequently been used in the context of racial and ethnic relations.

LEGALISM

"Thou shalt" and "thou shalt not" are vital aspects of the Judeo-Christian ethic. To *obey* is fundamental to success and divine approval. The tendency to orient one's life rigidly to laws may encourage the Christian to become a social conservative or advocate of the status quo. Unfortunately, the cycle common to all human cultures of expedience, custom, consensus, law, and conformity has had racist consequences again and again throughout the course of history.

NATIONALISM

A legalistic orientation creates the potential for obedience to laws, regardless of whether they are just or unjust. The sense of responsibility toward one's nation makes all laws seem just. The Christian who is convinced that all rulers are "ordained of God" may carry the teaching of Romans 13 to such an extreme that he begins to deify national leaders and their dictates, without questioning whether or not they correspond to a higher law. Even if the regime's actions are patently racist and unjust, such a person retreats to a passive "we must obey the powers that be" stance. Invariably the result is a racist Christian in a racist society.

LITERALISM

Many leading biblical characters such as Abraham and Elijah were slaveholders, while the nation Israel was commanded (or at least permitted) to enslave other ethnic groups (Lev. 25:44-46; Deu. 20:14-15). In fact, the institution of slavery existed throughout scriptural history and it is difficult to find a clear statement denouncing the practice. The unsophisticated biblical literalist assumes that the subordination of man by men is part of the plan of God, and to question this would be tantamount to questioning the validity of Holy Scripture itself.

DOGMATISM

"To contend for the faith which was once for all delivered to the saints" (Jude 3, RSV) can cause a conservative outlook which opposes new and different ideas. This kind of thinking can be carried over into other areas of one's experience, producing a union of political, social and religious conservatism. Christians may thus find themselves resisting new social trends, even when these are in the direction of greater justice.

CALVINISM

The teaching of predestination, God's control of human affairs, may mean that one does not try to change his society. Existing conditions were brought about by the sovereign hand of God, and the future can be entrusted to that same process. This can very easily result in racist behavior, if not attitudes. The task of effecting change is abdicated in favor of a laissez-faire approach. The Christian simply goes along with the stream of events, assuming that change will take place when God so wills it and therefore it will be by divine action.

OVERREACTION

Many liberal Christians believe that their faith is nothing more than glorified social work. For this group, redemption is solely physical, social, and economic. Certain conservative Christians have overreacted to that approach by rejecting completely any significant participation in the effort to meet the temporal needs of humanity. This attitude is reflected in such statements as "The material promotes integration in churches and that is not our job," or "We are too busy seeing that our children get a good Christian education to worry about these things." These comments, cited at the beginning of this essay, are racist to the core, and they totally ignore the teaching of the Scriptures about ministering to the whole man.

AUTHORITARIANISM

Certain child-training practices lead to a kind of personality which is characterized by prejudice and ethnocentrism. 10 Persons who in their childhood develop distrust of others, a readiness to condemn people, ambiguity about self-worth, rigidity, and related traits tend also to be more prejudiced. Many of the traditional "Christian" child-rearing practices, such as a heavy emphasis on physical discipline and uncompromising moral training, produce authoritarian personalities.

MATERIALISM

The Christian church constantly inveighs against materialism by referring to "seek ye first the kingdom of God," "lay up treasures in heaven," and "life is more than food, and the body more than clothing" (Mt. 6:33; Lk. 12:21, 23). This can be viewed as a prescription against seeking earthly gain for one's weaker and poorer neighbor. At the same time, the Christian church has profited by the arrangement of things in America, which is testified to by the multimillion-dollar edifices, prosperous ministers, and comfortable congregations in so many places. Why be concerned about those with less means, especially if they are of another race?

UNTANGLING A TWISTED KNOT

Inevitably Christians must face the question of what they can do. Such a complex problem defies easy answers, and only the combined efforts of a great number of concerned individuals will bring about the effective elimination of racism, both inside and outside of the Christian community. One may begin by developing a strong sense of responsibility and commitment to dealing with the problem of racial justice. To casually dismiss one's need to become involved by saying, "I am not responsible for what my ancestors did to yours" will contribute nothing to solving the problem. What present-day white America—of which white Christianity is an integral part—must recognize is that we have inherited a set of life chances which has been built upon and sustained by exploitation of other races. Thus, those who control and benefit from the arrangements must take the first step toward remedying the situation.

Christians must recognize that there is a divine imperative which requires that racism be eliminated from the nation as well as from the church. It is at this point that Christianity can make a unique contribution. When the question is raised, "Why should racism be eliminated?" acceptable replies are few in number and slow in coming, as racism offers many advantages to those in white society. In a world where resources are limited, why should men not seek gain at the expense of others? If economics is the principle by which societies thrive, why should men have any regard for others? Let the strongest survive!

The response that a Christian must offer is that the economic principle is not *right*. Christianity teaches in no uncertain terms that men must live by moral principles. It is not *right*—it is immoral—that some individuals should seek gain, regardless of what the cost or harm is to others. By injecting the principle of morality, the disciple of Christ is then able to offer justification for compassion and concern for the man who otherwise has no legitimate means of demanding public attention. Only when Christians appeal to moral principles can they argue against the escalation of advantage and the jockeying for power among individuals and nations.

Moral pronouncement is the business of the church. Oddly enough, then, those matters that many Christians have labeled as "social" problems, namely, issues which lie outside of the sphere of Christian responsibility, may in fact find their most satisfying solutions coming from the church. Unfortunately, the organized body of Christ has been as much a part of the problem as other institutions in society. Before it can begin to make pronouncements as to what others must do, it must judge itself. As 1 Peter 4:17 instructs, judgment must begin at the house of God. But the task of converting the church into the vanguard for racial justice ought not to be as difficult as other organizations. The church is, in fact, a natural point of beginning. After all, what other institution has such universal appeal, since its membership is drawn from all ages, social classes, and occupational groups? In contrast, other associations reach only relatively small and carefully defined segments of the total population.

There is a solid biblical basis for an open fellowship. Galatians 3:28 reveals that in Christ there is neither Jew nor Greek, slave nor free, male nor female. Christians are all one in Christ Jesus. Again, Colossians 3:11 states: "Here there cannot be Greek and Jew, circumcised and uncircumcised, barbarian, Scythian, slave, free man, but

Christ is all, and in all." The rendition of Ephesians 2:14 in Today's English Version (*Good News for Modern Man*) is particularly compelling: "For Christ himself has brought us peace, by making the Jews and Gentiles one people. With his own body he broke down the wall that separated them and kept them enemies."

Those who fail to comprehend the truth of these passages must be dealt with patiently and at length. It is necessary that Christians be able to set forth rational and biblical justifications for the elimination of racist practices. One must be prepared to wrestle with and counteract attitudes and arguments like those mentioned earlier in the essay. For example, it is profoundly disappointing to discover that many Christians who reject the "curse of Ham" rationalization for racial discrimination are unable to counter this notion with a discussion of the favorable references to blacks in both biblical and secular materials. It is not enough to deny that the Bible is ethnocentric, or that "Christianity is color blind." Positive alternatives must be offered in the context of particular attitudes and circumstances.

Through the centuries the church has again and again been a positive force for social change. The church laid the foundation for current expressions of social concern by its long-established custom of caring for orphans, widows, the sick, and disabled. The working class has churches and individual Christians to thank (along with labor unions) for improvement in working hours and conditions. Those are issues and activities of the past. The challenge of racism now confronts the Christian. He must determine to meet and find solutions to this grave problem.

Where shall we begin? Columbus Salley and Ronald Behm do not hesitate to offer an answer to this perplexing problem: "De-honkify [de-whiten] your church: its curriculum, its investment and purchasing programs, its leadership and its attitudes." [11] The choice is ours. Dare we delay any longer?

8

Evangelism and Social Concern

THE COP-OUT FORMULA

Evangelicals have a long-standing formula for the proper relationship between evangelism and social concern. We insist that society's problems, caused by individual sinners, will be solved only when individuals are converted. We should therefore sidestep social symptoms and attack sin, the disease, by persuading men to accept Christ. When people have become Christians, or enough of them anyway, they will heal the ills of society.

This formula holds undeniable appeal, and not a little Christian truth. The cause of social maladies is accurately diagnosed. The cure is truly placed in the person and gospel of Jesus Christ. The responsibility of believers to relieve suffering is clearly seen. The only trouble with this impressive formula is that it can scarcely ever be seen to *work* among today's Evangelicals.

Is the problem quantitative—that there have not yet been enough conversions? Perhaps so, but there are more evangelical Christians in today's America than ever in history;

estimates run to over 40 million, a fifth of the population. First century Christians, who "turned the world upside down," worked with much humbler percentages. In the great resurgence of evangelism since World War II many millions of Americans have been converted to Christ. But where are our social fruits? Social problems are compounding more obviously than our involvement is increasing. Rare is the evangelical congregation whose loving service in its community is distinguishably superior to that of neighboring theologically liberal groups, or of the local Kiwanis Club, for that matter.

It is time to expose our honored formula for what it is— a tragic cop-out, in fact, an active hindrance to the fulfillment of Christian social responsibility. We are left off the hook while awaiting the supposed inevitable. Our conscience is relieved of obligation even to cooperate with non-Christian reformers, since their work is outside the formula and the faith. The problem, of course, is that new Christians do not automatically begin to fulfill a social stewardship, and that they are too typically left untaught in such stewardship by evangelists, pastors, and fellow laymen. Converts hear commonly a partial gospel, persuasively designed to perform midwifery duty only with a minimum of theological instruction.

The newborn spiritual babe is often left cooing in the lap of a church so obsessed with its evangelistic function that Christian growth is pursued and defined in terms of preparation for evangelistic witness. So the child grows and waxes as one-sided as a starboard galley slave, qualified to share a a milk-fed faith and to parrot the formula as an insincere evangelistic gimmick: "Society will be cured when men are saved!" And if the child of faith is gifted in it, and if his earnest efforts are blessed by the patient Spirit of Christ, yet other Christians will too casually enter the fold without the instructive opportunity of "counting the cost," as we used to say.

An Evangelical Theology of Social Concern: Principles Without Practice

While the evangelical church is much more knowledgeable in the theology of evangelism than in the doctrines of social witness, it is not as though we are without principles and precedents in this latter field. The full scriptural analysis of the social implications of the gospel is presented brilliantly in recent evangelical writings, beginning with Carl F. H. Henry's *The Uneasy Conscience of Modern Fundamentalism* in 1947. "For the first protracted period in its history," Henry declared, "evangelical Christianity stands divorced from the great social reform movements."[1] He went on to enunciate a biblical theology of social engagement, to show isolated, monastic fundamentalists the way back to a world in need. At the time, the work was considered dangerously controversial, but it proved to be a turning point in modern evangelical thought.

Henry's call for evangelical social concern has been echoed by other scholars, while Christian social principles have been applied in the careers of such men as Senator Mark Hatfield, Paul S. Rees, Tom Skinner, and Leighton Ford, and in evangelical ministries like World Vision, Inc. A repeated theme of all these witnesses is the complementary and harmonious union of evangelism and social concern; or, as Sherwood Wirt put it, "To pit social action against evangelism is to raise a phony issue, one that Jesus would have spiked in a sentence."[2] Jesus, in fact, once enclosed in just a sentence all His rich social teachings and examples with a general evangelistic mandate:

> Go then and make disciples of all the nations, baptize them into the name of the Father, the Son, and the Holy Spirit, and teach them to practice all the commands that I have given you (Mt. 28:19-20, Williams).

While it is wonderful to have the theory, it is distressing

135

to see so little *practice* of these principles among Evangelicals. The gap between theological insight and practical demonstration is a recurring problem throughout church history, but it was never more painful than during the quarter century since Henry's book appeared, a time of unprecedented and highly publicized social change and challenge. Without the benefit of significant evangelical involvement and correctives, the United States distributed vast sums in international aid, mounted a war on poverty, sustained a delicate diplomatic contest with the Soviet Union, participated in a nuclear arms race, created and enjoyed wealth and leisure beyond precedent, and fought two undeclared wars for well-meaning purposes but with highly destructive results.

Yet our public defections may be less crucial than our failures as individuals, families, and congregations to alleviate the human distress—material, physical, psychological, spiritual—in our own communities. How many of the millions of breakdowns, addictions, divorces, suicides, and crimes during these years might have been averted by strategic applications of Christian love on the part of Evangelicals? But our simplistic socio-evangelistic formula, our unbiblical dualism isolating spiritual from temporal concerns, walled off the resources of Christ from centers of need. One trembles even for the spiritual results of such evangelism, recalling James' criterion:

> My brothers, what good is there in a man's saying that he has faith, if he has no good deeds to prove it? Such faith cannot save him, can it? (Ja. 2:14, Williams).

Even as no generation of believers has perfectly reflected the Spirit of Christ, so none has achieved a full biblical balance of evangelism and good works. Yet Evangelicals of the 1970s are laboring under a heritage of withdrawal from human suffering which began a hundred years ago, intensified during the first third of this century, and reached its nadir sometime before 1950. The slight recovery of evangelical involvement since then has in large part paralleled a general social awakening in America. A selective look at recent church history may help to clarify issues and explain present problems and prospects.

EVANGELICAL SOCIAL ACTION IN ENGLAND: A MODEL FOR AMERICANS

Many date the beginnings of modern Evangelism with the Wesley-Whitefield revivals in England during the decades following 1740. This spiritual awakening and its sequels provide a most dramatic example of Christ-inspired social reform. The list of major public reforms achieved by those early Evangelicals is impressive. Slavery was judicially excluded from England in 1772, as was the slave trade in 1807, and slavery in the empire in 1833. All European slave trade was prohibited by 1831 through England's international pressures and negotiations. Much legislation was passed in the years after 1833 regulating the unspeakable conditions of labor in industrial England, particularly that of children and women. Major gains were made also in the treatment of the insane, prison conditions, public education, honesty in government, army sanitation and health, medical care for the poor, and temperance.

Earle E. Cairns, who has studied the matter in depth, names the many Evangelicals who were the primary promoters of each of the above projects. "Nowhere and at no time," he declares, "can such a large body of reform be credited to any group as the social reforms which were brought about by the leadership of the Clapham Sect and their loyal evangelical and Dissenter supporters in both the clergy and laity." [3]

On the face of it, all of this appears to authenticate that maligned formula—reform followed evangelism in orthodox sequence. There was also a considerable delay between cause and effect, with major advances occurring decades

137

after Wesley's death in 1791, and with Lord Shaftesbury still crusading in the 1880s. There were, however, two significant variations. First, John Wesley set an influential example for his ministers and successors by accompanying his evangelistic preaching with a careful enunciation of the social principles of the gospel, and by commenting regularly upon public issues in sermons and pamphlets. He was not himself concerned about all the above issues, and his major energies were given to evangelism and church administration, but his spiritual allies and descendants, many of whom specialized upon certain ministries or problems, extended and applied his principles.

Second, the evangelical reformers developed sophisticated political strategies and tactics designed to generate wide publicity and maximum public pressure upon the seats of power. These practical Christian works began with careful fact-gathering by educated leaders, and dissemination of information through books, pamphlets, magazines, billboards, mottoes, songs, and public meetings everywhere. Ministers preached kingdom principles, conducted days of prayer, counseled loving action. Individual laymen, many of them accustomed to study and witness and leadership in Methodist class meetings, wrote letters to newspapers, signed petitions, cooperated in boycotts (especially of products produced by slavery), and worked in parliamentary elections for reform candidates. Temporary alliances were struck with non-Christians working toward the same ends, most notably with Jeremy Bentham's utilitarians. The remarkable follow-up and sustained dedication of a number of evangelical statesmen *after their legislative goals were achieved* insured permanent results. [4]

That so much was accomplished at a time when a high proportion of evangelical laymen could not even vote was testimony to extraordinary leadership, coordinated effort, and inspired Christian motivation at every class level. The fact that the most influential leaders had no difficulty with theological heresy or spiritual defection and that they maintained their interest in evangelistic witness, indicts the current tendency to separate faith and social action. Certainly, with their larger numbers, wealth, and democratic opportunities, American Evangelicals could do far greater works than these.

AMERICAN EVANGELISM FROM FINNEY TO MOODY: DECLINING SOCIAL CONCERN

Among American evangelists, Charles Grandison Finney most nearly approached the pattern of Wesley and the English Evangelicals. During the decade (1824-34) of his spectacular itinerant evangelism in the Northeast, he stressed social issues, especially temperance and abolition. His great successes, for example, in Rochester, New York, in 1830-31 where widespread conversions resulted in the closing of taverns, convinced him that revival alone would solve social problems. Let Christians go all out and expose slavery as "SIN!" he said in 1835, "and in three years, a public sentiment would be formed that would carry all before it, and there would not be a shackled slave, nor a bristling, cruel slavedriver in this land."5 However, he underestimated the complexity and tenacity of the social and political problems, and the need for direct organizational and political action. Although Finney did not consistently support the widespread American reform movement of the 1830s through the 1850s which his ministry had helped to launch, yet he joined social education to evangelism as no other major American has done.

Widespread evangelistic activity accompanied continued reform campaigns to the eve of the Civil War, culminating in the socially fruitful layman's revival that broke out in Eastern cities in 1858. Unfortunately, the Civil War and its aftermath saw a narrowing evangelical involvement in social reform. Many Evangelicals gave themselves too fully to the furies of that struggle, seeing it as a proud righteous crusade rather than a national tragedy and a divine judgment, as in Lincoln's discerning view. The postwar momentum of morally obtuse patriotism permitted most Christians to remain on the sidelines while the orientation of blacks to freedom and security was botched and betrayed in the so-called "Reconstruction" period and after. American evangelical abolitionists lacked the vigilant follow-through of their English brethren.

The triumphant, industrial Northeast, enjoying enor-mous business growth and political power after the war, presided over the most ruthless economy and corrupt state and federal governments the country has ever known. The period of 1865 to 1900 was a time in American history when the views and public actions of creative Christians were desperately needed. Unfortunately, the environment over-powered the faith, and the materialism of the time fastened itself upon both Evangelicals and evangelists. Also, the theo-logically liberal threats posed by higher critics, evolutionists, and students of comparative religion consumed much of the attention and energy of Evangelicals.

To be sure, they decried political corruption, assisted in the prohibition and feminist movements, and served in city rescue missions and the YMCA. Their most impressive social ministry, however, occurred overseas in medical missions and education which accompanied and stimulated evangel-ism. Far from fulfilling hostile stereotypes, American missionaries generally have been much more socially sensi-tive and active than their homeland supporters. Evangel-icals at home showed little more compassion than the rest of the complacent American establishment for those in need: Negroes, American Indians, immigrants, slum dwel-lers, and workers (including women and children) who suffered from long hours, low pay, and unsafe working conditions. Dwight L. Moody, the major evangelist from 1873 to his death in 1899, was a child of his socially apa-thetic time. Although he had experience working among the poor of Chicago early in his career, he came to identify with business interests and with the political and economic status quo. 6

BILLY SUNDAY AND THE PROFESSIONALIZATION OF EVANGELISM

Billy Sunday, Moody's successor after 1910 as America's best-known evangelist, appeals to some historians as a worthy if less dignified descendant of Finney in his concern for civic reform. Yet his vigorous attacks upon liquor merchants and fleshly urban sins obscured his silence concerning the oppressive policies of some of the industrial tycoons who supported him. His superficial hand-shaking, card-signing criteria for conversion may have made for impressive statistics, but they hardly produced the serious Christians demanded by the times. Like Moody, Sunday stressed a view of the second coming of Christ which implied that since in the last days "evil men and seducers shall wax worse and worse" (2 Ti. 3:13), it was no use giving one's energies to the hopeless task of reforming a doomed society.

Sunday publicly denounced theologically liberal Social Gospellers, most notably Washington Gladden. Their acrimonious exchanges during 1912-13 added an emotionally combative dimension to the Modernist-Fundamentalist struggle which the publication of the more scholarly *Fundamentals* had not done three years before. 7 Also, in popularizing a simplistic ethic of "thou shalt nots," and in preaching anti-intellectualism, Sunday contributed more than anyone else to the fundamentalist program of withdrawal from American society.

Billy Sunday and his many imitators left another unfortunate legacy to modern Evangelicals—they completed the professionalization of public evangelism. The evangelist became known as an attractive personality with gifts for entertaining oratory, a man who offers spectacular sermon topics and simplified explanations of deep Christian truths, and who creates a moving atmosphere conducive to decision. His coming to a congregation or community was associated with a certain style of preparation, advertising, schedule and financing, and people expected a particular kind of service and music and invitation. Fortunately many evangelists, divinely called to their work and spiritually prepared for it, have been able to minister effectively through this pattern and some have even departed imaginatively from it.

There are dangers, however, when a calling is reduced to a stereotype. Often the overpowering demands of method and expectation act to reduce the message to subbiblical proportions. "Converts" are robbed of an honest confrontation with the gospel because of the emotional tensions produced by crowd-manipulation techniques. Yet a natural or cultivated mastery of such methods is highly valued in evangelical circles, and this is often considered tantamount to an evangelistic calling. Most sincere undergraduates at Christian colleges and Bible schools from the 1920s through the 1950s seriously considered whether they were called to evangelize. Since many mistook ability and social pressure for a genuine call, the total ministry suffered. As one talented sophomore trumpeter said to a colleague of mine in the 1950s, in unwitting betrayal of his secularism, "I've got to learn to tell a story and give an invitation. It'll be my bread and butter!"

Many pastors, responding to revivalistic pressures, pattern their ministry after evangelists. They preach primarily for initial Christian decision, thus denying their congregations the careful biblical exposition that inspires Christlikeness. Few are as candid, however, as the pastor with a flair for evangelism who once declared: "I preach evangelistically because it takes so much less time to prepare!" Such ministers sometimes feel forced to schedule flashy and superficial professional evangelists in order to impress jaded congregations accustomed to a steady revivalistic diet.

One need not stamp evangelists with a hypocritical Elmer Gantry image to point out that the demands of public evangelism provide powerful temptations to violate basic Christian principles. The acclaim that goes with being a celebrity can glut an ego, which is fed further by the self-display and domineering ways that often confirm one's reputation as a "pulpit personality." Preoccupation with statistical "results" and dramatic illustrations tempts the evangelist to twist the truth; "evangelistic exaggeration" is a tragically unfunny evangelical byword. The combination of hero worship, hotel living, emotional drain, and long absences from home, offers temptations that most evangelists resist, but occasionally it does end in moral tragedy. Such a system demands careful scrutiny as to its effects, spiritual success and failure, and relationship to biblical principles of witness and evangelism.

The formalized suprascriptural methodology detracts from the message, and results in the preaching of a truncated gospel. With everything focused upon atmosphere and decision, the convert's responsibility to live a creative life of love in this world is omitted. Even the "results" for which the whole process exists are ambiguous, due to the fog of mythology created to justify the methods. Because many Evangelicals are converted through public evangelism, they automatically assume that it is highly successful. But what of the multitudes who could not be lured into a service, and other non-Christians who were repelled by these stylized culture patterns and gospel additives?

It is obvious, though seldom stated, that the evangelistic methods exist primarily for the benefit of our children, who are acculturated in evangelical ways. But this sort of tribalism—reminiscent of the Puritan New England halfway covenant, which gave the offspring of the elect a better chance at grace than the children of the unchurched—is something less than dynamic New Testament evangelism. Christians were never intended to keep the gospel in the family, nor to surrender their privilege of evangelistic witness to specialists.

BILLY GRAHAM'S INCONSISTENT BUT GROWING
SOCIAL WITNESS

Billy Graham, the contemporary heir of the Finney-Moody-Sunday tradition, clearly avoids the worst expressions of evangelistic professionalization. Graham's theology of social engagement goes much deeper than the simplistic formula that social change automatically follows conversion, although it is possible to ridicule his early statements on public affairs as naive and uninformed. Even today Graham, who is addicted to the language of crisis and superlative, has problems with his pronouncements on social issues. Many of his supporters are from time to time shocked by statements such as his offhand plug for American individualism in the Oakland crusade, televised in September, 1971. "Kill your own rats!" he advised the poor. "We had rats when I was growing up and we killed our own rats. We didn't ask the federal government to come in and do it." [8] How far the North Carolina dairy is from the Harlem ghetto!

Even more disconcerting is the fact that Graham permits himself to be used for partisan political purposes. Since 1955 he has appeared on the annual Gallup Poll list of the world's top ten "most admired men," and has been in the number two spot for the last three years. [9] Because of this he is actively courted by politicians, most notably Richard Nixon. Many observers think Graham's decision to feature Nixon in the nationally televised Pittsburgh crusade shortly before the 1968 election was a crucial factor in the Republican victory. [10] Such personal public involvement where Christian principles were not obviously at issue — after all, the dormant Quaker ran on a platform quite similar to that of the inactive member of the United Church of Christ — was an unfortunate misuse of power that would compromise Graham's influence on truly crucial issues. The apostle Paul's admonition to "stop forming intimate and inconsistent relations with unbelievers" (2 Co. 6:14, Williams) would seem to be directly violated by the evangelist's readiness to yoke himself to party purposes.

Despite all disappointments, the honest analyst must conclude that the important thing about Billy Graham is *not* the fact that he has been deeply affected by the socially negative aspects of his fundamentalist heritage. His significance lies rather in the fact that he has been leagues ahead of nearly all his evangelical brethren in both the principles and practice of social involvement. "We as Christians have two responsibilities," he writes in a typical statement. "One, to proclaim the Gospel of Jesus Christ as the only answer to man's deepest needs. Two, to apply as best we can the principles of Christianity to the social conditions around us." [11] As his social conscience and understanding developed, Graham has preached on a growing variety of social issues. For example, in 1967 he testified in Washington in favor of the "Great Society" poverty program, acknowledging that originally he was against it. [12] He still avoids certain social concerns thought to be "liberal," but he shows a capacity for honest self-criticism and growth, and hopefully he may yet come to rival Finney and Wesley in social as well as evangelistic fruitfulness.

Graham's greatest social ministry is undoubtedly his early and sustained efforts to combat racism. Consider the record in the 1950s of this man of conservative Southern background, when many of his present critics as well as supporters had not learned the ABC's of racial concern. Long uneasy about the segregated seating required in most Southern meetings, he had always refused to segregate his invitations, insisting, "The ground is level at the foot of the cross!" [13]

After careful study of biblical principles regarding race, he opened his first deliberately integrated Southern crusade at Chattanooga on March 15, 1953, more than a year before the Supreme Court decision on school integration, and more than a decade before the more directly applicable

Civil Rights Act of 1964. Professor Samuel Southard goes so far as to argue that "evangelism has been the major break through the ecclesiastical screen of silence" on the question of integration in the South, and he cites the activities of Graham in race relations as proof that evangelism is not necessarily in opposition to social action. [14]

During the 1950s over half (19 out of 34) of Graham's American crusades were held in the Southern states, even as racial tensions increased. He repeatedly criticized Jim Crow laws, offered biblical admonitions to both races, and appealed to all to accept the Christ who would empower them to love. He spoke on this theme before many denominational conferences in the South and privately to religious leaders of both races, counseling moderation and advocating an end to all public segregation. [15]

In October, 1956, *Life* published the first of Graham's several national articles applying Christian principles to racial problems. His courageous stand in that piece contrasts dramatically with the suspicious fears expressed by other Evangelicals in a symposium on the subject in the very same issue. [16] In 1957 Graham added a Negro associate evangelist, Howard O. Jones, to his team and another, Ralph Bell, in the early 1960s. Also, black musicians assist regularly in his meetings. Graham's fourteen crusades throughout Africa in 1960 gave worldwide publicity to his Christian program for race relations, and set precedents for public integration in some countries. [17] The impact of this reconciling socio-evangelistic ministry cannot be measured, but it carries an unmistakable prophetic air and savors of the Spirit of Christ.

Some believe that Graham's best prospects for a distinctive social ministry are through his chief associate evangelist, Leighton Ford. Ford's address, "Evangelism in a Day of Revolution" electrified delegates to the U. S. Congress on Evangelism in Minneapolis in September, 1969. He articulated a sound biblical union of social concern and evangelism on a more urgent and inspirational level than has yet been achieved. Rejecting the notion that conversion automatically produces social saints, he called for emphases upon Christian growth and social responsibility. Also, Ford's messages over Graham's "Hour of Decision" radio program serve as excellent scriptural models of a combined challenge to accept Christ and then, with new power and motivation, begin to confront specific problems in the world.

CONTEMPORARY EVANGELISTS AND SOCIAL ISSUES: 85 QUESTIONNAIRES

A questionaire on social issues filled out recently by eighty-five American evangelists revealed heroic struggles toward full-orbed social awareness amid persisting fundamentalist misgivings. [18] Several of the respondents, to be sure, thought and ministered in terms of the "formula," including one man who declared he never brought "such things as race problems, ecology, housing, etc., to the pulpit." People were weary of such things, he said, and he doubted the biblical grounds for that sort of preaching anyway. Not that this man *omits* socio-political issues from the pulpit; he advised his hearers to vote against John Kennedy in 1960, "frequently" denounces in public social sins such as pornography, and often urges congregations to be patriotic and loyal citizens. In other words, with like-mined evangelists, he confines his social ministry to issues popular with today's "silent majority."

Many such questions, of course, are entirely proper matters for Christian concern. The average response to a list of sixty-one current socio-political issues supported this extreme example to some extent, showing little concern about such "liberal" items as the military-industrial complex, the far right, and the cost of elections. Several problems usually perceived by socio-political conservatives, on the other hand, were generally considered very serious, including crime, marijuana use, abuse of welfare programs by recipients, Communism in America, black violence, and the rebellion of youth.

With a different selection of responses, however, it is possible to conclude that a genuine social awakening is under way. No less than 86 percent of the evangelists considered "evangelical apathy on social problems" to be either an "extremely serious" or "moderately serious" problem, as opposed to the one other option, "not serious." And certain "liberal" matters *did* rate as deeply important, including housing for the needy, hunger among the poor, and racial discrimination against blacks, Indians, and Chicanos. Then, too, some stereotyped "conservative" complaints scored low, such as antireligious court decisions, hypercriticism of the United States, and the erosion of capitalism.

Many evangelists seem to be breaking free from traditional socio-political alignments and are beginning to apply biblical principles to a wider range of social ills. Further, 29 percent of the evangelists "frequently" encourage congregations and groups of Christians to take public stands on social problems, and to work together in solving them. Another 55 percent do this "occasionally," with only 16 percent "never" urging such corporate action.

In answer to the question, "Do you find that bringing social concerns into evangelistic preaching increases or decreases the response of non-Christians to the Gospel?" a solid 59 percent declared "increases," with only 9 percent clearly negative. Some qualified their positive response, like an Oregon Quaker who observed: "People seem interested in solving social problems but are not too anxious to see personal disobedience to God resolved." "Some are offended," wrote Leighton Ford, but "increasing numbers, especially youth and young adults, seem to be attracted." Several contended unbelievers consider that a clear expression of social concern in an evangelistic appeal authenticates the message and makes it credible and appealing. A Christian Reformed pastor-evangelist reported that "when the gospel is brought to bear both with message and action on . . . life 'in need,' " a positive response often follows. Also, some people are service-motivated before conversion. A Church of Christ representative affirmed that he knew some people who at the time of conversion "were as much concerned about using their life to promote good as they were about personal salvation."

In response to the question whether American evangelists today stress social teachings more or less than twenty years ago, 77 percent voted "more," and 9 percent "less." Many explanations for this new social emphasis reflected refreshing candor. "The sad thing," wrote an Indiana American Baptist, "is that it may be because we are forced." Others agree that the pressures of new and intensifying urban problems, or "changing times and youth's social concerns," as Presbyterian Robert B. Munger put it, all leave the evangelist no alternative but to speak to the conditions of the age. An Assemblies of God district superintendent from Kansas added that social references are becoming "popular and expected. The larger crowds demand it." And Leighton Ford courageously exposed a delicate irony: "God has shamed us by the deep concern of humanists and unbelievers for those in need."

These external influences have been accompanied by an authentic rethinking and biblical criticism of inherited ideas and methods. Professor-evangelist Roy P. Clark of George Fox College poignantly summed up the issues and the process:

> The tragic realization that the evangelical church is still largely segregated, still steeped in traditionalism . . ., and has largely ignored the moral tragedy of war and militarism, is pathetically divided over non-essentials while apathetic to human need—this has given us cause for deep heart-searching.

The results of these questionnaires read movingly and testify to the capacity of a large sampling of leading evangelists for humble, healthy growth in Christlikeness. Many have related a spiritual Odyssey which began with the fundamentalist idea that in conversion "one swallowed some kind of big spiritual capsule that solved all of life's problems," as one evangelist of the Missionary Church put it. Then came the buffetings of life, the needs of people, and a new awareness of scriptural imperatives, all of which was part of their reeducation. This exciting process is continuing, and not all have reached identical or final conclusions. "I am convinced that the Gospel is radically social," asserted veteran Inter-Varsity Christian Fellowship staffer Paul Byer, speaking for the vanguard:

> *i. e.*, it commands the believer to take a new social position with all men. And if this is not done there is reason to question if the person has heard and is acting on the Word of God preached in the Gospel. . . . Actually I'm now convinced biblically, that not to teach the application of Christ's life and death to life is *not* to preach the Gospel.

Bruce Larson, creative head of Faith at Work, collided even more directly with "formula" preaching: "Years ago I believed that you only change a man's heart and then changed men change society," he wrote. "Now I see it is a both/and! Changed society can also help change men's hearts."

Following Jesus in Evangelism and Social Action

The socio-evangelistic opportunities of the 1970s require a revival of Christlikeness that will unlock resources of insight, motivation and faithfulness. Such revival will not come without a new emphasis upon the neglected message of the Spirit-filled life, one that is "hid with Christ in God" (Col. 3:3). Unfortunately, the doctrine of sanctification has often been distorted through controversies over theoretical points or charismatic gifts. We need to follow the command, "Ever be filled with the Spirit" (Eph. 5:18, Williams) by a continuing consecration and faith, permitting God to act sovereignly upon us, releasing love through our lives. Baptist Bernard Ramm has put it well, bridging the old Calvinist-Arminian contention:

> Every Christian takes two looks at the cross. In the *first look* we see Christ dying for us, for our salvation, for our justification, for our redemption. In the *second look* we see ourselves dying with Christ for our sanctification. 19

This continuing relationship fits us for deepening fellowship and identification with Jesus Christ and empowers us to follow His example. The Lord repeatedly urged that we do this, and He even promised that our works would surpass His. In one instance, especially meaningful for present purposes, He combined an invitation to discipleship with a promise to produce evangelists: "Follow me, and I will make you fishers of men" (Mt. 4:19). What does it mean to follow Jesus in light of combined evangelistic and social responsibilities?

Let us follow Jesus, first, in His careful differentiation between doctrine and tradition. Jesus quoted Isaiah in indicting His contemporary fundamentalists, the Pharisees, for "teaching for doctrines the commandments of men" (Mk. 7:7). Conservative Protestants have an unerring eye for the suprabiblical rituals and dogmas of high-church and Roman Catholic groups, but are blind to their own accretions. The policies, methods, and attitudes of every evangelical church and organization, which are sometimes held as precious and inviolable as the faith, deserve periodic review in the light of Scripture and a changing world.

Have we conditioned ourselves to be hostile to the "liberal" old-line denominations and their "deluded" members? Applying love to our unChristlike attitude, we will be surprised by the opportunities for fellowship with true "renewed" Christians, cooperation in worthy projects, and fruitful ideas for worship and ministry.

Have we habitually avoided the social side of Christian education? Annual thematic Bible studies and discussion of such books as David Moberg's *Inasmuch* would begin to restore balance.

Have our churches traditionally remained on the political sidelines except for "safe" conservative issues? Biblical injunctions against materialism, injustice, racism, and pride of status deserve new emphasis, and this would result in significant individual involvement as well as congregational stands on selected issues.

Do we tend to draw unbiblical lines between clergy and laymen and their responsibilities? Are we silent at social ignorance and neglect on the part of Christian leaders?

Do we support and reschedule popular evangelists who fail to preach the whole gospel, or who are unduly professionalized? Every congregation could multiply such queries.

Let us follow Jesus, further, in His freedom from binding worldly allegiances. Despite all pressures, Jesus refused to commit Himself to any of the politico-religious factions of His day—Pharisees, Herodians, Sadducees, or Zealots. We, too, must wear all party, philosophical, and personal loyalties loosely, remaining free to express fully a higher commitment to God in Christ. This will modify sociopolitical alignments, as Moberg suggests:

> The Christian ideally is both a conservative who tries to conserve all that is true, honest, just, pure, lovely, and gracious (Phil. 4:8) in society and a liberal who tries to liberate mankind by changing the conditions of society that violate those criteria of excellence. [20]

Jesus was a loyal Citizen of an imperfect government, but He did not let this keep Him from fulfilling His own purposes. No one can improve on His finely balanced "Pay

Caesar what belongs to Caesar, and pay God what belongs to God" (Mk. 12:17, Williams). This statement urges loyalty to government as divinely sanctioned authority, a point which Evangelicals stress. But they neglect the equally essential truth that the province of Caesar is limited, that government deserves prophetic, corrective censure when it violates God's standards.

Christians are obliged—particularly in a democratic republic responsive to citizens' views and needs—to help government rise to its responsibilities. As Carl Henry concluded, the principle of the lordship of Christ over the state (Col. 1:16) has prepared the way "for the gradual rise of political science whereby man may shape and use civil government under God in constructive ways." [21]

Let us follow Jesus, also, in His authentic, understanding involvement in the world. "Just as you have sent me into the world," Jesus prayed the night before the cross, "I have sent them into the world, too" (Jn. 17:18, Williams). The parallel is direct. The pattern for our life "in the world" is Jesus—the one who learned a trade, respected social customs, was in demand as a guest and a companion to publicans and sinners, "well knew what was in human nature" (Jn. 2:25, Williams). Yet the testimony of Christ was twisted by both medieval monks and modern fundamentalists who professed love for Him but insulated themselves thoroughly from the world He died to save.

Jesus' example shows the need for a deep knowledge of the world, and this alone will prepare Evangelicals to follow the admonition that our basic corrective role in society is "to identify why a situation is wrong, when and why it demands public confrontation, and precisely what the right alternative is." [22] Our unscriptural separation, emphasis upon the "great gulf" between saved and unsaved, and cliquish subculture with its special vocabulary and ways have made it easy to undervalue unbelievers, and difficult to form genuine friendships with them. Thus countless opportunities to love and minister are lost. The need for recovery of genuinely personal relationships is well stated by Bruce Larson:

> Nothing was more impersonal than the old "personal" evangelism, which really meant scalp-hunting or doctrine-pushing or decision-card signing. Nobody knew anybody. The old social action was just as impersonal. It was a group of bleeding-heart liberals dreaming up a program for some ghetto and going down and pushing it on them. . . .I think we're coming into a deeply personal age where there's going to be a new kind of social action and a new kind of evangelism where people get involved with one another. 23

Let us follow Jesus, finally, in His loving service to those in need. By acts of compassion Jesus illustrated the principles He preached. His acts of physical healing, words of counsel and comfort, sharing of food and drink, and dramatic foot-washing all fit together naturally with His teachings about the welfare of the soul. Jesus posed no secular-spiritual dichotomy. He ennobled love of neighbor by proclaiming it the best evidence of love for God. He reached out warmly to the poor, prisoners, children, women, aliens, and outcasts. This dynamic pattern is totally relevant to evangelism as well as to social concern, and it binds them together in essential union, as Leighton Ford makes clear:

> God wants to give through our lives as Christians a kind of preview, an advance demonstration, of the love and peace and justice that will mark his eternal kingdom. Then, when from a platform of love in action we ask men to be reconciled to God, the church's message will sound with the ring of truth. 24

It is not that we should reduce social action to an evangelistic ploy; it should emerge rather as a sincere response to our understanding of God's will and purpose. In the opinion of Gilbert James of Asbury Theological Seminary, it will lead Evangelicals to infiltrate "the major social,

154

political, and professional groups as ministers of reconcil-iation! Not starting new movements, but letting Christian love, and the gentle, understanding heart of Jesus be felt."[25] Evangelism in such a context would naturally accompany our desire to serve the best interests and meet the deepest needs of all human beings.

As such followers of Jesus increase, evangelism will speak more and more to social as well as personal needs. Christians will be able to escape or modify the influence of the conformist pressures of American materialism. Growing confidence will free Evangelicals from dissipating so much energy to prove their innocence of heresies, such as salvation by works or the Social Gospel. And most important, with humanistic and radical approaches to life and its problems proving increasingly to be inadequate, this new positive vision will reveal an age particularly ripe for evangelism with a dynamic social witness.

9

Evangelical Christianity and Poverty

POVERTY IN AMERICA

How can the plight of a group of people whose life expectancy is seventeen years, whose infant death rate is 258 out of every 1,000 and whose yearly income is less than $500 be assessed? Most readers would assume that these people reside in one of the underdeveloped countries of the world. As a matter of fact, these statistics apply to a group of present-day American Indians dwelling in the most affluent society history has ever known.

Who are the poor? Poverty is a relative term which is intertwined with a concern for a minimum amount of goods and services. In 1904 it was estimated that a family of five in America would need $460 per year to survive. That figure has continued to rise so that in 1964 the Office of Economic Opportunity defined the poverty line as being $1,540 for one person, $3,130 for four, and $5,090 for seven or more. In 1972 the figure is about $4,000 for a family of five.

The Christian faith, of course, has had a concern for not only poverty but also the conditions that bring it into being. For example, the Christian has to be concerned with certain basic questions. Is impoverishment caused by direct action from God? Is man to be blamed in any way when poverty is present? Has God ordained this to teach man a lesson or to serve some wider purpose? Is poverty the result of man's fallen state—individually or collectively? How should Christians view programs to help the poor? Should a program be an act of love with no strings attached, or should it be designed to accomplish some kind of reform? Is there a harmful aspect to actions undertaken by Christians to alleviate poverty? Does the church have a responsibility beyond that of preaching the gospel? Should the churches try to influence public policy by promoting the adoption of legislation designed to alleviate and/or abolish poverty?

Reactions to poverty on the part of those within the church have varied historically from a position of apathy to the traumatic shock expressed by Walter Rauschenbusch after his experience in a place called Hell's Kitchen in late nineteenth-century New York City. Although the role of the church in history relating to poverty would be a profitable venture for an essay, the nature of this volume precludes such a study. Therefore, this work focuses on the problem of poverty as it exists in the United States, except for some brief comments on the world outlook in the concluding portion.

The Treatment of the Poor: A Historical Survey

In Puritan New England the poor were reduced to an inferior class, both socially and morally. Part of this was because of the philosophy of rugged individualism which became closely identified with life in America. The early Protestant settlers blended religion and capitalism to form what Max Weber later identified as the "Protestant ethic." According to Weber, the Puritans strengthened the capitalist system with their doctrine of election and the divine calling wherein God was identified with the interests of those who were successful in life. The man who proved

to be diligent in his calling, thrifty with his goods, successful in his business, and impeccable in his character was
assumed to be demonstrating the obvious blessing of God.

Consequently, misfortune became almost as much of a
sin as laziness or vice. The poor—good or bad, lazy or unfortunate—were treated as a class somewhat the same as criminals, since it was doubted that an impoverished person could
be one of God's elect. Hence, the poor were reduced to an
inferior class socially and morally; and in order that they
might be encouraged to help themselves, any relief or aid
extended to them was kept to the barest minimum. All of the
colonies held some aspects of this view of the poor, ideas
which had been carried to America from Europe and England. In the Middle Colonies, where a greater degree of
tolerance would be expected, those receiving any relief
payments were known to all. For example, in New Jersey
the pauper was required to wear a badge on the right sleeve
with a blue or red "P" along with the first letter of the
name of the city or county in which he resided. [1]

Of course, at the same time, colonial America offered a
great many opportunities for the ambitious person. Land
was cheap and labor was scarce. Even in the urban centers
there were opportunities for those possessing a craft or who
were willing to work hard. Consequently, rugged individualism yielded dividends to those who followed the prescribed
formula.

In the early years of the nineteenth century in the United
States the rural agrarian society still placed great confidence in the philosophy of individualism. There were many
ways in which the Protestant ethic could be applied since
so much of the frontier still awaited a conquering hand.
Those individuals who protested about not receiving their
just shares of the economic fruits, such as the mill workers
in New England, were still a minority. The evangelical itin-
erants, such as Charles G. Finney or Lyman Beecher, did not
evidence any great concern about the problem of poverty.

159

It was in the post-Civil War years, however, that forces emerged which have a bearing on the church and poverty today. Not only was the philosophy of rugged individualism challenged, but disintegrative pressures were brought to bear on the agrarian views of the antebellum period. This era was one of change and transition, with the growth of industrialism and the phenomenal increase in urban areas as the major forces affecting the problem of poverty. In order to encourage the maximum growth possible under the free-enterprise system, an approach stressing minimum state intervention, known as the laissez-faire policy, was encouraged.

A group of thinkers emerged who defended laissez-faire in a rather sophisticated manner. Herbert Spencer, a British author, introduced the concept in the English-speaking world, although it was William G. Sumner who popularized Spencerian ideas in America. Sumner joined together three lines of thought—the Protestant ethic, Darwin's biological theory of natural selection, and the ideas of the classical economists. The resultant philosophy, known as Social Darwinism, provided a rationale for laissez-faire doctrine and fortified the position of the industrial capitalists. According to Sumner, the man on top had struggled to get there, and his superior position was explained by the process of natural selection. He argued that although millionaires recieved high wages and lived in luxury, the bargain was a good one for society.

Like other precepts of laissez-faire economics, the natural selection thesis was given an allegedly scientific basis by the Social Darwinists. If the Social Darwinists were right, there was no remedy for poverty except individual self-help. The poor, if they could not change their status, must pay the price exacted by nature from all the unfit. Any interpositions on their behalf, either by benevolent philanthropists or the state, were pointless and dangerous. Spencer taught that it was unfortunate that the poor should die, but it was better that they perish rather than live to perpetuate an unfit species. To prevent such from taking place would be an unwarranted interference in nature's plan.

The subject of laissez-faire economics caused some division in the churches of America. Andrew Carnegie, John D. Rockefeller, and other industrialists were often lauded from the pulpit. Russell Conwell, a popular Baptist preacher, repeated a lecture entitled "Acres of Diamonds" over five thousand times. "I say that you ought to get rich," said Conwell, "and it is your duty to get rich." [2] William Lawrence, an Episcopal bishop, stated it even more strongly: "Godliness is in league with riches." [3] Henry Ward Beecher, one of the leading clergymen of the era, gave scant comfort to the poor when he stated that any working man who really tried could support his family on a dollar a day, providing he did not drink or smoke. If the rumor was true that Beecher's income was in the neighborhood of $20,000 a year, his condemnation of the poor would seem unfair. [4] Hence, the traditional Protestant ethic, blended with laissez-faire economics, seemed to be all that the Protestant churches had to offer to the poor of that period. This "gospel of wealth" was obviously an attempt to justify the accumulation of riches rather than to correct poverty.

It was particularly difficult for that generation to accept the fact that in a complex economy individuals were not as independent as they had been some decades earlier. Because an impersonal element had entered into economics, individual virtue or the lack of it no longer determined whether men were to be rich or poor. Rather, it was increasingly apparent that individuals suffered as often from the aberrations and miscalculations of others as from their own failings. Many were poor in spite of the fact that they were doing the best that they were able to do. Several of the characters in Upton Sinclair's novel, *The Jungle* (1906), kept losing the struggle to be free from want, no matter how hard they tried. The laissez-faire doctrine came under attack from such individuals as Jane Addams, Edward Bellamy, Lester Frank Ward, and Henry George. Many of these individuals stated, in different ways, that one could not remain passive in the face of so much suffering and want and support a theory which claimed that the state should not intervene to help the needy.

As dissatisfaction with unbridled capitalism increased, the so-called personal causes of poverty appeared insignificant in comparison with the larger problem of a system of economics which was deficient. "What other result can we expect under our present organization," asked George Herron, "than that great numbers of persons should be poor? Our economic order is not intended to serve any social purpose, but only to enrich individuals." [5] The emerging thesis was obvious: devise a more "Christian" system of production and distribution that was better equipped to meet individual needs.

THE SOCIAL GOSPEL

The dilemma of finding individual moral improvement in the midst of an amoral society was met head-on by a group of clergymen who formulated an idea known as the Social Gospel. These individuals said that since rugged individualism did not provide the answers to the new problems, a new system of ethics was needed. In other words, they were trying to reorient the historical Christian faith of America to an industrial society. The pietistic individualism stressed by traditional American Protestantism was one of the phenomena against which the champions of the Social Gospel reacted. Their aim was to awaken the churches to their responsibility for the social needs of their communities, and the conversion of society in its entirety was the eventual goal. Washington Gladden told his Yale divinity students that "one man can no more be a Christian alone than one man can sing an oratorio alone" and his view, shared by many contemporaries, was that society, even more than individuals, needed a conversion experience. [6]

Many respected clergymen joined the ranks of the Social Gospel movement, among whom were Gladden, Lyman Abbott, Shailer Mathews, and Walter Rauschenbusch. At the age of twenty-five, Rauschenbusch accepted the pastorate of the Second German Baptist Church on West 45th Street in New York City where he spent eleven years ministering to a poverty-stricken congregation. This proved to be the great dynamic experience of his life as he was sickened by the disgusting conditions in which many people were forced to live in the New York slums. [7]

Most Social Gospel advocates had a very optimistic view of human nature and the ability of men to find rational solutions to their problems. In contrast to the Calvinist view of human depravity held by the Puritans, they assumed that the kingdom of God could and would become a reality in human history. Social progress, in other words, would come about as social programs were implemented, both hastening the fulfillment of the kingdom of God.

Although leading evangelical preachers such as Dwight L. Moody and Billy Sunday were not primarily concerned with the problems of the poor, there were some efforts by Evangelicals to ease their suffering. The rescue missions and the Salvation Army worked among the destitute of the inner city and tried to alleviate poverty as much as they could. Many churches established orphanages and hospitals so that the poor, as well as those who could afford to pay, could receive care.

As the twentieth century was ushered in, the Social Gospelers soon discovered that the Progressives were their natural allies. Progressive leaders suggested that poverty could be cured by instituting corrections of the unjust and degrading conditions of work and living. Among other things, they proposed legislative action to establish and maintain fair standards of wages and hours; the prohibition of child labor; compensation for unemployment, sickness, accidents, and old age; public health programs; and a more adequate system of public education.

The Progressives were disturbed by the practice of child labor, particularly among the poor. They felt that the industrial system was robbing the nation of one of its most valuable assets—childhood. John Spargo estimated the number of working children in the United States around the turn of the century at 2,250,000, and blamed the evil on the social system that created it. The normal progression was that poverty-stricken parents were forced to send their children to work. Then the employer found that it was cheaper to hire the children than the adults, who then became permanently unemployed. Indeed, the objective of child-hiring, according to Spargo, was the increase of the employers' profits. [8]

The most shattering book on human need in the early twentieth century was Robert Hunter's *Poverty*. Hunter chided his generation for their apathy toward the poor. Poverty, he said, was a breeding ground for criminals, paupers, vagrancy, and for various kinds of social deviancy. The poor, he noted, were fighting a losing struggle and did not receive any mercy or help from society until they were beyond help. Some said that poverty was irremedial since Christ stated that the poor would always be on the earth, but Hunter replied that these people made no distinction between those who were poor because of their own folly and vice and those who were forced into poverty by social conditions. The poor of this latter class, he said, are the mass of poor; they are bred of miserable and unjust social conditions which punish the good and the pure, the faithful and industrious, the lazy and vicious alike.

Hunter's book was intended to show the need for help among the poor. "I am at a loss to understand," he wrote, "why well-known and generally recognized poverty-breeding conditions, which are both unjust and unnecessary, are tolerated for an instant among a humane, not to say a professedly Christian people." [9] Hunter's questioning of the age-old assumption that poverty was the normal condition of the masses typifies the thrust of the Progressive era. If social conditions were the cause of poverty, they should be removed or changed so that progress could continue.

Heavily influenced by Progressivism, Theodore Roosevelt called his program of social reform the New Nationalism, while Woodrow Wilson referred to his as the New Freedom. Both were concerned with the goal of social justice, although each chose a different route to the destination. Still, the rumbles of social discontent were in the land. Many individuals remained poor largely because the rate of wages paid by the industries of the United States would not permit them to be anything but poor.

The Social Gospel lost ground with the coming of World War I. The war with all its cruelty and inhumanity seemed to vindicate the more orthodox Christian view that man was not perfectible and progress was not inevitable. In practical terms, this meant that the experiment in finding a gospel ethic to fit social problems was to be set aside during the following decade. However, there persisted in this period of unparalleled prosperity a national faith in the possibility of overcoming poverty. In fact, conservatives boasted that the American dream of material abundance was being realized. Herbert Hoover, accepting the Republican nomination on August 11, 1928, said: "We in America today are nearer to the final triumph over poverty than ever before in the history of any land. The poorhouse is vanishing from among us. We have not yet reached that goal, but given a chance to go forward with the policies of the last eight years, we shall soon, with the help of God, be within sight of that day when poverty will be banished from this nation." [10]

FROM INDIVIDUALISM TO THE WELFARE STATE

A little more than a year later the great depression shook America. The crash of the stock market on October 24, 1929, ushered in the worst economic disaster in the nation's history. It idled millions of persons who could not be considered indolent or lazy. Factories were forced to close, banks failed, and the list of unemployed grew to unbearable lengths. Americans who previously had thought of unemployment as the problem of the inefficient and the indolent now saw things in a different light. Most individuals no longer had the family farm as a buffer against economic misfortune but were dependent on a weekly paycheck. Private agencies now could not cope with the problem of widespread unemployment, and the Red Cross refused to accept 25 million dollars that President Hoover offered it, stating that the task was beyond its resources.

Likewise, the Protestant churches of America found that they did not have the resources to meet the problems of human need in this emergency. Some Christians decided to reevaluate their whole approach to the problem. One religious journal, *The Baptist*, stated: "We can be . . . sure that in any fair conflict between rich and poor, Jesus could be found on the side of the poor." [11] The depression increased man's understanding both of his own vulnerability and of the fact that the world could be cruel and unfair. Perhaps the most significant change arising from the experiences of the depression was a new willingness of most Americans to accept government intervention to meet human economic needs.

Franklin D. Roosevelt's New Deal, inaugurated in 1933, was the first large-scale government attempt to solve the problems of the depression. In some respects, the New Deal was reminiscent of earlier reform efforts, but it was also a major departure from the past in that laissez-faire was abandoned. President Roosevelt made this clear when he said that the government was going to use affirmative action to realize its objectives. The direction of the New Deal became evident with the passage of the Federal Emergency Relief Act of May 12, 1933. This legislation repudiated the old poor-relief philosophy and stated that in a complex industrial society the individual was no longer in control of his economic destiny. After the attempt to meet basic human needs and some beginnings at reform were made, F.D.R. emphasized in the campaign of 1936 that one-third of the nation was "ill-housed, ill-clad, and ill-nourished." In his State of the Union message of 1944, Roosevelt outlined an Economic Bill of Rights which was designed to combat poverty.

Although some of the New Dealers were influenced by the teachings of Christianity, not all churchmen were enthusiastic about New Deal programs. One New York clergyman said that aid to the unemployed was unchristian because it robbed people of their responsibility and opportunity to give aid to the needy. Another minister stated that the government handouts would cause a situation where it would be years before the "lazy, dole-seeking laborer will again 'look' for work." He continued, "Thank God, there are some folks left who know that real happiness comes from earning one's own bread by the sweat of the brow." Someone else thought that the government was punishing the hard-working citizens by passing "their hard-earned savings over to mendicants and dead-beats, who never worked when they had work and who won't work after the administrative socialistic schemes finish squandering the money of the taxpayers upon them." [12]

The Second World War interrupted Roosevelt's economic policies, but the Fair Deal of President Harry S. Truman supplemented and enlarged the New Deal. In one of his early economic reports, President Truman rejected the laissez-faire philosophy that certain unchangeable economic laws must direct the nation's paths. Chairman of the Council of Economic Advisers, Arthur F. Burns, presented a similar view when on October 19, 1954, he said that "it is no longer a matter of serious controversy whether the Government should play a positive role in helping to maintain a high level of economic activity. What we debate nowadays is not the need for controlling business cycles, but rather the nature of governmental action, its timing and its extent." 13

In 1958, Professor John Kenneth Galbraith published his important book, *The Affluent Society,* in which he claimed that poverty in America has been reduced from the problem of a majority to that of a minority. Nevertheless, the crux of the matter was the fact that there could be poverty in the midst of such great affluence. With this in view, President John F. Kennedy, in his inaugural address, noted that if a free society could not help the many who are poor, it could not save the few who are rich.

It was Michael Harrington, however, who in 1962 graphically revealed the problem of poverty in the United States in his book *The Other America.* He began by saying there is an America familiar to all, the one celebrated in speeches and in the media as the nation which boasts the highest mass standard of living the world has ever known. This implies that the poverty problem is either solved or shortly will be. "While this discussion was carried on," Harrington continued, "there existed another America. In it dwelt somewhere between 40,000,000 and 50,000,000 citizens of this land. They were poor. They still are." He advanced the thesis that the welfare state was created in the New Deal and Fair Deal programs and that it catered to the needs of those other than the poor. Therefore, a type of "socialism for the rich and free enterprise for the poor" philosophy evolved. The huge corporation farms received the real benefits while the poor farmers go on being poor, and the construction of luxury housing with public funds continues while the slums are left largely untouched. Harrington claimed that "as long as the illusion persists that the poor are merrily free-loading on the public dole, so long will the other America continue unthreatened." 14 In his opinion, the poor are getting less out of the welfare state than any group in America.

According to Arthur Schlesinger, Jr., President Kennedy was profoundly influenced by *The Other America*. The book demonstrated not only the fact that poverty and affluence had a parallel existence but that few of the existent programs ever reached those in real need. However, before he could act to correct the situation, Kennedy was struck down by an assassin's bullet. But his successor, Lyndon B. Johnson, almost immediately declared an "unconditional war" on poverty. In a ringing appeal he said, "Unfortunately many Americans live on the outskirts of hope, some because of their poverty and some because of their color, and all too many because of both." [15] The new President proceeded to secure the necessary legislation from Congress to fashion the Great Society's antipoverty program.

Today, however, the poverty problem remains and President Richard M. Nixon has proposed a program to guarantee a certain level of subsistence to all needy families. The national floor of $1,600 per family represents a major breakthrough, and now an application for this kind of relief will be comparable to that for social security. It can be said that the Nixon program represents an advance in the structure of the welfare system, but it has not yet touched the basic problem of poverty in America.

Presently, in superaffluent America, the criterion of poverty is not absolute in itself, but rather is measured in terms of the affluence of others. In 1904 Robert Hunter put the dividing line at $460 for a family of five, while today the federal government draws the line for a similar family at $3,960. Thus, "In dollar terms the 'poverty line' reflects the constantly rising threshold of poverty as defined by government and welfare officials." The paradox of this is that the poor today are materially better off than those in the past, but they may be poorer in spirit because they have so little hope of deliverance. Poverty currently erodes the spirit more than the body. Poverty in the U.S. means that its victims are unable to participate in the good life which is available to the majority of its citizens as a matter of course. The poor today include the aged, families on relief, the uneducated, the unskilled, and many members of minority groups. [16]

Furthermore, the current poverty problem in the United States has been aggravated by certain recent socioeconomic developments such as automation and migration to the suburbs. For example, Edward Banfield in his recent book, *The Unheavenly City*, states that the subculture of poverty among the poor in the inner city causes them to lose their will to work. Banfield's critics point out, among other things, that the poor do want to work but find few opportunities and that many of the poor are unemployable because of age or disabilities. Most programs have been designed merely to alleviate poverty rather than to abolish it. The poor in America today are more urban, more Negro, more unemployed, more fatherless, and more difficult to help than ever before. Added to this, of course, is the fact that there are some individuals involved in trying to cheat the system. [17]

It seems obvious that private charitable institutions and local governments cannot handle today's poverty problems. It is even more evident that the churches cannot effectively alleviate the situation. Perhaps as many as one in eight Americans are living in poverty. As a matter of fact, the high cost of poverty is perhaps the most serious problem in New York City. The federal government appears to be the only institution in the society which has the capability to act in a way that will eventually solve the problem of poverty. Why, then, does it not act to do so? According to Harrington, "At precisely that moment in history where for the first time a people have the material ability to end poverty, they lack the will to do so." [18] The will of the people is lacking!

The stimulation given the economy by the Vietnam War, in one sense, served as an antipoverty program. On the other hand, Chairman J. William Fulbright of the Senate

Foreign Relations Committee stated that from 1946 through 1967 the nation spent 904 billion dollars of its national budget on military items and only 96 billion for such things as education, health, labor, welfare programs, housing, and community development. Surely a drastic change in emphasis at the national level is in order! Since the annual gross national product has passed the trillion dollar mark, this makes any further delay in shifting national priorities so as to aid the poor utterly inexcusable!

The remarkable feature of poverty in this country is its endless capacity for reincarnation. It dies off in one form and comes to life in another in spite of an ongoing succession of antipoverty programs in the twentieth century. A report issued in 1968 revealed that in order to make four-fifths of a nation more affluent than any people in history the one-fifth has been degraded. Perhaps even more devastating is this recent comment on the moral stance of the church: "Brotherhood was a vacuous exercise reserved for incantation on Sunday mornings, and appropriately forgotten the other 167 hours of the week." [19]

What Are Christians Doing on the Contemporary Scene?

"Many an honest Christian," declares Alan Keith-Lucas, "is troubled by the welfare picture as he sees it in America today." [20] He sees vast, expensive tax-supported programs, some of which are undoubtedly necessary, but others which seem to maintain people in idleness or even put a premium on shiftlessness and immorality. On the other hand, those acquainted with individuals who are receiving aid from the state are shocked that anyone is expected to make do with so little.

One of the obstacles to any involvement by evangelical Protestant churches in a poverty program is the fact that they are often identified with the rich, the employer class, and the local establishment. The churches are not usually thought of today as the haven of those who were the objects of the first beatitude, "Blessed are the poor" (Mt. 5:3). The common people have had a genuine attachment to their churches in times past. Today, however, the average congregation does not seem to enter into the daily life of the masses. Poverty programs are not generally the subject of discussion at board meetings or Bible studies. Perhaps this is because many Christians believe that religion is a personal matter and therefore not a proper subject for social action.

There was a time when belief in the idea of progress—that is, things are continually improving—could explain away certain miseries by holding that the future would eventually resolve most of them. Those naive and optimistic theories do not square with the realities of today's world. If nothing else, the fact that two World Wars have occurred in such a short space of time has given pause to this concept.

Some American churches have adjusted to the times and are attempting to help the poor in new and innovative ways. Instead of using only the traditional paths to fight poverty, such as orphanages, hospitals, and homes for the aged, they are moving into the ghettos in an attempt to supplement the war on poverty being fought by the federal government. For example, the American Lutheran Church recently invested $1,250,000 in programs to assist minority groups; the United Presbyterian Church made one million available for investment in New York City ghetto housing and businesses; and the Roman Catholic Archdiocese of Detroit has engaged in an experimental housing program. The National Council of Churches of America has rallied to the defense of the Community Action Programs sponsored by the Office of Economic Opportunity. The Friends (Quakers) of Philadelphia initiated a program of self-help housing in which they aided in buying and renovating old homes for families willing to do part of the work. [21]

Unfortunately, evangelical participation in programs of this kind has been rather limited. Often evangelical Protestant churches are no longer located where poverty needs are evident. Protestants are abandoning the declining transitional areas of the inner city to follow a select constituency to the more attractive residential suburbs. Furthermore, inter-faith cooperation many times is needed in order to pool the resources necessary to be of any vital assistance in a poverty-blighted area. Frequently the only church remaining in an inner city is Roman Catholic, and the parish priest is the only religious contact that the residents have.

Evangelicals regularly take a back seat to labor unions and other concerned people where the poor and the needy are concerned. In reality, wherever there is human need, that is where evangelical Christians should be. Instead, the people living in poverty scarcely know that they exist, and probably the same is true regarding the evangelical view of poverty. It is not unusual to hear sermons condemning the vast amounts of money spent each year in America on liquor, cigarettes, and cosmetics. But what Evangelical ever hears a sermon that condemns the small amount of money being spent to help the poor in this country?

Opponents of the War on Poverty often quote the words of Jesus—"The poor you shall always have with you"—to support their position, but that grossly distorts the meaning of this Bible verse. A careful reading of the entire passage from which it is taken clearly indicates that Christ was not institutionalizing poverty when He said this, but instead He made a historical statement in a historical context, the point of which was His forthcoming crucifixion (Jn. 12:1-8). Let those who want to know what Christ taught about poverty read the four gospels, particularly Matthew 25:31-46. They will find that He moved regularly among the poor, instructed them, made Himself available to them, and in general lifted their spirits. At the same time He condemned the dishonest rich and challenged all wealthy people to be better men and not merely better off. Twentieth-century evangelical Christians who desire to be as faithful as possible to the teachings of Christ might well ask themselves, not how much the poor enter into the life of their churches, but how much their churches enter into the life of the poor.

Since the churches apparently do not have the means to win the war on poverty, perhaps they should accept a role of attempting to define and arrange priorities for action. Once these priorities are established, they then could work much harder to make believers aware of the social implications of their faith. A protest regarding the maldistribution of wealth in modern society and a demand for reforms to assist the poor would show those living in poverty that Christians really care about them. This kind of attitude in the churches might at least make it more difficult for members to listen to a sermon on Sunday proclaiming that Christ fed the hungry and helped the hopeless, and then on Monday write to their congressman to ask that the budget be cut for poverty programs.

The evangelical churches, then, should seek to become the friend of the poor. A higher standard of morality should not be required of the poor than of those who are self-sufficient. Christians should not judge all public-assistance programs by the few who attempt to beat the system or who are unwilling to work. Perhaps the reason for compulsory Social Security, welfare taxes, and a legally established right to assistance for those in need is that personal giving has proved in the past to be both inadequate and far too capricious to meet the needs of the people.

It is also a fact that some ministers face difficulties if they take a stand on social issues, and there may be instances in which a clergyman could find himself looking for another job. Nowadays, church boards are more likely to keep a closer watch on the social views of their minister than his private morals, especially in comfortable, middle-class, suburban churches. Thus, a pastor often is financially dependent on those who would least likely approve of any criticism of the existing economic order.

The churches and the clergy working with federal and state programs in an attempt to alleviate poverty is not a perfect solution to the problem, but this approach should be utilized until a better answer is found. Some have even urged that Christians move beyond humanitarianism to a theology of welfare. That, of course, is what the formulators of the Social Gospel had tried to do. One important criticism of their position was that man should not try to make God in his own image, even the finest image that he could conceive, and this warning must be repeated to those who seek to develop a theology of welfare. Man is not to enlist God as sponsor for his fallible human endeavors but to accept Christian precepts as he searches for solutions to the problem of poverty. "Modern welfare," asserts Keith-Lucas, "was in fact born of the church's failure and of the failure of the small community which acted almost as if it was a local church with all the church's exclusiveness and parochialism." [22] Many churches also have failed to accept any guilt in connection with their part in the creation of the poverty conditions which exist in the world.

Some Christians attempt to avoid responsibility and guilt by going back to the Elizabethan Poor Laws for answers regarding the punitive thrust of some of current welfare legislation toward the poor. They should take note of the fact that Americans for the most part still measure success or failure today in terms of economic mobility. In this regard, many of the poor have never even had a chance to put their foot on the bottom rung of the ladder leading upward. In addition, Christians are prone to judge sins in a qualitative manner, thus, the sin of sloth is much more harshly punished than are avarice, gluttony, envy, or pride. The church recognizes that both sloth and gluttony are sins. But the difficulty, according to some, lies in the fact that church leaders are more inclined themselves to gluttony

175

than they are to sloth, and the old situation arises again that it is much easier to condemn the sins which one does not practice himself.

POVERTY ON THE WORLD LEVEL

The nineteen richest countries of the world represent only 16 percent of the population but control about 75 percent of the world's income. In human terms, this means that the vast majority of the people of the world are poor, hungry, subject to disease, and living in conditions that can only be called inhuman. Furthermore, this stark poverty and hunger in the world have no relation to the Christian ideal of voluntary poverty, that is, giving up of this world's material goods for the service of God.

Many of the poorer nations have not benefited from the technical and industrial transformation that provided the base of prosperity for the richer nations of the West. Most modern Western colonialists showed little awareness of the plight of the ordinary peoples who came under their jurisdiction. Rather, they were concerned with their own trade, their own prosperity, and had a very impersonal and businesslike view of the colonial areas. Since the end of World War II, there has been a "revolution of rising expectations" in the former colonies. This reaction to imperialism resulted in some overemphasis of its evil effects, but at least it has made the poor of the world aware of the possibilities of a better life. Moreover, it has made prosperous countries realize that justice and prudence require that they share their wealth with the peoples whose poverty they have helped to perpetuate.

What can Christians do in the face of such overwhelming problems? The present per capita income of Americans compared to that of the average Asian is approximately 40 to 1; and at the rate the gap is widening, it could possibly be double that figure by the end of the century. This dreadful prospect could and must be reversed. "The obstacles to relieving the degrading poverty afflicting a large part of mankind," according to one writer, "although immense, are more cultural than economic." 23 In effect, for the first time in history, man has the resources and skills to provide a truly human existence for most of the earth's inhabitants.

Therefore, sufficient concern and imagination among the affluent countries is a place where a beginning can be made. In this regard, the Christian population must provide the moral force which is sorely needed to overcome the fatalism and apathy that now blocks progress. The evangelical churches must be willing to overcome their handicaps. One of the obstacles in the past has been the otherworldly orientation that refuses to take this world and its problems seriously. "In a world that has become a planetary village," states one religious leader, "every man is my neighbor— especially every man in need." 24 This same author states that the churches in general simply have not yet determined that the people living in poverty deserve the very highest priority.

Economist Barbara Ward warns that in a time when the wealth of the Western world surpasses the resources of the rest of the world by ten to one, heed must be taken by the Christian community. She writes: "If these profoundest insights of the Christian faith do not energize the Western conscience and make the great work of world-aid and world-development a first responsibility of its overwhelming wealth then its material frame may survive but it will house a failing spirit." 25 In her view, the acid test for pure Christianity is the willingness to care for the needs of those who are suffering from the conditions brought on by poverty.

If evangelical Christians can justify their support of government programs to combat poverty in America, then surely Christian compassion for starving mankind should lead them to see that they must act politically to combat poverty in the world. Government assistance programs to underdeveloped nations as well as support for United Nations projects would be a good place to begin. Hence, the prophetic role of the church should be to lead the way in worldwide programs designed to distribute wealth more equitably and to achieve real social justice. Jesus deliberately chose to be poor, lived with the poor, and showed preferential love for the poor. How many Christians think of this when they sing "More Like the Master" on Sunday morning?

The churches then must manifest their love in more concrete ways. They must assert that any system which allows one of God's creatures to suffer must not be tolerated. God wants His creatures to live, not to die or needlessly suffer while there are resources available to give them life. If the world is moving along a course where the rich are getting richer and the poor are getting poorer, then the churches must protest this drift. There is a theory, rooted in Marxism, which states that the development of the industrialized nations is dependent upon exploitation of the underdeveloped nations. Related to this is the belief that the vast Third World will rise up in violent revolution unless this exploitation ceases. Up to this point, the Christian community has not shown empathy, as have the Communists, for the "Third World."

Perhaps the struggle against Communism is more of a bread-and-butter issue than heretofore has been admitted. As one Christian has observed, "The question of bread for me is a material question. The question of bread for my neighbor is a spiritual matter." [26] At the same time, many missionary agencies close to the National Association of Evangelicals maintained they could not work with the World Council of Churches on social matters because it "viewed missionary work as social and economic help for the underprivileged rather than stressing the Christian message and view of personal salvation through regeneration." [27]

Samuel Escobar declared at Urbana 70 that in some regions of the world Communism has become synonymous with a committed, disciplined, sacrificial way of living, while Christianity has become synonymous with a gay, unconcerned, and irrelevant selfishness. [28] Thus, if the Communists are the only ones who champion the poor and wretched of the earth, then American Christians should not be surprised if these people are attracted to that ideology. The good news of the gospel is that Christ came to set people free from their sins, but should it not be a part of this good news that Christians protest poverty where it is to be found? Undoubtedly one of the best antidotes to Communism is a standard of living that lifts people out of poverty and into hope.

It is true that Jesus rebuked those who cared only for material goods (Mt. 6:30), and that He told of the difficulties in the way of a rich man's salvation (Mt. 16:22-26). But Jesus also commended those who helped to alleviate the suffering of the poor. This does not mean in any way that poverty is a desirable condition nor that Christ was implying that all men should be poor. The implication that the evangelical churches should take a stand in favor of a decent standard of living for all men is hard to resist.

Billy Graham in a 1967 speech in Washington, D. C., announced that he had become a "convert" to the nation's antipoverty program. Declaring that he had changed his mind on the subject, he said, "I was once against it, but now I am for it." The evangelist cited numerous Bible passages which advise care for the poor and stated that the antipoverty effort was in line with biblical teaching. [29] Likewise, David O. Moberg, perhaps the best-known evangelical Christian sociologist in the United States, caught the essence of the Christian concern for the poor and devoted an entire book, *Inasmuch*, to the subject of evangelical social responsibility. [30] If poverty is one of the most persistent conditions facing humanity today, the efforts of the evangelical

179

church to alleviate these conditions must be equally persistent. 31 In the words of Christ, "Truly, I say to you, as you did it to one of the least of these my brethren, you did it to me" (Mt. 25:40, RSV).

10

Evangelical Christianity and the Ecological Crisis

THE ECOLOGICAL CRISIS

The heavy, stinking, stifling, acrid pall of smog that chokes the air of cities and spreads a red-gray shroud over the countryside and the sluggish, putrid offal that fills our rivers and streams and reaches into the vast open space of the oceans have combined with television, articulate scientists, and questioning youth to force all men, including comfortable Americans, to recognize the interrelatedness of life on the spaceship planet earth.

Concern with the disposal of human waste and an awareness of man's impact on the environment in which he lives is not new. Even the oldest urban civilizations sought to develop adequate sanitary facilities, and the descriptions of the squalor of tenement life in ancient Rome sound uncomfortably familiar today. Indeed, one who reads the description of ancient urban life is impressed with how little real progress modern technology has made in dealing with the basic processes of life. But even though the problems of pollution and environmental contamination are as old as man, a new awareness and a new urgency are facing ecologists today. The sheer growth of human population, accompanied by urban sprawl and technological change, threatens to accelerate the contamination of the environment beyond its ability to recover or to sustain life.

One of the most urgent voices in the battle for ecological awareness was that of Rachel Carson in her landmark book

Silent Spring. In this work she sounded a clear warning to the public concerning the dangers involved in the increased dependency on chemical pesticides. The very title of the book hammered home her belief that poisoning insects would also poison the birds that feed on them, and the pesticides would enter the complex link that spreads modern contaminants to all parts of the environment. [1]

Since the publication of *Silent Spring* in 1962 *ecology* has become a household word. And yet, like many such words, its meaning may be vague and fuzzy, even to those who use it. Herbert C. Hanson in his *Dictionary of Ecology* defines it as "the study of interrelationships of organisms to one another and to their environment." [2] Other definitions place more emphasis on broad systematic concepts. Lynton Keith Caldwell, for instance, speaks of the *ecosystem* which is "the totality of the interacting entities and systems, physical and social, that comprise every environment [and which] must be taken into account in any decision regarding the environment." [3] This definition, however, is too broad to use as a framework for analysis and action. Caldwell, therefore, borrows the symbol of "Spaceship Earth," which has been used by Barbara Ward and Adlai Stevenson, as a paradigm or model of the ecosystem.

> What are the ideas that the spaceship integrates into one comprehensible image? The essential ideas are these: The spaceship (Earth) is a unified system dependent upon the coordinated and continued functioning of interrelating systems and parts. It has surpluses, redundancy, and back-up capacity, but its resources are nevertheless limited. Because carrying capacity is one of its limits, it must so far as possible recycle its resources unless it can obtain them at feasible cost from external sources. Changes in the system must be studied in relation to their total effects, because altered relationships among the parts, even intended improvements, may adversely affect the performance of the whole. Maintenance of the system and its subsystems must be watched, for failure at any critical point could lead to the destruction of the entire enterprise. [4]

Once one recognizes the total interrelatedness of the environment, he begins to see the importance and urgency of the crisis created by the polluting and despoiling of the limited atmosphere and resources of the little spaceship earth. This essay briefly reviews the challenge of the pollution of water, air, and land, and then examines some of the possible responses to this problem. Particular attention is devoted to the question of a Christian perspective on the ecological crisis.

WATER

In many ways water pollution is the most vivid and frightening form of ecological destruction. Life without water would be inconceivable.

> Water is the basis of the blood of animals, the sap of trees; and the very texture of life at its rawest and most ancient (in single-celled protozoa) consists of structures in which water is used as mortar, as a miniscule pool for digestion, and as a means of carrying chemical and electrical information from the outside world to the nucleus, so that even the tiniest bit of life may be organized and may strike its small spark of struggle against the oblivion that surrounds all creatures. [5]

Some forms of water pollution are inherent in nature and have always been present. The problem of mud being washed from the fields into rivers and streams at flood time is as old as the earth itself. And the gradual silting of rivers and lakes and the contamination of fresh water by salt, whether from the ocean or from underground salt deposits, are both natural processes that occur whether man is involved or not. But even these natural problems have been made more serious by human activity. The despoiling of land in watersheds by removing trees and grass has increased both the danger of flood and the amount of mud which is carried off by floodwaters. Further, man's attempts to respond to these dangers in a nonsystematic way often result in "solutions" that create new problems. The attempt to control floods by building big dams may greatly increase the problem of silting of riverbeds.

One of the most dramatic examples of this type of unintended side effect is the Aswan Dam in Egypt. The dam represents a desire to change the traditional cycle of flooding by which the Nile kept the land surrounding it fertile and productive and to replace it with a controlled system of irrigation. However, the dam has created massive silting problems which threaten grave damage to this traditional source of life.

In addition to exacerbating natural pollution problems, man has added new sources of contamination. The first of these is the disposal of human waste. Prior to the eighteenth century there were no separate sanitary sewers, and human waste was allowed to remain in the streets where it was eventually washed away into the surrounding streams and rivers. Some attempts had been made in antiquity to develop more sanitary arrangements for disposal of human waste, but these were limited to the elite. Following the fall of the Roman Empire, even these attempts at sanitation were abandoned. In addition to the lack of sewers there was an absence of any real understanding of sanitation. As no effort was made to protect water supplies, disease ran rampant. In the later Middle Ages the Black Death wiped out anywhere from one-fourth to three-fourths of the population in the years 1348 and 1349. [6]

The problem remains unsolved even though improvements have been made in the technological process for removing the waste from homes. In sanitation processes man has not advanced far beyond what was available to the patricians of Mohenjo-Daro in India who lived 3,000 years before Christ. Partially treated waste is still dumped into the streams, and most rivers are totally unfit as sources of drinking water and even for recreational use. Most modern cities still rely on a single sewage system that mixes sanitary sewers with storm water runoff. As a result, the sewers back up or overflow after heavy rains. Donald Carr cites an example in one major city where during a recent storm "pollutants were entering the receiving stream at a rate of nine times that which would have occurred *if the city had discharged all its sewage untreated.*" This occurred because the storm waters not only bypassed the sewers but flushed them out as well. 7

Although chlorine is used to sterilize drinking water, the discharge of raw or partially treated sewage into rivers still presents serious problems. In addition to the stench and the ugliness of flooding feces, fats, and vegetable matter, the sewage, when dumped in large enough amounts, uses up the oxygen supply in the water and kills the fish and aquatic plants. Scientists have made the disturbing discovery that otherwise pure water samples from various American rivers contain microscopic worms called nematodes. These worms may carry pathogenic bacteria and viruses, and they are able to withstand chlorination and other forms of water treatment. Therefore, these parasites can pass through a water-purification system, carrying in their stomachs undigested bacteria, and they have even been known to breed in sewage-disposal treatment plants. 8

The second major source of man-made water pollution arises from industrial activity. Carr notes that "modern man has introduced a new spectrum, a new life of merchandise, in water pollution." This is a by-product of industries which locate on the banks of rivers or on the shores of lakes because they need significant quantities of water for their manufacturing processes, a place to dispose of the dirty water that is not consumed in the process, and the availability of water-transport facilities for their products. Industry, therefore, uses vast quantities of water but actually consumes very little of it. Most of it is returned to the streams and rivers, carrying with it pollutants ranging from paunch manure and other animal fats to chemicals, oil, and solid wastes. One of the worst polluters is the pulp and paper industry which pours "sulfite liquor" into rivers. This cooking liquor contains the nonfibrous material removed from the wood chips during the cooking process and is not toxic in the sense that it would poison an animal. It can be broken down by bacterial attack in the water, but in order for this to happen a large amount of oxygen is required. Therefore, the "effect of paper- and pulp-mill wastes is to send the BOD [Biological oxygen demand] soaring so high that fish and other water creatures are suffocated." [9]

In addition to actual contaminants, industrial water use creates the problem of thermal or heat pollution. This phenomenon is especially noticeable in the production of electricity, whether the power source is fossil fuel or nuclear energy. These plants use great quantities of water as coolants and it is then returned to sources up to 25°F. hotter than before. If these installations are located on an open coastline, the enormous volume of cold sea water helps to dilute the heated discharge. Even here the heat may damage kelp beds and other inshore biological communities, but when it is discharged into more restricted areas, such as estuaries, bays, inland lakes, and rivers where dilution is much less effective, the heated water may have a serious impact on marine life.

> It is estimated that by 1985 fully one quarter of the total annual runoff by the United States will be cooling power plants. Since much of the total actually occurs during a relatively short flood season, the fraction will be closer to half for most of the year. This will mean the virtual extinction of much of the flora and fauna which inhabit our rivers today, including a number of valuable food species. It should be noted that part of the threat which warm water poses to aquatic life is its reduced content of dissolved oxygen. Since other pollutants already discussed consume waterborne oxygen, we can expect destructive reinforcement of these effects to hasten the demise of freshwater life. [10]

The third major source of man-made pollution is modern chemical products, especially detergents and insecticides. The detergents are not susceptible to normal sewage disposal by bacterial decomposition, and the suds created by them produce vast clouds of foam which clog sewage-treatment plants, seep into underground water supplies, and even periodically cover some rivers and streams. At present, considerable research is being devoted to developing biodegradable detergents or substitutes that will meet cleaning needs without causing pollution.

Rachael Carson warned in 1962 that the use of modern insecticides was not only killing insects but also birds which ate the poisoned insects. She pointed out that various pesticides were being used with little or no consideration as to their impact on the total environment. Her argument was not against insecticides as such but rather that they were being used indiscriminantly by people ignorant of their potential for harm. One of the most controversial of the pesticides is the popular DDT. Once hailed as the almost ultimate answer to insect infestation, DDT is now regarded as a significant threat in its own right. This is because it breaks down very slowly and thus is not eliminated by dilution into water or air. The DDT content of wildlife that is used as food for human consumption has raised the specter of the poisoning not only of animals but of man himself.

Frank Graham notes that scientists are continually finding pesticides in foodstuffs. They are omnipresent in fish and game, and in 1969 the Food and Drug Administration seized nearly two million pounds of imported cheese because of excessive pesticide content. Even mother's milk is not exempt from contamination, and in fact the Ecology Center at Berkeley dramatized this buildup of DDT by issuing a poster, bearing the likeness of an attractive nude and obviously pregnant young woman with a label on her bosom reading: "Caution, keep out of the reach of children." [11] Certain birds and fishes are already being poisoned as a result of the concentration of chlorinated hydrocarbons passing up the biological food chains.

> Some species of birds, particularly fish-eating hawks, eagles, and sea birds (which eat four or more steps up from the base of the food chains), may be threatened with complete extinction. Part of the difficulty is that the pesticides interfere with the birds' calcium metabolism in such a way that the eggshells are too thin and thus are easily crushed. Coho salmon, which also feed high on the food chain, have been passing pesticide residues into their eggs. In 1968, almost 7,000,000 young Lake Michigan salmon died as they absorbed the last drop of DDT-rich oil from their yolk sacs, and DDT concentrations are now rising ominously in such important food fishes as tuna, mackerel, and hake. . . . [These] birds and fish are cited here because the problem is already quite visible. . . . There is good reason to believe that the birds and fish are only the *first* victims. [12]

AIR

Air, like water, has suffered from various forms of contamination. Dust particles and volcanic ash have always been present, and even areas of rich vegetation create their own special "airs."

> In a state of nature with man not around, there is still a gentle sort of air pollution. A great deal of poetic nonsense has been written about country and mountain air but the truth is that, until one gets above the timber line, the air of well vegetated mountains and hills is miasmic with the exudation of plants. . . . On the banks of streams, when the ecological equilibrium between plants struggling for favorable locations is established, each stream and in fact each length or curve of a stream may be redolent of its own private blend of essential oils depending on the plants that have established themselves on the banks. [13]

But the advent of man and his use of fire added a new dimension to the problem of air pollution. This was especially true when coal became the dominant fuel in the cities of Europe. The wide usage of coal which began in the sixteenth century represented a major victory for the commercial instinct over aesthetics and health. Before that time England and the other European countries had prohibited the use of coal, and in some places people were punished by torture for filling the air with so-called pestilential odors. But, in Elizabethan England the restrictions were removed and London was virtually drowned in coal smoke. Travelers to London "were astonished and revolted at the filthy smoke from tens of thousands of domestic fires and workshops. They had seen no spectacle like it on earth. Breweries, soap and starch houses, brick kilns, sugar refineries, etc., were pouring out smoke. London seemed unfit for human habitation." [14]

In the present time, with the tremendous increase in population and industrial development, vast quantities of pollutants spew into the atmosphere daily. In the United States, automobiles fill the air with "66 million tons of carbon monoxide, 12 million tons of hydrocarbons, 7 million tons of sulfur and nitrogen oxides, and 1 million tons of miscellaneous particulate matter" every year. Further, heavy industry, refineries, chemical plants, power stations, the heating of homes, and burning of trash add more matter, resulting in a grand total of 140 million tons of filth and assorted poisons annually. [15]

In addition, these various pollutants interact with each other creating a whole that is worse than the sum of its parts, while the traditional reliance on dispersal of the pollutants into the atmosphere is producing a worldwide pall. There are reports of lichens in Lapland that are blighted by the air pollution of Western European industrial centers, and the "smog" which was once synonomous with Los Angeles is now found in most major cities throughout the world. The problem strikes areas such as Los Angeles with a special intensity because of certain climatic conditions, especially the phenomenon of temperature inversion. In an inversion all of the particulates from countless sources of pollution remain at ground level, and the poisons which normally dissipate are concentrated.

Since the cause of temperature inversions is unknown and their occurrence unpredictable, it is impossible to say that any particular place is immune from them. Mile-high Denver has smog problems that rival those of Los Angeles. It is advisable to heed Donald Carr's warning that every community "must live as if it expected judgment day tomorrow, since inversion may turn all its sloppy little sins suddenly into mortal ones." Occasionally such judgments do come and it may be with a vengeance as, for example, the "Black Fog" of London on December 5-9, 1952, which caused over 4,000 deaths in its four-day seige. Although the exact number of fatalities attributable to the fog is difficult to determine, the 4,000 figure represents the number of so-called "excess deaths" from heart failure, chronic bronchitis, emphysema, and other respiratory diseases. [16]

Of all of the pollutants in the air, none is more insidious or pervasive than carbon monoxide (CO). "When man invented charcoal, carbon monoxide glided into both the home and the work-place. When man invented the blast furnace it swirled over heavy industry, and when man invented the automobile, it . . . took its pale refuge in all the streets and all the tunnels of the world." [17] Because of the sheer number of cars in the United States, automotive exhaust has become the single most significant source of air pollution in the country. Although in theory the gasoline used as fuel in an automobile is turned into carbon dioxide and water, in actuality engines always produce some carbon monoxide. The stop-and-go pattern which characterizes city driving merely increases the proportion of CO in the exhaust. Carbon monoxide in a confined place—such as inside an automobile with a faulty exhaust system—can be deadly. And, because CO is produced in such vast quantities in modern cities, it cannot adequately be diffused into the atmosphere and thus becomes a major component of the acrid blanket of smog hovering ominously overhead.

Soil

Like water and air, the soil is basic to life. Man is dependent on the soil as the ultimate source of most of his food supply, but yet his careless use of land has been as irresponsible as that of water or air. Of course, floods and windstorms have been eroding soil since time immemorial, and the land masses of earth have been rearranged by geological forces on numerous occasions. But, here again, man has greatly added to the natural processes of erosion. Agricultural development, with its cutting of trees and breaking up of sod, has left the soil exposed to the forces of wind and rain. Even where trees were reintroduced as a conservation practice, such as shelter belts, they often were plowed under during the good years in a desperate attempt to exploit every last inch of land for wheat production. Such a concentration on "this year's crop" can have devastating results in times to come when drought or flood strike.

Soil is not just a collection of crushed rock arranged to keep plants from blowing down in the wind. It is complicated collection of organisms—bacteria, fungi, protozoa, worms, and insects, to name a few—all of which participate in the retention, conversion, and processing of the nutrients used by plants. The biological community of fertile top soil is "produced" as it were, at the rate of about one inch every three hundred to one thousand years. The dispersal of the same amount by wind or water, aided by the shortsighted logging, grazing, and cultivation practices of man, may take as little as a day or even an hour. The process of erosion is of course not deterred by the use of fertilizer, nor can the addition of these few inorganic chemicals be expected to compensate for long for the loss of the top soil itself.

191

At a time when population growth demands ever increasing areas of productive land, the record of our essentially permanent losses to erosion is most discouraging. The fraction of the Earth's land surface classified as desert and wasteland has increased from less than ten to over twenty-five percent in the last century. [18]

A second major threat to the land is the continued expansion of urban sprawl which now stretches out for miles from the major cities. Victor Gruen charges that such a development, exemplified by Los Angeles, but characteristic of metropolitan areas generally, is creating giant "spread cities." Every year, he points out, millions of acres of landscape and natural beauty are indiscriminantly taken for industrial, residential, and other urban land uses. The pattern is the same throughout the entire United States, from north to south and east to west. "We are cutting down hills and filling valleys; we are felling our trees; we devastate fields and meadows, desecrate ocean and lake beaches, and the banks of rivers and brooks, blanketing all with mass-produced sameness." [19]

Moreover, Lewis Mumford warns that this sprawl will grow into a vast megalopolitan wasteland, unfit for human habitation. His solution is the establishment of regional reservations of green space, which will remain in a state of natural growth or useful cultivation. The most important public task of every urban center, he contends, is the maintenance of permanent open areas available for agriculture and horticulture. These green spaces should surround American cities and separate one urbanized area from another. [20] In the meantime, the ever increasing population of metropolitan areas continues to spill out into the countryside and overwhelm even the increasingly inadequate national parks, while the desert and Arctic areas find their already fragile ecologies threatened by the wave of recreational and industrial expansion.

Is Christianity Responsible for the Ecological Crisis?

As was pointed out, in each of the major areas of ecological crises—water, air and land—there has always been pollution, erosion, and natural contamination. Forests have been destroyed by fires started by lightning, while windstorms and floods have scoured the land and filled the air and water with dust, silt, and mud. However, the advent of man, with his increasing population and his sprawling cities, has brought about a great acceleration of these natural processes, and the very basis for life is now threatened with annihilation. In fact, man's record of mindless destruction is so great that it reveals the basic threat to the environment is not from technology but from human nature itself. In reviewing the causes of pollution, Caldwell recognized that the "cardinal question regarding man's future is whether, as a species, he is capable of bringing his destructive tendencies under control." He adds, "In order to improve the quality of man's environment, the quality of man himself also must be improved." [21]

But how can man be induced to change? Is it sufficient simply to point out the consequences of his actions and then hope he will learn? Caldwell, for one, believes that man is capable of meeting the crisis if he can be made to understand it. But others are less sanguine, noting that all of the health warnings have had little impact on man's use of tobacco. And, a man's devotion to his automobile and the other conveniences of modern life is likely to prove just as strong.

> Men make politics; political institutions influence human behavior; but behavior is also influenced by attitudes, beliefs, and values. Purposeful shaping of the environment involves the purposeful shaping of outlooks on life. The quality of the future environment depends therefore upon the shaping of attitudes, beliefs, and values through present education. [22]

But how will these values be shaped? Is Christianity relevant to this area of life? Does it provide a value system that can effect a positive response to the ecological crisis? Interestingly, Caldwell suggests that Christianity is indeed' relevant, but as part of the problem, not part of the solution. He charges that Christianity profoundly influenced the American frontiersmen who had no conception of a balance of nature. They regarded nature as an enemy to be conquered, and their "immediate self-interest" was reinforced by their Old Testament Christianity." He further emphasizes this point in a rather tortured passage where he charges that religious thought in general and Christianity in particular tended to separate man from his earthly environment.

> The separability of man from Earth was a theological concept, and the universality of a tolerable, although not necessarily agreeable, environment was assured by divine intent. Wherever there were men, whether on Earth, in heaven, or in hell there was an environment in which the human personality, in some form, could exist. The separability of man from the earthly environment was, however, seldom joined to the equally valid proposition that the Earth was separable from man. Theologies pictured the world as created for man; they had no reason to postulate environments or, more precisely, natural conditions totally unrelated to man or to his destiny. Not until the time of Darwin did man begin to perceive the meaning of vast geologic epochs in a world without man. This meaning, reaffirmed by the discovery and probing of outer space, was that all life, including the life of man, is contingent upon the fitness of the environment.[23]

The best answer Caldwell can advance for correcting man's destructive tendencies is a call for effective environmental management based on a better technique of cost accounting. Ultimately he places faith in man's rationality and ability to see that all actions carry with them certain costs in energy and opportunity. "Therefore, all policies for the environment represent value judgments; they are, in effect, decisions as to the worth of specified properties or conditions of the environment."

To begin it is necessary to gather and interpret the facts which are needed to make the proper assessment of the real cost of various alternative environmental policies. Moreover, he warns, the policies that may emerge from this approach to preserving "our life support base" could require powers "that would have been unthinkable in the simpler past. A highly technoscientific culture must be paid for by a discipline that some sectors of a free-enterprise economy will find it hard to accept." [24]

Caldwell has struggled with the problem of developing an adequate frame of reference which will make environmental management possible. Although he obviously recognizes the importance of religious teaching in the development of values, he maintains repeatedly that the world religions have an anti-ecological bias based upon a conviction that man is prior to and outside of nature.

In Caldwell's opinion, there are three basic points of conflict between Christianity and contemporary ecological concern. First, man has dominion over nature and thus he may subjugate and exploit the environment as long as it is for his benefit. Second, Christians reject the inherent worth of nature, as exemplified by "Christian Zealots" chopping down "druidic oaks." This, in Caldwell's view, reveals the hostility of Christianity to "Pantheistic nature worship" and indifference to the natural world. Finally, the Christian conception of this world as temporary, merely a place in which one prepares for eternity, means that it has no inherent worth in and of itself.

He does, however, acknowledge that Christianity is not a monolithic ideology and that there are different streams of thought. For example, the teachings of Saint Francis of Assisi illustrate a more positive approach to nature. He also is encouraged by recent church declarations that the desecration of nature is inconsistent with the concept of

195

God as Creator, and urges the formulation of an ethic based on a "profound and genuine respect" for creation and a sense of wonder uncorrupted by arrogance.

Other writers have also accused Christianity of being a major cause of the ecological crisis. Historian Lynn White, Jr., in an address to the American Association for the Advancement of Science meeting on December 26, 1966, maintains that the problem is a result of the "orthodox Christian arrogance toward nature." White's basic argument is similar to that of Caldwell. He charges that Christianity is the "most anthropocentric religion the world has seen," and that it "insisted that it is God's will that man exploit nature for his proper ends." By "destroying pagan animism," Christianity made it possible for man to "exploit nature in a mood of indifference to the feelings of natural objects." [25] White sounds a call for the creation of either an entirely new religion or the drastic rethinking of the existing one. And like Caldwell he finds an inspiration for this in Saint Francis:

> The key to an understanding of Francis is his belief in the virtue of humility—not merely for the individual but for man as a species. Francis tried to depose man from his monarchy over creation and set up a democracy of all God's creatures. With him the ant is no longer simply a homily for the lazy, flames a sign of the thrust of the soul toward union with God; now they are Brother Ant and Sister Fire, praising the Creator in their own ways as Brother Man does in his. [26]

White's critique of Christianity was essentially repeated by Richard A. Means, a sociology professor, in a *Saturday Review* article entitled "Why Worry About Nature?" [27]

THE CHRISTIAN RESPONSE TO THE PROBLEM

These ideas have not gone unchallenged. Noted evangelical scholar Francis Schaeffer has submitted the opinions of

White and Means to a detailed examination in his recent book *Pollution and the Death of Man: The Christian View of Ecology*. Schaeffer acknowledges that the record of the church in ecological matters is little better than that of unbelievers. But, those who look to pantheism for a solution to the ecological crisis will be disappointed. For example, Christians cannot accept the false and unwarranted romanticizing of nature in pantheism. Since nature is not inherently benevolent, if a person projects his feeling into a tree, he has surrendered his ability to distinguish between benevolence and terror. [28]

Both Means and White assert that Christians have no conception of a tree as more than a physical fact and, like Caldwell, they are disturbed by Christian missionaries who for two thousand years have supposedly been chopping down sacred groves because they were regarded as idolatrous. Schaeffer's response is that this argument only points out modern man's lack of categories and standards for judgment:

> For him the fact that a Christian would cut down a sacred grove when it has become an idol proves that Christians are against trees. It is rather like arguing concerning the Bible and art. The Bible is not "against" art. But supposing somebody argued that the Jews broke the brazen serpent which Moses had made (2 Kings 18:4). Here one has a serpent made of brass which the godly king broke, so therefore God is "against" art. Of course, from the biblical viewpoint, it is not a statement against art at all. They were against the brazen serpent, which God had originally commanded to be made, *only when it became an idol.* God commanded this work of art to be made, but when it became an idol it was to be destroyed. . . . This means that one has categories. [29]

The pantheistic approach which views nature as normal is unable to come to grips with abnormality in nature. And because of its inability to respond to abnormality, pantheism results in the abasement of man. This is particularly evident in India where the basic economic problems are complicated by a pantheistic system in which the rats and cows are allowed to eat food needed for human consumption. "Instead of man being raised, in reality he is lowered. Rats and cows are finally given preference to man himself, and man begins to disappear into the woodwork in economics as well as in the area of personality and love." [30]

Is there, then, a Christian approach that can provide a basis for ecological concern? Schaeffer responds with a resounding *yes*, but he also warns that the Christian does not automatically have an answer. It must be "the right kind of Christianity." It cannot, for example, be a platonic, "two story" form of religion which is concerned only with "saving the soul" and thus views this world with contempt. The basis for a Christian view of nature rests on the concept of creation. The believer should treat a tree with integrity not because it has a soul but because God made it. This is explicitly set out in God's agreement with Noah in Genesis 9. In establishing the covenant relationship, God includes not only man and his seed but "every living created thing," and He speaks of the rainbow as a token of His covenant with the earth. Thus the covenant covers all creation, and man must respect it. As Schaeffer forthrightly affirms, "What God has made I, who am also a creature, must not despise." [31]

Christians must recognize the natural world as a fellow creature, and their dominion over the natural world is not that of a conquering monarch but of the steward. This world belongs to God, and men are to exercise control over mundane things, not as though they have the inalienable right to exploit them but as stewards who hold them in trust for the true Owner. Christians must not deify the physical world nor exalt nature above man and deny him the right of wood for shelter or meat for food. But, in satisfying these needs, man is required to approach the natural world with respect.

When we consider the tree . . . we may chop it down, so long as we remember it is a tree, with its own value *as a tree*. It is not a zero. Some of our housing demonstrates the practical application of this. Bulldozers have gone in to flatten everything and clear the trees before the houses are begun. The end result is ugliness. It would have cost another thousand pounds to bulldoze *round* the trees, so they are simply bulldozed down without question. And then we wonder, looking at the result, how people can live there. It is less human in its barrenness, and even economically it is poorer as the topsoil washes away. So when man breaks God's truth, in reality he suffers. 32

Each Christian must examine his own understanding of man's relationship to the natural world around him. He must recognize that the exploitive, contemptuous attitude toward nature that Caldwell, White, and Means attribute to Christianity is, in fact, just as anti-Christian as the pantheistic worship of nature. The world of nature is a jungle as well as a garden, a flood as well as a sparkling brook. Nature in the raw is not necessarily benevolent, and man can play a positive role as a cultivator and husbandman. Cutting trees and cultivating fields can be life-giving rather than destructive. But, he must remember that his dominion is to be that of the steward and not of the conqueror. He approaches fields, trees, and wildlife with respect, taking only that which is genuinely needed to support life, and not wantonly slaughtering or plowing them under.

Further, it is necessary to be cognizant of the balance of nature. Each usage, each change, each cutting of a tree, each breaking of the sod or diffusion of waste into air or water affects the total balance. It is inconceivable that human life can continue if nothing is done to halt those who pillage and pollute the environment. Vague concepts of "economic need" as a justification for exploitation are absolutely unacceptable to a Christian with even a minimal sensitivity for the environment.

Congested megalopolises which cannot "afford" open space or the conservation of aesthetic amenities, exemplify this aspect of the nonsense of economic necessity. For example, the value of land in mid-town Manhattan is no more than what the society that controls its use wishes to impute to it. . . . One could argue that human needs for open space in the heart of a popular city could make some land too valuable to be built upon. 33

Christians can and should engage in political action to call attention to ecological crises and seek solutions in law and regulation. But, in the final analysis, laws will only be as successful as the value system of the society permits. If so-called "economic need" is not to be considered the ultimate arbiter of ecological action, then an alternative is needed. This means that we who are Christians must begin with ourselves. If we would deny other men "the right to ravish our land, just as we refuse them the right to ravish our women," we must see to it that we do not ourselves "ravish our 'fair sister' for the sake of greed, in one form or another." 34

And beyond this, Christians must take the lead in establishing a value pattern that can shape the response of others in the society. Schaeffer uses the symbol of the "pilot plant" to illustrate this point. He indicates that when a corporation sets out to erect a major new factory, they begin by building a pilot plant to demonstrate how the full-scale one will work. The church should serve in the role of a pilot plant to demonstrate "that in this present life men can exercise dominion over nature without being destructive." 35

If Caldwell's concept of the planet "Spaceship Earth" is combined with Schaeffer's pilot plant, the concerned believer can better understand both the urgency of the current ecological crisis and the importance of his own response. The Christian's God is infinite, but the world He has entrusted to His created beings is not. The scriptural warning,

"Whatsoever a man sows, that he will also reap" (Gal. 6:7), must not be ignored. If man continues the present pattern of senseless exploitation, then he will reap the destruction of the earth whose care has been entrusted to him. The warnings have been sounded by scientists, young people, and an increasing number of other concerned groups. Ecology has become a cause. But, it is a cause that may well flounder in futility unless the Christian pilot plant can help to establish a set of values that places life and its support system ahead of convenience and supposed economic need. [36]

11

Christian Attitudes Toward Israel

The existence of the nation of Israel is an extremely perplexing problem for the Christian community. As
long as there was no political entity, one could argue
abstractly about a restored Israel and what part it would
play in relationship to the Christian church. Many Christians have held that the church is the New Testament equivalent of the Old Testament nation of Israel. In other words,
God's dealings with the nation under the old covenant
economy are paralleled by Christ's relationship to the new
covenant "Nation of Israel," the church.

There is in a certain sense a biblical basis for this teaching, but unfortunately many have carried the equation of
the church with Israel too far. This is nothing new, for a
steady stream of sermons, articles, and books on the subject
of the church as the kingdom of God appeared throughout
the Christian era. A notable example of this interpretation
is the comment of Geerhardus Vos that Christ's reference
to "*my church*" meant "the church which by recognizing me

(Jesus) as Messiah will take the place of the present Jewish church (i.e. Jewish nation)." [1]

MODERN ISRAEL

With the establishment of a modern national state, however, Israel is no longer merely an academic or theoretical question. Israel has engaged in three major wars with neighboring Arab states and has come out of these encounters militarily and geographically stronger than many thought possible. There are a number of reasons for this phenomenal growth, but perhaps the most important one is immigration. The anti-Semitism which Jews experienced in both Christian and Muslim lands has caused them to desire a national homeland. [2] The "Law of Return," which guarantees citizenship for any Jew who immigrates to Israel, has caused many Jews to come seeking a fresh start in a political system with which they can identify. Although some could not adjust to this new system and returned to their former homes, the majority stayed and furnished talents and skills for building the new order. In the early days of the nation most of the immigrants came because of religious and political persecution in the lands of their birth. With the possible exception of Soviet Jewry, this is no longer the case and the new arrivals now come voluntarily. Professional and skilled individuals are to be found in great quantity. In fact, Golda Meir has recently stated "that Israel cannot exist, and has no right to exist, without *aliya* [immigration]." [3]

Statistics indicate this phenomenal growth. For example, during the last twenty years Israel's irrigated acreage has increased from 75,000 to 428,000 acres, and the value of its agricultural production has risen from 11 million to over 445 million dollars. During the past two decades the number of employees in industry has expanded from 73,000 to over 260,000, and production from 170 million to over 2 billion dollars. Israel's exports have grown from 28 million dollars in the late 1940s to 683 million dollars in the early 1970s. At the time of the founding of the nation, exports were only 11 percent of the percentage of imports. This had risen to almost 60 percent in early 1970. [4]

Israel's economy is a mixture of socialism and private enterprise. The roots of Eastern European Jewry and the *kibbutz* heritage have produced the socialist ideology of the government.[5] The influence of Western Jewish capitalism and investment has given rise to private and corporate enterprises. This mixture, along with rising immigration, has led to remarkable economic growth in which unemployment is virtually nonexistent.

A pamphlet has recently been published by the Israeli Department of the Treasury to attract foreign investments in Israel. It was prepared for the Prime Minister's Third Economic Conference scheduled for May, 1973. If there is even a 75 percent degree of accuracy in these estimates, it is still startling and will undoubtedly cause concern in the neighboring Arab states. The population is projected to rise to at least four million by the end of 1980, of which over 1,100,000 will be of school age. The student population in universities and technical schools will increase to 85,000 by the end of the decade as compared to 50,000 presently. [6]

These data reveal that Israel is no transitory political phenomenon, and the Jewish religious community both within and outside of the country is very much aware of this. Disapora Judaism is faced with difficulty in deciding how to relate its religious beliefs, forged largely outside of an Israeli national context, with the new state. Judaism has always held that one of the chief roots of persecution was nationalism, but now Jews themselves espouse this ideology. Western Reformed Judaism is particularly faced with the problem of relating to Israeli Judaism. In other words, not only Christians, but Jews as well, are having to reexamine their positions. [7]

The question of Israel's moral right to exist has caused sharp divisions among American Christians. To separate the opinions into liberal and conservative camps is of no value, for these camps are not united on the question. It is probably true that the more conservative or evangelical Protestants tend to support Israel, but this is not necessarily true of the more conservative elements in Roman Catholic circles. The more liberal wings of Protestantism have often sided with the various Arab positions, but it is difficult to make simple categorizations.

Roman Catholic, Greek Orthodox, and Armenian Christianity have deep roots in Palestine. In the early fourth century Armenia accepted Christianity as a state religion and the Roman Empire followed soon after this. The Christianity of the empire was largely Greek in its expression. The church acquired much land in Palestine for its church structures and monasteries in the fourth and fifth centuries. As the gulf gradually widened between Latin Christianity and Greek Orthodoxy, the two churches competed fiercely for the acquisition of "authentic" holy places. Under Ottoman Turkish rule in Palestine during the last four hundred years, the French were instrumental in helping different Roman Catholic orders to acquire properties. After the expulsion of the Turks in World War I, the Orthodox and the Catholics had favored status, first with the British Mandate government and then with the Jordanian government.

In 1947 the United Nations Special Commission on Palestine recommended that Jerusalem be internationalized.[8] This met with approval from the Vatican and most of the Eastern Orthodox churches. The churches did not wish to negotiate with a local government, but after the 1948 war these groups accepted the authority of the Jordanian government. A reasonably congenial relationship with the

Arab authorities developed in the next few years, and once Israel took over all of Palestine in 1967 the Greek Orthodox and the Roman Catholic churches were reluctant to accept this turn of events. The Catholic Church has accommodated itself to the Israeli government, but the Greek Orthodox Church has been reticent to cooperate with the new regime. This Orthodox reluctance is due in part to a desire to retain the choice property which they own in Jerusalem and elsewhere in Palestine.

The American branches of these churches have tended to side with their brethren in Israel. Some of the more liberal Catholic churchmen have supported the Israeli government's handling of the holy places in Jerusalem. This can be seen in a document issued by a group of twenty-four Catholic and Protestant leaders in New York stating that historically the internationalization of a city has never worked satisfactorily. [9] Other Catholics, however, have been very critical of the Israeli takeover. The editor of *The Tablet,* a London Catholic weekly, states:

> No one would question the sincerity of the Jewish people's feeling for Jerusalem in the long centuries of exile. Nor can there be any legitimate reason for Jews to disregard the feelings of others or to question the rights of the Muslim and Christian Arabs after thirteen centuries of unbroken occupation. If sentiment and ancient prophecy are to be invoked to justify military conquest, the world will find itself in a disorderly and dangerous situation. . . . Israel's claim to sovereignty over Arab Jerusalem has no more solid basis than the fact that the Israeli army captured it by force of arms in 1967. . . . The Arabs will never renounce their claim to a city which has been theirs for more than a thousand years. If the Israelis insist on keeping it, the conflict in the Middle East will be indefinitely prolonged. [10]

The Greek Orthodox in the West have been relatively silent on this issue, but generally most Orthodox spokesmen have been sympathetic to the pro-Arab position that their church has taken in Israel and in other places in the Middle East.

PROTESTANT CHRISTENDOM

In a recent issue of the *Christian Century*, W. G. Oxtoby calls for Protestants to adopt a stance between "pro-Arab" and "pro-Israel." [11] He feels those terms have become so emotionally loaded that when a person is tagged with one of them, he is categorized as an extremist on the issue. Oxtoby sets forth his position in a fourfold statement: (1) The Palestinians as a people have been wronged and deserve justice. (2) Israel's occupation of the west bank of the Jordan River is unacceptable because it was the result of military conquest. (3) Doves are to be preferred to hawks in the Israeli political system, and the external threat to Israel has not been sufficient enough to justify the harsh measures taken. (4) It is morally right to give the Arab views more sympathetic attention than the American government and news media have done so far. He is concerned both about the suffering of the Palestinians and the fact that this has not been recognized in the West. [12]

A. Roy Eckardt, a liberal theologian like Oxtoby, opposes the moderate position toward the Middle Eastern question. His thesis is: "No reconciliation or compromise is possible between antagonists one of whom rejects the reality of the other. The life of a nation is not negotiable." [13] Because the Arabs are unwilling to admit the existence of the state of Israel by refusing to enter into direct negotiations with it, there can be no settlement in the Middle East. In fact, Eckardt believes that opposition to the Israeli position on the question is tantamount to anti-Semitism. "It is impossible to separate Arab anti-Israelism and anti-Zionism from anti-Semitism. They are mutually reinforcing." [14] The hate literature now emanating from Muslim Arab sources is nothing more than a new form of the hate propaganda of classical Christian anti-Semitism, Eckardt feels.

Recently the American Friends Service Committee published a study of the Israeli-Arab problem. Its four major points are: (1) Israel is a sovereign state and must be recognized by Arab governments as such and guaranteed security by the world community. (2) Israel must abide by U.N. Resolution Number 242 and return all annexed territories except for minor border changes. (3) Palestinian refugees must receive compensation or be allowed to return to their homes, and they must maintain the right of political self-determination. (4) Each side has made tragic mistakes. [15] This report clearly affirmed the right of the Palestinians to reclaim the lands that are presently held by the state of Israel.

The document proved to be highly controversial and was praised by some Christian groups and condemned by others. Most Jewish organizations denounced it as anti-Semitic, and a Jewish refutation was quickly released. [16] These critics contend that the Friends made demands of the Israelis that they did not make of the Arab governments involved, for example, the insistence that Israel should not demand direct negotiations because they were "not feasible." An objective consideration of the report would reveal that it is naive concerning the subject of compensation or return of the Palestinians' land. Ownership can be determined for only a small percentage of the refugees, as the bulk of the uprooted Arabs were landless peasants. So much change has taken place in the last two decades that it would be impossible for the refugees to return to their old way of life.

On the conservative or evangelical side of the theological spectrum there is a division of opinion, but of a different nature. More Evangelicals than liberals support the existence and development of Israel. An excellent recent example of this is the Billy Graham film *His Land,* which presents the modern state of Israel in the most favorable light possible. There are those, however, who are concerned with the growing nationalism of Israel. This concern is related to two factors: the Palestinian refugees, and Christian missionary activity in Arab lands. Elisabeth Elliot, who visited Palestine shortly after the 1967 war, wrestled with the problem of the Israel of prophecy as contrasted with the actual conditions in the state of Israel following their recent victory.[17] As she interviewed both Arabs and Jews, she questioned that if this is indeed the fulfillment of Scripture, how could God condone one people persecuting another people?

Mrs. Elliot's book beautifully expresses the frustrations of any war between two peoples. On which side was God between the wars of the Greeks and Romans? Was God on the side of the white man in the United States as he pushed west, conquering Indian lands? Is He always on the side of the winner? These are questions which do not have simple answers. War and the results of war are never attractive. The weakness of Mrs. Elliot's book is that it was written in the immediate aftermath of the June, 1967, war. Her emotions, along with those of many others, were aroused because of the suffering that had taken place, and rightly so. But one cannot evaluate history from such a platform, as cruel as that may sound.

Many Christians concerned about God's work in Arab lands feel that there must be an about-face in the minds of American evangelical Christians regarding Israel. This was recently expressed in a forceful way in a student newspaper which published interviews with several Christian Lebanese students. One statement, though rather strong, is quite representative of Arab thinking:

> In the Arab world we are suspicious of any foreigner. The average person looks on an American as an imperialist, a person who has come to try to influence the Arabs to sur-

render to Israel. We can't help it because American policy has been for Israel. Particularly on campuses in strong Moslem circles scepticism of missionaries is rampant. They are viewed as being dragged to the Middle East by the Western powers to act as fifth columnists. [18]

Although some points in this statement may be debatable, such as what is American policy toward Israel, that was no issue as far as this student was concerned. Whether these impressions are right or wrong is not the problem, for the fact is that most Arabs feel this way. Middle Eastern Christians and Muslims alike think that the American mass media is in the control of adherents to the Zionist position. Because of this suspicion of Westerners, the only successful Christian missionary activity will be that which is conducted under the direction of Arabs themselves.

There is another group of evangelical Christians who tend to support Israel, not necessarily because they agree with all its policies, but because they consider this important for the fulfillment of biblical prophecies. Many conservative theologians have long felt that the nation of Israel occupies a pivotal role in the future as revealed in the Bible. [19] The most recent popularizer of this view has been Hal Lindsey, whose book *The Late Great Planet Earth* has sold hundreds of thousands of copies in the English-speaking world. [20] He has won a large following among the Christian youth who are disenchanted with the institutional church. Where theologians are abstract, Lindsey becomes concrete with specific names of nations which will be involved in the eschatological events. He states:

> To be specific about Israel's great significance as a sign of the time, there are three things that were to happen. First, the Jewish nation would be reborn in the land of Palestine. Secondly, the Jews would repossess old Jerusalem and the sacred sites. Thirdly, they would rebuild their ancient temple of worship upon its historic site. . . . This restoration would take place after a world wide dispersion and long term deso-

lation of the land of Israel. However, it would occur shortly before the events which will culminate with the personal, visible return of the Messiah, Jesus Christ, to set up an everlasting Kingdom and bring about the spiritual conversion of Israel. [21]

One of the reasons Lindsey's work is so popular among youth and adults is because he is very certain about the future. Theologians and biblical scholars are generally more careful in their discussions of prophecy. Many young people, caught in the prevailing anti-intellectualism, have become disillusioned with the learned and have been seeking for authority.

The problem with Lindsey's book is that people will study it and accept it as gospel truth. Many statements in the book are only interpretations of events which are not clearly set forth in Scripture. An example of this is the statement that the false prophet will definitely be a Jew, which may be true, but the Bible does not speak so unequivocally. [22] An assertion like this can have a definite effect on the way people relate to Jews or to Israel. Lindsey's training at Dallas Theological Seminary is obviously reflected in remarks of this nature. Professor J. Dwight Pentecost of Dallas Theological Seminary has written a textbook on biblical eschatology in which he too, but in a more scholarly manner, makes the same identification of the false prophet. [23]

A much more healthy sign of evangelical interest in eschatology was the international Jerusalem conference on Biblical Prophecy in June, 1971. Christian leaders from many segments of the evangelical world gathered to discuss the subject of the return of Jesus Christ. Although the conference participants were of one accord about the fact of the second coming itself, there were many differences on the details surrounding this future event. Even a number of Jewish leaders were invited to present the side of Israeli Judaism on the matter of the Messiah and Israel. [24]

IS THERE A CHRISTIAN POSITION?

Several years ago this author wrote about the dilemma facing the Christian who was attempting to be fair in his evaluation and relationship to both peoples. 25 The dilemma still exists, but there are certain political realities which have to be taken into account in this present time. Regardless of one's theological position on the Israeli-Arab conflict, there are certain basic criteria which must be recognized.

The first is the right of Israel to exist as a state; the Jews possess that right just as much as any other group of people with similar cultural traits who wish to have their own nation-state. The United States and other Western nations should strongly protest the position of the Arab governments who will not officially recognize that an Israeli government exists. If the Arab regime will not accept this basic premise, there seems little chance for a peaceful settlement.

The second issue is whether Israel has a right to exist in the geographical area of Palestine. One may ask: "Where could the nation of Israel exist if not in Palestine?" In the early part of this century the British suggested that a Jewish state be established in East Africa. To the Zionist this was unthinkable because it omitted a major part of his religious and traditional identity—the land of Palestine.

However, the indigenous Palestinian responds that he, too, has an identity in the land of the Bible. His ancestors have lived there for over a millennium. Is this not his home as well? The only reasonable answer is that it is the home of both. The Romans destroyed the nation of Israel in the first century A.D. Those Jews who remained eventually intermarried with the various conquering peoples and did not reestablish an autonomous Jewish political entity. The Byzantines, Persians, Arabs, Crusaders, and Turks, who ruled portions of Palestine at one time or another during the past two thousand years, have contributed to the creation of a Palestinian people. Certainly they have just as much of a right to exist as a nation, but not to the exclusion of the state of Israel. Some feel that the Palestinians might agree to this if it were not for the pressure of neighboring Arab brothers. From a historical standpoint, it is obvious that there could be no other place for either a Palestinian state or an Israeli state.

The third issue involves the Israeli seizure of Palestinian territory during the three Middle Eastern wars. Unfortunately, the neighboring Arab governments have used the Palestinians as pawns in their dealings with Israel. There would not have been so many Palestinians displaced had it not been for these conflicts. Many Palestinians were poor peasants with little education who believed the promises of the politicians which, of course, were never fulfilled. They were the tragic victims in the wars, not the leaders of the neighboring Arab states.

Wars always cause agony and suffering, especially for the innocent who are caught between opposing sides. The Palestinians are in this unenviable position today. Does one condemn them for losing the conflicts, or does one denounce the Israelis for winning? Neither is the answer. Instead, the Christian must look at the situation realistically, and begin the process of rebuilding from there. To tear down what has taken place and create the possibility of still another war would bring more heartache and pain to the region.

Although the United States government has in actuality supported neither Israel or the Arab states very strongly, the American position is somewhat more favorable to the Israelis. This can be demonstrated by looking at the speaking and voting patterns of the American delegation at the United Nations as well as the State Department's policy decisions. American foreign policy in regard to Israel and Palestine parallels that of the British government during the Mandate period. This practice of "fence-straddling" resulted in neither side being satisfied and then a tragic war.

214

It is time for some bold moves in foreign policy like those that have recently been made in the case of China. The first step in the right direction would be to change the location of the American embassy from Tel-Aviv to Jerusalem. Such a move would eliminate doubts from the minds of the Israelis concerning the intentions of the United States. No major power has an embassy in Jerusalem, but only consulates. This is an insult to the Israeli Jews who believe that there can be no other capital than the city of David. At the same time the U. S. government should support King Hussein's proposed plan or one similar to it, with the possible exception of Jerusalem. 26 Primary negotiations to accomplish these goals cannot take place in the United Nations because of the loss of confidence in the organization by Middle Easterners. The major powers must make bold strides to bring a peaceful settlement to this troubled area.

The Evangelical, whose interest in the region is heightened by biblical prophecy, must remember that the main focus of the biblical prophet was not on the future, but on his own day. The bulk of the message was a denunciation of spiritual failure, government ills, and social problems. The future was brought into the prophetic message as an illustration for the present or as an offer of hope in the face of discouraging times.

Jesus tried to dissuade His disciples from asking too many questions about the future (Ac. 1:7), for their responsibility was to proclaim the gospel in the present (Mt. 24:14). An awareness of future events would serve to prevent slothfulness in the ministry. For believers to be so concerned about the details of eschatology that they neglect the needs of people in the world was never in harmony with Jesus' message. It behooves the Christian to adopt the same careful approach and to be very cautious in his use of the Scriptures as a crystal ball.

12

The Christian, War, and Militarism

The Grim Threat of Militarism

The Indochina war has brought sharply into focus for Americans the grave danger of an emphasis on militarism. Evangelical Christians must confess to their shame that they have not been willing to stand against the war mentality that has brought the nation to the point of spiritual and psychological exhaustion. Since World War II, Evangelicals have generally supported a hard line toward Communism, perhaps because Marxism is a competing ideology to the Christian faith. Anti-Communism has helped to bring into being a military establishment which has hitherto been quite uncharacteristic of the United States. To combat the uncritical evangelical support of the present militarist attitude of the United States, it will be helpful first to notice some of the effects of American militarism, then to trace various Christian opinions toward war, and finally to indicate options other than military action which are available to the United States to exert influence in international affairs.

The most obvious effect of the present military emphasis of the nation is the large commitment of resources to the "defense" effort. The scale of these expenditures is staggering! For example, the United States is estimated to have spent 387 billion dollars to fight World War II, as compared to only 32 billion for World War I. All the powers involved in World War II made direct expenditures of 1,167 billion, compared with 211 billion in World War I. Prior to World War I the United States never spent more than one billion dollars annually or $8 per capita for war materials in time of peace. However, during the 1960s the annual defense budget rose to over 70 billion or $350 per capita, more than the total expenditures of all the powers in World War I. Previous to 1914 the United States per capita military expenditures approximated the world average and were only about one-third of the average for the other major nations. But in the 1960s its per capita expenditures were over six times the world average. [1]

Spending on such a grand scale has caused the Defense Department to become so entwined in the national economic system that it is nearly impossible to separate them. To put these billions of dollars into more comprehensible terms, it should be pointed out that the defense establishment has 470 major installations with over 6,000 lesser facilities covering a combined area larger than the state of Tennessee. Approximately one of every ten Americans owes his job to defense spending, while about 22,000 prime contractors and 100,000 subcontractors produce defense products. Huge industries, such as ship building and aircraft, earn over half of their income from military expenditures.

The allocation of such large amounts of the society's wealth for war purposes is particularly tragic because it keeps America from dealing with a wide variety of pressing problems. It is not possible to have both "guns and butter," hence America, the richest nation on earth, has one-fifth of its population living in poverty, decaying cities, financially endangered educational systems, foul air, polluted rivers and streams, crime, and racial unrest. To alleviate these problems will require both the expenditure of vast sums of money which must be taken from the defense budget and the utilization of much of the manpower currently employed in war-related industries. In a recent Senate discussion of military expenditures it was pointed out that a missile meant to fire at enemy planes, presumably Russian, cost $400,000 apiece, while the plane it is supposed to shoot down costs $800,000. If it would require two missiles to do the job, the expense of destroying a plane would be as much as that of building it. Some years ago President Eisenhower said that the cost of one bomber would pay for thirty new schools or two fully equipped hospitals. (With the inflationary rise in the prices of military hardware, one bomber would now pay for forty schools or four hospitals.) He added that this is no way of life at all. It is humanity hanging from a cross of iron. [2]

If militarism affects America physically, it has had an even greater impact psychologically. Before World War II, American attitudes were generally isolationist, pacifist, and antimilitary. The peacetime military establishment had little prestige and influence on national affairs. However, the vast scale of World War II and the realignment of international relationships that resulted created a military machine in America. Following the conflict, distinguished leaders from the armed services filled many important government posts. Further, the United States had assumed a new and unprecedented role in international affairs, and the firm views and problem-solving experiences of the military seemed to offer the ideal solution for national problems.

Civilians, also, were frequently influenced by a martial outlook. Millions of young Americans matured during their years in uniform, and they brought the views they had learned during their service experience into civilian life. To the 14.9 million veterans of World War II were added 5.7 million during the Korean War, and by the early 1970s over 20 percent of the adult population were veterans.

Many of these men have risen to positions of leadership in government, civic, and professional life.

> Whether they liked it or not, their military training and experience have affected them, for the creeds and attitudes of the armed forces are powerful medicine, and can become habit-forming. The military codes include all the virtues and beliefs used to motivate men of high principle: patriotism, duty and service to country, honor among fellowmen, courage in the face of danger, loyalty to organization and leaders, self-sacrifice for comrades, leadership, discipline, and physical fitness. For many veterans the military's efforts to train and indoctrinate them may well be the most impressive and influential experience they have ever had—especially so for the young and less educated. [3]

As these men grow older, they tend to romanticize and glorify their own military experiences and manifest chauvinistic and pugnacious attitudes such as those reflected in organizations like the American Legion, Veterans of Foreign Wars, and Amvets. These groups generally favor the use of force to solve international problems and believe their military service forms a useful pattern to be repeated by the younger generation.

The military establishment also cooperates with industry in the campaign to keep defense "needs" constantly before the American people. Each of the four armed services has its own association which engages in public relations work to influence thinking on matters of national policy. For example, the Air Force Association publishes and distributes to its members *Air Force and Space Digest*, a slick-paper magazine which echoes the service line. Its message is the strengthening of air power, an interpretation of international affairs in terms of the use of air power, the need for larger quantities of every type of aircraft, and an affirmation of the effectiveness of bombing in warfare. All of this is well coordinated with the efforts of the aerospace industry which thrives on air force business and advertises regularly in the magazine. Among the 96,000 members of the Air Force Association are active, reserve, and retired air force personnel and leaders in government and industry. Since most of those who receive the magazine are not careful in balancing their reading, they tend to believe its propaganda.

Another impetus to militarism has been the fact that since World Wat II Americans have become accustomed to a violent, gun-toting, military outlook on life. This attitude has been created through war movies ("heroes" like John Wayne are especially influential), comic books, toys, and television programs with military settings. War news on television and in newspapers has also been a staple commodity in the formative years of Americans.

Yet another and, according to Marine Corps General David Shoup, the most important encouragement to militarism, has come from the hard-core professional military leaders.[4] They are the products of a rigorous selection system which equips them to take the lead in planning, organizing and directing society with a single-minded determination to achieve their ends. Because of the nature of competition in the armed forces, the combat experience which only a war can offer is necessary for promotion since it gives officers the opportunity to exhibit the qualities that attract the attention of superiors and results in advancement. Moreover, the training that the military offers includes a high component of anti-Communism coupled with a stress upon the values found in the American civic religion.

This military emphasis has already distorted the American attitude toward other nations of the world. Take, for example, her behavior in the Indochina war, the most brutal one in which the United States has ever engaged. That land has been blasted with a severity unequaled in the history of warfare. Napalm, white phosphorus bombs, rockets, debilitating gases, anti-personnel bombs, B-52 bomber raids, defoliation chemicals—an entire science-fiction arsenal has been unleashed on Southeast Asia. Not only have American troops been involved in fighting an armed enemy, but they have also been concerned with "pacification" efforts. In the course of subduing the countryside, they have burned villages, shot chickens, ducks, and water buffalo, and even killed innocent civilians. The massacre at My Lai was no isolated incident in the war.

There has never been much doubt about what happened on March 16, 1968, in the South Vietnamese hamlet designated My Lai (4) on American military maps. On that day the first platoon of Charlie Company, 11th Infantry Brigade, America Division, swept through the village in pursuit of the forty-eighth battalion of the Vietcong. However, there were no Vietcong soldiers in the village; only women, children, and old men. Nevertheless, the first platoon, under the command of Lt. William Calley, proceeded to go berserk, raping young women and murdering groups of civilians that offered no resistance.[5] When the incident was finally brought to light (the military had tried to conceal it) and Lt. Calley was put on trial, it was shocking to see how many veterans of World War II sprang to his defense and confessed that they, too, had committed atrocities in their day. Some even suggested that they should be tried along with the lieutenant, while the Reverend Michael Lord announced in Columbus, Georgia, that the sentencing of Calley was like the crucifixion of Jesus. The Gallup Poll estimated that eight of every ten Americans sympathized with Calley. If such a mentality is allowed to thrive it might one day be possible to have American versions of Dachau and Buchenwald!

Another change that militarism has brought to the American outlook is the attitude of wishing to police the world. It is one of the ironies of history that the United States, a nation born in revolution, has come to be the great bulwark against revolution. The desire seems to be to support the status quo in foreign lands ideologically sympathetic to the United States by the establishment of a Pax Americana. Since unrest and the possibility of revolt exist in many countries today, this may mean that American soldiers will have to be deployed every time an uprising occurs against a "friendly" government. (Some of these friends include Franco of Spain, the Greek military dictators, and the Shah of Iran.) Given this antirevolutionary mentality, is it not conceivable that American forces may someday be called upon to fight in such places as Spain, Greece, Iran, Bolivia, or Colombia?

Evangelicals and Militarism

It is clear that, on the physical and psychological level, America is now heavily influenced by a militarist emphasis. But, how shall Evangelicals react to this? Historically, Christians have held widely varied views on the problem of war. The New Testament has little to say specifically on the matter, and it is difficult to generalize from its remarks. However, principles have been developed by theologians and philosophers, and these have varied among the different periods of Christian history as well as among individuals in the same era. The distinguished scholar of Christian thought, Roland Bainton, has classified these attitudes into three categories: pacifism, the just war, and the crusade. [6] Generally, the early Christians took a pacifist position, but when Emperor Constantine made Christianity the most favored religion of the state and the barbarians invaded the Roman Empire, Christians found it necessary to condone violence. Consequently, during the fourth and fifth centuries the church took from classical thought the teaching of the just war and remodeled it into a Christian doctrine.

As propounded by Augustine, this type of conflict must have as its objective the establishment of justice and the restoration of peace. It was to be waged only under the authority of the ruler and should be conducted in a just fashion. Justice meant that the enemy was to be dealt with in good faith and there was to be no looting, massacre, or profaning of church edifices. Also, clergy were to be exempt from participation in warfare.

During the Middle Ages, the crusading ideal arose. This was a holy war fought under the auspices of the church, not on behalf of justice conceived of in terms of life and property, but for an ideal: the Christian faith. In this type of war the enemy was thought to be the representative of evil, and consequently the just war codes concerning the treatment of the opposition tended to break down.

The pacifist, just war, and crusading positions were well established by the close of the medieval period. During the Reformation era the Wars of Religion again caused Christians to articulate theories about war. The Lutherans and Anglicans adopted just-war ideas, the Reformed churches emphasized the crusade, and pacifism was advocated by the Anabaptists and the Quakers. Because eighteenth and nineteenth-century wars were more limited, they did little to stimulate Christian thought on the matter. However, during the twentieth century, with the use of large conscript armies, modern technological weapons, and the spread of war to all corners of the world, all three Christian positions on war have been topics of wide attention. World War I was treated as a crusade by many Christians; pacifism was prevalent between the two world wars; and the mood of the just war was present duing World War II.

At present, the historic peace churches, the Quakers, Church of the Brethren, and the Mennonites stand adamantly against any military action. The Augustinian view of the just war is held by the Roman Catholic Church as well as by the major Protestant denominations. Some Christians still preach the ideal of the crusade, with the enemy being the Communists rather than the Albigensians or the Muslims. Many Evangelicals agree fully with John R. Rice's claim that

America sinned through our government in holding back General MacArthur and preventing outright victory in the Korean War. I believe our government sinned against God in holding back and letting Russian troops occupy Berlin and divide Germany. I believe that before that, the American government greatly sinned in being soft on communism, and turning the mainland of China principally over to the Communists and thus betraying our friend, Chiang Kai-shek. I have no doubt that if there is ever holy and righteous cause for war, it is to prevent godless communism with its murder and torture and persecution from taking over other lands which ask our help. [7]

Most Evangelicals, however, do not follow either the pacifist or the crusade position. Instead they attempt to maintain the just war or, as a recent article termed it, "the mediativist position." This teaching holds with pacifism

the value and importance of human life and the need for the exercise of love rather than hatred as the believer's motivation. It also recognized the fact that there have been, and indeed may again be, times when morality demands the call to arms. The mediative view also acknowledges, however, that there is no simplistic "rule of thumb" which will always and in every case provide a handy guide to personal action with regard to involvement in a given war. [8]

In a day when war may lead to nuclear holocaust, many Christians are modifying the just-war theory in the direction of pacifism. Substantial data is now available to show the folly of allowing nuclear explosions to take place in the atmosphere. For some time the destructive possibilities of nuclear warfare have been familiar to Americans. One has often heard details such as the fact that a twenty-megaton H-bomb could blast out Washington, D.C., and devastate the adjacent area from Norfolk, Virginia, to Harrisburg, Pennsylvania. Now, Ernest Sternglass' research on the effect of strontium 90 on children reveals the stark probability that the explosions of enough ABM warheads to defend against a Russian first strike would result in a sufficient amount of radioactive pollution to insure that few, if any, children in the world would survive to maturity, thus meaning the human race would perish from the earth.[9]

Even if this prediction is overdrawn, no one questions that thermonuclear warfare would entail the slaughter of everyone in the attack area, regardless of the degree of their participation in the war. Also, the long-range effects of atmospheric radioactivity would have serious consequences for the neutral powers, future generations of all mankind, and the very earth itself. The specter of destruction that emerges from this consensus makes the rational aim of the just war meaningless.

When the Christian considers the risks involved in the arms race and the policy of containment of Communism, the just-war theory no longer seems adequate. What the nations of the world need and Christians can give is the New Testament emphasis on peace. This message is so consistently woven throughout its twenty-seven books that a Christian "hawk" is a contradiction in terms. The Lord was styled "the Prince of Peace," and He counseled His followers to live as peacemakers. A person must start by being at peace with God by the removal of sin's enmity through faith in the sacrifice of Jesus Christ (Ro. 5:1; Col. 1:20). Inward peace will follow (Phil. 4:7) and will extend in an outward fashion between man and man (Eph. 2). Peace is thus viewed as one of the initial products of the work of God's Holy Spirit (Gal. 5:22-23). Since Christ and the apostles never limited this fruit of the Spirit, a Christian should not confine it merely to inward experience. Hence, Christians today must be found on the side of the peacemakers to a much greater degree than they have been in the past.

With the advent of modern technology, war has become too expensive a commodity, both in a physical and moral sense. Evangelicals are peculiarly suited by their faith to deal with the current war mentality, and indeed, it may be that they have been called for such a time as this. To the detractor who argues that war is necessary to the economy, the Christian ought to respond that man does not live by bread alone. There is another alternative to the poetic lines of Auden:

> The expert designing the long range gun,
> To exterminate everything under the sun;
> Would like to get out but can only mutter,
> What can I do? It's my bread and butter. 10

The Christian can suggest that government expenditures be shifted into rebuilding cities, mass transportation, developing the resources of the oceans, and a hundred and one other fields that would improve the quality of human life. Middle-class people in the Western nations desperately need to hear this word, since they have always been more prepared to spend money on weapons than welfare.

The extremes of American militarism can be noticed by the Evangelical more readily since his faith has taught him to judge the culture in which he lives. Clarence Jordan in his own inimitable style pointed out the folly of sending the society's finest young men to die on the battlefield:

> "The 18- to 26-year-olds may be the best killers, but they're too reckless, too flighty, and too sexy" and too much time and money has to be spent training them. . . .Middle-aged men would be good, but they're too productive. They have to stay home and make the bombs and planes and napalm, "without which there can be no peace." But senior citizens? They wouldn't even have to be drafted. If we gave them the opportunity they would volunteer in droves. No man is more anxious to fight than one who is sure he's too old. . . .
>
> The morale of such an army would be boundless. "Unlike the youngster at 19, the senior citizen would have had long years to reflect on the bliss of private enterprise and the

gross evil of communism. Without any hesitation, he would know what's worth dying for, and would gladly and eagerly spill his iron-poor blood." Many of the troops would be directors and chairmen of the boards of huge corporations with war contracts. "Given the opportunity to execute the wars they've helped plan and that have made them rich, their zeal would have no limits. . . ."

"This army would have no equal in the art of pacification. In its ranks would be retired bankers and insurance company executives who could completely rebuild the crude economic structure of any foreign country. In mere weeks after storming the beaches, all these mighty architects of the American Dream, these wrinkled but wise GIs, would transform alien lands into prosperous territories ready for statehood. With prospects of such affluent bliss, most countries would actually invite us to invade them. It might be necessary to have a war waiting list." 11

CHRISTIAN ALTERNATIVES TO WAR

What options are open to the country as substitutes for militarism? The Evangelical can point to several of these. A most important project should be the reeducation of young Americans. It is almost self-evident that present educational systems do not prepare young people for the "global village" in which they will live. The shrinking of the world has caused Americans to be nearer in travel time to Asia than they once were to other Americans. Christians, of all people, should be aware of and able to cope with this situation.

Christ's words in the Great Commission, His story of the good Samaritan, and the apostle Paul's bold statements all emphasize the value of every human being. 12 In sharp contrast to these emphases, most American Christians have come to identify their faith with Western civilization and have shown little sympathy with the outlook of other lands and cultures which vary from the Western Christian norm. Young people must spend more time studying the various world civilizations and developing an appreciation for non-Western cultures. Then they will appreciate and share the experience of Elisabeth Elliot, the well-known former missionary to the Aucas, as she explains:

> So here are "heathen" people, I told myself. And here is the Word of Truth. There must be evidenced among them a recognition of the difference, for example, between good and evil. Would it be the same for them as it was for me? What did God say about it? What would "Christian" conduct mean to the Aucas? I came to see that my own understanding of these subjects was not nearly as clear as I had supposed. I kept balancing the Auca way of life against the American, or against what I had always taken to be the Christian. . . . A comparison did not convince me of the superiority of any other group. I had come from a society where polygamy was illegal to one where it was permissible. . . . I observed faithfulness and a strong sense of responsibility on the part of the Auca husbands. . . . The Aucas were unhampered by clothing and the caprices of fashion, but stuck firmly to a code of modesty which did not change with the seasons. In their nakedness they accepted themselves and one another for what they were, always abiding by the rules. . . . I saw the Indians live in a harmony which far surpassed anything I had seen among those who call themselves Christians. I found that even their killings had at least as valid reasons as the wars in which my people engaged. [13]

Another aim of evangelicals should be an attempt to reduce the international sale of American weapons. Almost 10 percent of the national income of the United States is devoted to military purposes, while at the present time it is the largest supplier of weapons to the nations of the world. It is well known that the encouragement for the armaments trade has come from a desire to gain a favorable balance of trade and to aid certain industrial empires. [14] The United States is responsible for allowing the introduction of unneeded sophisticated weapons systems, such as jet fighters, tanks, and submarines, into relatively tranquil places like Latin America. Thus, it has permitted the creation of mini-arms races among poverty-stricken nations who have few or no reasons for conflict with one another.

Evangelicals should also be in the forefront of those encouraging bilateral disarmament. The cause of arms limitation needs the kind of dedication and encouragement that God's people can bring to it, for it has hitherto been characterized by long, hard, and mostly fruitless efforts. Beginning in 1946 with the meetings of the United Nations Atomic Energy Commission, there has been a long series of conferences between the delegates of the Eastern and Western powers in an attempt to halt the arms race. In 1952 and again in 1954 and 1955, the United Nations Disarmament Commission initiated a series of meetings that proved fruitless. These meetings, including the Geneva conferences and the current SALT talks, have produced libraries of books and learned articles but few tangible results in the reduction of the levels of military hardware by the major powers. These efforts are frequently attacked by conservative spokesmen on the grounds that "realism" demands the pursuit of military preparation rather than "useless talk."

In order to gain widespread American support for disarmament, the Christian must help to overcome the popular fear that the Soviet Union is determined to conquer the world for Communism and that if the United States disarmed even in a limited way, Russia would be all the more eager to accomplish her objectives. In reality, those scholars and statesmen who are best informed about Soviet intentions argue that the Russian revolution, as designed by Lenin and Trotsky, is no longer operative. The victory of Stalin and the execution of almost all the old Bolsheviks brought about a decisive change in the nature of Soviet Communism. The system which Stalin built was neither socialist nor revolutionary, but rather a form of state capitalism based upon authoritarian methods of planning and economic centralization. Instead of leading the anti-Communist forces, Evangelicals should be in the vanguard of promoting a proper understanding of the nature of the Russian system so that they may aid their fellow citizens in overcoming the national paranoia concerning Communism. [15]

Those who are committed to seeking peace on earth must try to find new political directions. Perhaps America needs a "peace" party or a "peace bloc" within one of the existing parties. This group could then work for disarmament and encourage America to share its wealth rather than its weapons with the poor nations of the world. The problems that help to cause wars of liberation might be alleviated if the United States would give perhaps 5 percent of its gross national product to the social and educational arm of the United Nations for helping the have-not nations. An examination of the situation in these lands dramatically demonstrates the need for this kind of aid and how it would help to decrease international violence. Roughly two-thirds of the world's people have an income of about $200 per capita or lower, while the remaining one-third have incomes as high as $2,400 in the case of the United States. The gap between the rich and poor countries seems to be increasing, as evidenced by the fact that lands with an annual per capita income below $200 have a growth rate of two percent per year while the richer countries normally grow at double that rate.

Several reasons could be given for the disparity in the global distribution of income. One of these is the difference in the growth of population. Generally speaking, the poor lands have high birth rates and the rich ones low rates of increase. Projections indicate that unless there is a change in the current pattern of growth, in sixty years India and China will have a combined population of ten billion. Another reason for the global disparity in income distribution is the terms of international trade which discriminate against the underdeveloped countries. Their economies are based largely on extractive industries, and the economic reality is that the prices of the food and raw materials produced by them tend to fall while prices of manufactured goods which they must purchase from the developed countries are steadily rising.

These difficult and, in most cases, declining conditions are, without doubt, involved in the desire for revolution. In thirty-two of the poorest countries of the world with a per capita income of $90 a year there were on the average two serious outbursts of violence per year from 1958 to 1965. During the same period, the twenty-seven richest nations of the world with 75 percent of the earth's wealth but only 25 percent of its population experienced only one important internal uprising.

A CHRISTIAN APPROACH TO REVOLUTION

Evangelicals through a peace party might also be able to help America adopt a more positive attitude toward revolution. Despite the publication of Christian books with titles such as *Jesus the Revolutionary,* most believers have come down solidly on the side of the status quo. One writer expresses the well-worn argument closing the door to revolution in this fashion:

> The tolerance expressed by the New Testament towards an institution like slavery does not prove that God approves of of it. *It does prove that the Christian has no Christian mandate for violent social change.* If there was no call to first-century Christians to free their own slaves, much less to revolt to abolish slavery everywhere, certainly we must be hesitant about saying that Christ would have his twentieth-century disciples engage in revolutionary violence to overthrow what are clearly lesser social evils than slavery.[17]

Vernon Grounds has summed up the reasons for this attitude in his thought-provoking work, *Revolution and the Christian Faith.* Among the causes he mentions is the other-worldly emphasis of most preaching, or to use an old but not irrelevant cliche, Evangelicals have "become so heavenly minded that they are no earthly good." A second reason is the evangelistic emphasis of contemporary orthodox Christians. Grounds points out:

> It has concentrated entirely on changing individuals, refusing quite universally to undertake the task of changing institutions. Quite universally, moreover, it has treated individuals as if they were disincarnate atoms moving privatistically in a spiritual vacuum where the massive evils of unemployment, racism, inflation, poor housing, political corruption, and bad sewage are nonexistent. [18]

Further, many have allowed their faith to become identified with the middle-class outlook on life. The "good" Christian shares with the bourgeois the virtues of decency, respectability, legality, industry and prosperity. Being a good church member became synonymous with being a good American. In this outlook, the status quo with all its inequities must be maintained, and whatever course of action the government chooses to pursue is deemed correct. This has caused Evangelicals to stand firmly on the side of reactionary movements against innovation and change.

> Conservative, otherworldly, individualistic, bourgeois, even reactionary—this is the indictment its critics level against evangelicalism. . . . To attempt a dispassionate evaluation of the possible exaggerations and errors in this sweeping indictment would prove useless. Substantially, however, it is irrefutable. An evangelical, therefore, ought not waste time in nitpicking with these critics. Accepting their brief of Christian failures as a pride-shattering word of judgment, he ought, instead, to take any insights thus painfully gained and apply them to his present situation. [19]

Many Christians outside the framework of American evangelical churches have begun to see the need for a more favorable relationship to revolution. Recently, sixteen Roman Catholic bishops in the so-called Third World countries issued a manifesto in which they declare that revolutions are at times necessary and that these upheavals often abandon their original opposition to religion and produce good fruits. They point especially to "the French Revolution of 1789, which made possible the declaration of human rights." [20] A rethinking of traditional attitudes has become necessary since the prospect of violent revolution characterizes the struggles of many emerging nations. Such a course of action is a natural response to Western imperialism which historically was violent in its implementation. Indeed, as Jacques Ellul has pointed out, all governments use violence through police power to perpetuate their authority. [21] What makes status quo violence so correct but revolutionary violence so wrong? Although the state is the instrument ordained by God in Romans 13, it also may become the beast of the Apocalypse which denies man his essential human rights.

The scriptural writers show clearly that the state's obligation is to insure justice. This includes the equality of all before the law; respect for the individual, his family, and property; impartial execution of the law, with punishment for dishonest practices such as fraud and the victimization of the innocent; and proper regard for widows and orphans who represent the poor of society. [22] What should Christians do if the state adamantly refuses to give justice to its citizens? Certainly in dealing with such a situation violence should always be the last resort. It should be used only after petition, public demonstrations, and passive resistance have proven futile to correct abuses. When all of these fail, however, Christians will be forced into the unpleasant position of having to approve of revolution. Such approval would have to be modeled on just-war theories. Even though there is extreme difficulty involved, Evangelicals must still try to articulate such a position. [23]

They must not line up with those who romanticize revolution, but rather, call attention to the fact that it is a bitter medicine for social ills. Christians must point out that such internal disturbances result in a profound reorientation of the operational values of a society. What was once respectable and in conformity with social mores is not considered proper behavior in time of revolution. For example, during peacetime a day's work for a day's wages is moral. However, during a rebellion it might be a social virtue to slow down and sabotage machines used in production. What normally would be dishonest acquires the attribute of honesty. Also, after the outbreak of conflict, both sides seem to reject the prospect of a peaceful solution, and violence becomes the accepted way to solve all social problems. Often the original causes of violence are forgotten and the struggle turns into an outlet for personal vengeance.

Considerations of this type give the evangelical teaching of the just revolution a melancholy cast. Still, when the established government completely fails to do its duty, justice demands that it be overthrown. The means used by the revolution should be as humane as possible and not motivated by hate. The Christian who cooperates in a rebellion should not engage in indiscriminate slaughter, torture, and wanton destruction of property. Also, the violence should be in proportion to the wrong inflicted and ought to result in more just conditions than those which existed before the revolution.

Applying principles such as these would help Americans justify their own revolution as well as those of other lands in the twentieth century. Every revolution could not fit these criteria but some would. The Vietnam War has demonstrated that a revolution accompanied by guerrilla warfare can be suppressed only by the use of genocide. [24] Undoubtedly a more positive attitude toward wars of liberation might help the United States to avoid becoming engaged in similar actions in the future.

However, violence is seldom the answer to man's problems, and Christians must affirm this truth. Moreover, the real antidote to revolution, war, and militarism was presented in a memorable fashion by Samuel Escobar at the Inter-Varsity Christian Fellowship Urbana missionary conference in 1970. In his major address he stated that Evangelicals must change their attitude and become more positive toward the social message of the gospel. He accused them of being wedded to conservative ideals so that the gospel "which was in the past an agent of dynamic renewal in society . . . serves now as a preserver of the status quo." Because of this, Evangelicals believe "politics is worldly, business is not. Active membership in a labor union is worldly, active membership in an association of real estate owners is not. Giving alms to the poor is acceptable, organizing them to fight the causes of poverty is not."[25]

Let believers in Christ stand for justice for the world's people and include in their struggle an encouragement of both the physical and psychological dismantling of American militarism.

NOTES

Chapter One

1. These are cogently summarized by Paul B. Henry in *Three Young Laymen: A Symposium* (New York: Ministers and Missionaries Board, American Baptist Convention, 1970).

2. Reported in *Christianity Today* 14 (June 19, 1970), p. 38.

3. Harold O. J. Brown, *The Protest of a Troubled Protestant* (New Rochelle, N.Y.: Arlington House, 1969), p. 64.

4. Vernon C. Grounds, *Revolution and the Christian Faith* (Philadelphia: Lippincott, 1971), p. 208.

5. Calvin Redekop, *The Free Church and Seductive Culture* (Scottdale, Pa.: Herald, 1971), p. 59.

6. Sherwood Eliot Wirt, *The Social Conscience of the Evangelical* (New York: Harper & Row, 1968), p. 9.

7. David O. Moberg, *Inasmuch: Christian Social Responsibility in the Twentieth Century* (Grand Rapids: Eerdmans, 1965), pp. 96, 53.

8. Carl F. H. Henry, *A Plea for Evangelical Demonstration* (Grand Rapids: Baker, 1971), p. 120.

9. Myron S. Augsburger, "Revolution and World Evangelism" in *Christ the Liberator* (Downers Grove, Ill.: Inter-Varsity, 1971), p. 123.

10. Harold John Ockenga, "Resurgent Evangelical Leadership," *Christianity Today* 5 (Oct. 10, 1960), pp. 11-14.

11. Paul Benware, "The Social Responsibility of the Church," *Grace Journal* 12 (Winter, 1971), p. 15.

12. E. Mansell Pattison, "Closed Mind Syndrome: An Analysis of Current Data," *Christian Medical Society Journal* 17 (Spring, 1966), pp. 7-11.

13. Moberg, p. 21.

14. John W. Montgomery, "Evangelical Social Responsibility" in *Our Society in Turmoil*, ed. Gary R. Collins (Carol Stream, Ill.: Creation House, 1970), p. 15. For a more extensive discussion of this general subject see, in addition to the works by Collins, Moberg, and Wirt, the following: Carl F. H. Henry, *Aspects of Christian Social Ethics* (Grand Rapids: Eerdmans, 1964); H. F. R. Catherwood, *The Christian in Industrial Society* (London: Tyndale, 1964); T. B. Maston, *The Christian, the Church and Contemporary Problems* (Waco: Word, 1968); R. G. Clouse, R. D. Linder, and R. V. Pierard, eds., *Protest and Politics: Christianity and Contemporary Affairs* (Greenwood, S. C.: Attic, 1968); and J. N. D. Anderson, *Into the World—The Need and Limits of Christian Involvement* (London: Falcon, 1968).

15. C.S. Lewis, "The Christian Hope," *Eternity* 5 (Mar. 1954), p. 50.

16. Henry, *Plea for Evangelical Demonstration*, p. 115.

17. Billy Graham, *World Aflame* (Minneapolis: BGEA, 1965), pp. 172-13; W. David Lockard, *The Unheard Billy Graham* (Waco: Word, 1971), chap. 6.

18. W. Maxey Jarman in *Christianity Today* 16 (Jan. 7, 1972), p. 16.

19. Anderson, pp. 56-57.

Chapter Two

1. These are true incidents. However, I have refrained from using names and changed the details of the stories somewhat in order to protect the individuals involved.

238

2. This, likewise, is a true story with the name of the Christian leader omitted for obvious reasons.

3. "Most Respected Professions," Report no. 14 in *Gallup Opinion Index* (Princeton: Gallup International, 1966), p. 26; and "Political Ethics," *New York Times* (Apr. 14, 1967), pp. 1, 22.

4. For similar tales and other Daley memorabilia, see Mike Royko, *Boss: Mayor Richard J. Daley of Chicago* (New York: Dutton, 1971).

5. Niccolo Machiavelli, *The Prince* (New York: New American Library, 1952), originally written in 1513; and William Ebenstein, *Great Political Thinkers* (New York: Holt, Rinehart & Winston, 1960), pp. 278-86.

6. Ebenstein, pp. 1-12, 64-75, 209-22, 280; and H. F. R. Catherwood, *The Christian Citizen* (London: Hodder & Stoughton, 1969), pp. 32-47.

7. J. N. D. Anderson, *Into the World—The Need and Limits of Christian Involvement* (London: Falcon, 1968), pp. 14-17. For a further and more detailed discussion of this subject, see the introduction to this volume; David Moberg, *Inasmuch: Christian Social Responsibility in the Twentieth Century* (Grand Rapids: Eerdmans, 1965), pp. 21-58; and Sherwood E. Wirt, *The Social Conscience of the Evangelical* (New York: Harper & Row, 1968), pp. 6-26.

8. Mark O. Hatfield, *Conflict and Conscience* (Waco: Word, 1971), pp. 50, 63, 65; and Mt. 22:34-40.

9. The same admonition would apply to the international scene where some Evangelicals fret about the activities of such political figures as Bernadette Devlin, Ian Paisley, and Enoch Powell.

10. Hatfield, "How Can a Christian Be in Politics?" in *Protest and Politics: Christianity and Contemporary Affairs*, ed. R. G. Clouse, R. D. Linder and R. V. Pierard (Greenwood, S.C.: Attic, 1968), p. 13.

11. Donald D. Wall, "The Lutheran Response to the Hitler Regime in Germany" in *God and Caesar: Case Studies in the Relationship Between Christianity and the State*, ed. Robert D. Linder (Longview, Tex.: Conference on Faith and History, 1971), pp. 85-100; David T. Priestley, "The Baptist Response in Germany to the Third Reich," in *ibid.*, pp. 102-3; and Robert D. Linder and Richard V. Pierard, "Christianity in East Germany Today," *Christianity Today* 16 (Jan. 21, 1972), pp. 12-13.

12. An alarming example of this sort of thing was the now-famous CBS-TV news poll of March 20, 1970, which revealed that a majority of adults in America seemed willing to restrict some of the basic freedoms constitutionally guaranteed by the Bill of Rights. Even more disconcerting was the follow-up poll on the same topic conducted by the Christian Life Commission and Research Services Department of the Baptist Sunday School Board which showed that a cross-section of church leaders in Southern Baptist churches for the most part agreed with the national sampling done by CBS. In particular, more than half of the Baptist leaders contacted in the Christian Life Commission's poll said they would be willing, in certain circumstances, to restrict the right to peaceful assembly, the right to a free-press, the right to free speech, the right concerning double jeopardy, the right of privacy, and rights concerning freedom of religion. (Lynn McMasters, "Southern Baptists and the Bill of Rights" [Dec. 7, 1971]).

13. Moberg, p. 22.

14. Earle E. Cairns, *Saints and Society* (Chicago: Moody, 1960); Charles I. Foster, *An Errand of Mercy* (Chapel Hill, N.C.: U. North Carolina, 1960); and Timothy L. Smith, *Revivalism and Social Reform* (New York: Abingdon, 1957).

15. John B. Anderson, "American Protestantism and Political Ideology" in *Congress and Conscience*, ed. John B. Anderson (Philadelphia: Lippincott, 1970), p. 179.

16. Wirt, pp. 76-77.

17. Christopher Dawson, quoted in Alec R. Vidler, *The Church in an Age of Revolution* (Baltimore: Penguin Books, 1961), p. 273.

18. John W. Montgomery, "Evangelical Social Responsibility in Theological Perspective" in *Our Society in Turmoil*, ed. Gary R. Collins (Carol Stream, Ill.: Creation House, 1970), pp. 13-23.

19. Billy Graham, *Peace with God* (Garden City, N.Y.: Doubleday, 1953), p. 190; and Mt. 10:42.

20. Billy Graham, *World Aflame* (Garden City, N.Y.: Doubleday, 1965), p. 187. See also the important works of Carl F. H. Henry on this subject: *The Uneasy Conscience of Modern Fundamentalism* (Grand Rapids: Eerdmans, 1947); and *A Plea for Evangelical Demonstration* (Grand Rapids: Baker, 1971).

21. Albert H. Cantril and Charles G. Roll, Jr., *The Hopes and Fears of the American People* (New York: Universe Books, 1971), pp. 15-30, 51-53.

22. Linder and Pierard, "Christianity in East Germany Today," pp. 12-13.

23. At this writing, there exists no sound, balanced, up-to-date history explaining the present situation in Northern Ireland. However, the Christian reader can glean a great deal of helpful information from a careful perusal of the following works: J. C. Beckett, *Protestant Dissent in Ireland* (London: Faber & Faber, 1940); Tim Pat Coogan, *The I.R.A.* (London: Fontana Books, 1970); Liam de Paor, *Divided Ulster* (Baltimore: Penguin Books, 1970); and Martin Wallace, *Northern Ireland: Fifty Years of Self-Government* (New York: Barnes & Noble, 1971). For a recent, brief assessment of the current situation from an evangelical perspective, see J. D. Douglas, "Wish You Could See . . .," *Christianity Today* 16 (Dec. 17, 1971), p. 38. Billy Graham's visit to Northern Ireland in May, 1972, is a hopeful sign that Evangelicals are going to become involved in working for reconciliation there.

Chapter Three

1. See also Thomas Howard, "What Not to Tell Your Child About Religion," *Redbook* 135 (June 1970), pp. 67, 131-38, 144.

2. Some useful works on the historical origins of Christian America include: Martin E. Marty, *Righteous Empire: The Protestant Experience in America* (New York: Dial, 1970); Thomas Sanders, *Protestant Concepts of Church and State* (Garden City, N.Y.: Doubleday, 1965); and Anson Phelps Stokes and Leo Pfeffer, *Church and State in the United States* (New York: Harper & Row, 1964).

3. The idea of Christian America is evaluated by Robert N. Bellah, "Civil Religion in America" in *The Religious Situation 1968*, ed. Donald R. Cutler (Boston: Beacon, 1968), pp. 331-93, and Richard V. Pierard, *The Unequal Yoke* (Philadelphia: Lippincott, 1970), pp. 106-30.

4. For some recent examples of this type of behavior see Billy Graham, "The Unfinished Dream," *Christianity Today* 14 (July 31, 1970): 20-21; "Billy Graham and 'Civil Religion,'" *Christianity Today* 15 (Nov. 6, 1970), pp. 56-57; Reinhold Niebuhr, "The King's Chapel and the King's Court," *Christianity and Crisis* 29 (Aug. 4, 1969), pp. 211-12.

5. *Traditionalist* has in this context no pejorative connotation; it merely means people who hold to the Christian description of things as understood and interpreted through the course of church history. Nineteenth- and twentieth-century theology represents a distinct *re*-interpretation of Christian dogma.

6. An excellent book that stresses the difference between Christianity and American culture is Elisabeth Elliot, *The Liberty of Obedience* (Waco: Word, 1968).

7. Many today deplore the whole missionary enterprise because of its identification with imperialism and capitalism; but the Word of God was preached in many places where it would not have otherwise reached, and much good was done to improve the physical and social conditions of other peoples.

8. Several evangelical historians have recently discussed the role of Christianity in a number of different political situations where the faith was not established, in Robert D. Linder, ed., *God and Caesar: Case Studies in the Relationship Between Christianity and the State* (Longview, Tex.: Conference on Faith and History, 1971).

Chapter Four

1. Martin, Marty, *Righteous Empire* (New York: Dial, 1970), p. 98.

2. Statistics on the working woman are published periodically by the Women's Bureau of the United States Department of Labor. Figures given here are from the 1970 report as reported in *Time* 98 (July 26, 1971), p. 56. An excellent analysis of the problems of the working woman is Caroline Bird, *Born Female* (New York: Pocket Books, 1968).

3. Billy Graham, "Jesus and the Liberated Woman," *Ladies' Home Journal* 87 (Dec. 1970), p. 42; David Hubbard, "When Man Was Human," *His* 32 (Oct. 1971), p. 3; Herbert J. Miles, *Sexual Understanding Before Marriage* (Grand Rapids: Zondervan, 1971), p. 177; James Montgomery Boice, "Marriage by Christ's Standard," *Eternity* 21 (Nov. 1970), p. 21.

4. 1 Co. 12:11. Although the King James Version uses the word "man" in this verse, there is no word for "man" or "male" in the Greek; rather, it is the indefinite pronoun "each" or "anyone." A very profitable study could be made of this and other passages such as Eph. 4 concerning what is expected of *every* mature Christian and how the Spirit equips each one individually without respect to sex for the task of serving God. An equally worthwhile study could also be done on the "fruits of the Spirit" as listed in Gal. 5:22-23 and how they correspond with what society traditionally claims to be a mature man and a mature woman.

5. For many detailed expositions of the Scripture passages involved, see Nancy Hardesty, "Women: Second Class Citizens?" *Eternity* 22 (Jan. 1971), pp. 14-16, 24-29; Letha Scanzoni and Nancy Hardesty, *Christian Woman's Liberation* New York: Harper & Row, 1970); Russell Prohl, *Woman in the Church* (Grand Rapids: Eerdmans, 1957); Sidney Cornelia Callahan, *The Illusion of Eve* (New York: Sheed & Ward, 1965); Mary Daly, *The Church and the Second Sex* (New York: Harper & Row, 1968); Krister Stendahl, *The Bible and the Role of Women* (Philadelphia: Fortress, 1966).

6. For a short and beautifully articulated statement of Jesus' attitude toward women, see Dorothy Sayers, *Are Women Human?* (Grand Rapids: Eerdmans, 1971).

7. See the book of Acts (5:14; 8:12; 9:36-42; 12:12; 16:12-15; 17:4, 34), Ro. 16; Col. 4:15; Phil. 4:2; as well as other verses dealing with women. Ruth Hoppin suggests in *Priscilla: Author of the Epistle to the Hebrews* (New York: Exposition Press, 1969) that the woman mentioned in Ac. 18:2-3, 24-28, and Ro. 16:3, as well as elsewhere, was the author of Hebrews. Her arguments merit consideration. Also interesting is the possibility that 1 Ti. 3:11-13 refers to female deacons rather than the wives of deacons.

8. A good discussion from a more secular and philosophic viewpoint of the whole feminist issue is found in John Stuart Mill and Harriet Taylor Mill, *Essays on Sex*

Equality, ed. Alice S. Rossi (Chicago: U. Chicago, 1970). Philosopher Mill suggested seeing marriage as egalitarian and analogous to a business partnership in his essay, "The Subjection of Women," written in 1869. See pp. 168-71 of the Rossi edition.

Chapter Five

1. President's Commission on National Goals, *Goals for Americans* (New York: Prentice-Hall, 1960).

2. Clinton Rossiter, *Conservatism in America*, rev. ed., (New York: Vintage Books, 1962), p. 237.

3. Barry Goldwater, *The Conscience of a Conservative* (Shepherdsville, Ky.: Victor: 1960).

4. Michael Harrington, *The Other America* (New York: Macmillan, 1962).

5. To many Americans, the term "political conservativism" refers to that seventeenth- and eighteenth-century liberalism which believed the role of the state should be restricted as much as possible insofar as is compatible with the necessity for society to establish order. The term "political liberalism" has come to refer to that nineteenth- and twentieth-century liberalism which seeks a more active role for the state in managing the overall affairs of society.

6. On this see Philip G. Altbach and Patti Peterson, "Before Berkeley: Historical Perspectives on American Student Activism," *Annals of the American Academy of Political and Social Science* 395 (May 1971), pp. 1-14.

7. See Philip M. Burgess and C. Richard Hofstetter, "The 'Student Movement': Ideology and Reality," *Midwest Journal of Political Science* 15 (1971), pp. 661-86.

8. This statement is available in Robert A. Goldwin, ed., *How Democratic Is America?* (Chicago: Rand McNally, 1971), pp. 1-15.

9. *Ibid.*, p. 4.

10. Charles A. Reich, *The Greening of America* (New York: Random House, 1970), p. 4.

11. A fascinating study of how new left activists have been drawn into the Jesus movement is provided by Edward E. Plowman, *The Jesus Movement in America* (New York: Pyramid Books, 1971).

12. Michael Novak, *A Theology for Radical Politics* (New York: Herder & Herder, 1969), pp. 17-18.

13. See Sherwood E. Wirt, *The Social Conscience of the Evangelical* (New York: Harper & Row, 1968) and Carl F. H. Henry, *A Plea for Evangelical Demonstration* (Grand Rapids: Baker, 1971).

14. Leighton Ford, "Evangelism in a Day of Revolution," *Christianity Today* 14 (Oct. 24, 1969), pp. 6-12; Mark O. Hatfield, "American Democracy and American Evangelicalism—New Perspectives," *Theology, News and Notes* 14 (Nov. 1970), pp. 8-11.

15. Goldwin, p. 15.

16. Daniel P. Moynihan, commencement address at Notre Dame University, quoted in the *Wall Street Journal,* June 20, 1969, p. 16.

Chapter Six

1. David B. Stevick, *Beyond Fundamentalism* (Richmond, Va.: John Knox, 1964), p. 178; William G. McLoughlin, "Is There a Third Force in Christendom?" *Daedalus* 96 (Winter 1967), p. 61; James Nolan, "Jesus Now: Hogwash and Holy Water," *Ramparts* 10 (Aug. 1971), p. 22.

2. Benton Johnson, "Ascetic Protestantism and Political Preference," *Public Opinion Quarterly* 26 (Spring, 1962), pp. 35-46; "Theology and Party Preference

Among Protestant Clergymen," *American Sociological Review* 31 (Apr. 1966), pp. 200-8; Jeffrey K. Hadden, *The Gathering Storm in the Churches* (Garden City, N. Y.: Doubleday, 1969), pp. 82-83; Leland Harder, "The Political Behavior of Northern Indiana Mennonites," paper delivered at the Indiana Academy of Social Sciences, Terre Haute, Ind., Oct. 30, 1970; Mark Chesler and Richard Schmuck, "Social Psychological Characteristics of Super-Patriots" in *The American Right Wing*, ed. Robert A. Schoenberger. (New York: Holt, Rinehart & Winston, 1969), p. 183; Ezra Earl Jones, *Where United Methodists Stand on Extremism: Attitudes Toward Political and Social Issues* (New York: Board of Missions, The United Methodist Church, 1971).

3. James McEvoy, III, *Radicals or Conservatives? The Contemporary American Right* (Chicago: Rand McNally, 1971), pp. 2-3.

4. This scheme has been suggested by Keith R. Sanders in "An Empirical Study of the Integrity of Evidence Used in John A. Stormer's *None Dare Call It Treason,*" Ph.D. dissertation, U. Pittsburgh, 1968, p. 7. I have replaced his term "extreme" with "moderate" in the first category, as that is a clearer designation.

5. William P. Strube, Jr., *Communism—A Monopoly*, undated pamphlet, pp. 8-9.

6. This is discussed in greater detail in my essay, "Christianity, Democracy, and the Radical Right" in *Protest and Politics*, pp. 39-64, and chap. 2 of my book, *The Unequal Yoke: Evangelical Christianity and Political Conservatism* (Philadelphia: Lippincott, 1970).

7. Georgh Thayer, *The Farther Shore of Politics: The American Political Fringe Today* (New York: Simon & Schuster, 1967), p. 147.

8. *Ibid.*, p. 276; Irwin Suall, *The American Ultras* (New York: League for Industrial Democracy, 1962), pp. 36-37. A devastating expose is Greg Walter, "Snow Job at Valley Forge," *Philadelphia Magazine* 59 (Feb. 1968), pp. 70-75, 148-54.

9. *Group Research Reports* 9 (June 25, 1970), p. 48.

10. "The Fragility of Freedom," *Decision* 11 (July 1970), p. 2.

11. See Pierard, *The Unequal Yoke*, pp. 53-68, for a description of these organizations.

12. *Homefront* 5 (July-Aug. 1971), p. 51.

13. Erling Jorstad, *The Politics of Doomsday: Fundamentalists of the Far Right* (Nashville: Abingdon, 1970), pp. 120-24.

14. Henry Stob, "Fundamentalism and Political Rightism," *The Reformed Journal* 15 (Jan. 1965), pp. 12-14.

15. Rodney Stark and Charles Y. Glock, *American Piety: The Nature of Religious Commitment* (Berkeley: U. California, 1968), p. 75.

16. Stevick, p. 211.

17. E. Mansell Pattison, "Closed Mind Syndrome," *Christian Medical Society Journal* 17 (Spring, 1966), p. 8; Ira S. Rohter, "The Genesis of Political Radicalism: The Case of the Radical Right" in *Learning About Politics*, ed. Roberta S. Sigel (New York: Random House, 1970), pp. 638-39.

18. Patricia J. Harrison, "An American *Kulturkampf*: Factors in the Development of Anti-Intellectualism among Evangelicals in America," *Studia Biblica et Theologica* 1 (Mar. 1971), pp. 50-61.

19. E. Mansell Pattison, quoted in Joseph T. Bayly, "Why We Have Lacked Creativity," *Eternity* 16 (Oct. 1965), p. 47; Rohter, "Genesis," pp. 639-41.

20. Timothy L. Smith, *Revivalism and Social Reform* (Nashville: Abingdon, 1957); Bruce L. Shelley, *Evangelicalism in America* (Grand Rapids: Eerdmans, 1967).

21. David S. Gotaas, *The Preservation of Our Freedom* (Chicago: Moody, 1970).

22. Dick Hillis, "The First Communist," *Christian Economics* 21 (Feb. 11, 1970), p. 5.

23. Dixon Gayer, article in *Dixon Line* 7 (Sept. 1970), p. 12.

24. Raymond E. Wolfinger et al., "America's Radical Right: Politics and Ideology" in *Ideology and Discontent* ed. David E. Apter (New York: Macmillan, 1964), p. 267; Fred W. Grupp, Jr., "The Political Perspectives of Birch Society Members" in Schoenberger, pp. 96-97, 93; and McEvoy, pp. 68-70, 104.

25. Ralph Lord Roy, "Conflict from the Communist Left and the Radical Right" in *Religion and Social Conflict*, ed. Robert Lee and Martin E. Marty (New York: Oxford U., 1964), p. 62.

26. Dudley Morton Lynch, "The General and the Christian College: Where Was the Dissent?" *Christian Century* (June 9, 1971), pp. 724-26; see also his article in *Mission* (Abilene, Tex.) 3 (1970), p. 305ff.

27. Ted Ward, *Memo for the Underground* (Carol Stream, Ill.: Creation House, 1971), p. 95.

28. Samuel Escobar, "The Social Impact of the Gospel" in *Is Revolution Change?* ed. Brian Griffiths (London: Inter-Varsity, 1972)..

29. These arguments are succinctly summarized by John H. Redekop, "Evangelical Christianity and Political Ideology," *Christian Living* 17 (May 1970), pp. 26-27.

30. Franklin H. Littell, "Christians in a Violent Age," *Dialog* 8 (1969), p. 35.

31. In a challenging article, Baptist seminary professor Leland D. Hine suggests that failure to break with the subculture may soon result in the demise of evangelical Christianity in America ("Is Evangelicalism Dying of Old Age?" *Eternity* 23 [Mar. 1972], pp. 21-23).

Chapter Seven

1. A widely disseminated account of the incident is in *Newsweek* 77 (Nov. 15, 1971), p. 105.

2. See Don and John Ottenhoff, "Timothy Christian Schools," *The Other Side* 7 (Mar.-Apr. 1971), pp. 22-25.

3. *Christianity Today* 11 (Jan. 6, 1967), p. 43; and 16 (Feb. 4, 1972), p. 36.

4. Angus Campbell, *White Attitudes Toward Black People* (Ann Arbor: Institute for Social Research, U. Michigan, 1971), p. 48.

5. Billy Graham, *World Aflame* (Garden City, N. Y.: Doubleday, 1965), p. 7.

6. *Christianity Today* 15 (Sept. 24, 1971), p. 48.

7. Charles Carroll, *The Negro a Beast* (St. Louis: American Book & Bible House, 1900). For other expressions of this view see David M. Reimers, *White Protestantism and the Negro* (New York: Oxford U., 1965), pp. 27-30.

8. The curse of Ham is effectively refuted in J. Oliver Buswell, III, *Slavery, Segregation and Scripture* (Grand Rapids: Eerdmans, 1964). Useful accounts of slavery and the slave trade are Daniel P. Mannix and Malcolm Cowley, *Black Cargoes: A History of the Atlantic Slave Trade, 1518-1865* (New York: Viking, 1962), and Winthrop Jordan, *White over Black: American Attitudes Toward the Negro, 1550-1812* (Chapel Hill: U. North Carolina, 1968). For a general overview of black history, consult John Hope Franklin, *From Slavery to Freedom: A History of American Negroes* (New York: Knopf, 1967), and Lerone Bennett, Jr., *Before the Mayflower: A History of the Negro in America* (Chicago: Johnson, 1964).

9. I have dealt with these points in greater detail in the following two articles: "Racist Use of the Old Testament," *The Other Side* 6 (May-June, 1970), pp. 11-12,

23; and "Christians and Conservatives," *The Other Side* 7 (Jan.-Feb. 1971), pp. 26-29.

10. See Gordon W. Allport, *The Nature of Prejudice* (Garden City, N. Y.: Doubleday, 1958).

11. Columbus Salley and Ronald Behm, *Your God Is Too White* (Downers Grove, Ill.: Inter-Varsity, 1970), p. 114. This book as well as the following works by Evangelicals will be of assistance to the Christian who is trying to combat racism in his own life and in the church: Tom Skinner, *Words of Revolution* (Grand Rapids: Zondervan, 1970) and *How Black Is the Gospel?* (Philadelphia: Lippincott, 1970); William E. Pannell *My Friend the Enemy* (Waco: Word, 1968); and Robert D. Linder, "A Christian Approach to the Contemporary Civil Rights Movement" in *Protest and Politics*, pp. 121-49. Of particular merit is the hard-hitting Christian magazine, *The Other Side*, published bimonthly in Savannah, Ohio.

Chapter Eight

1. Carl F. H. Henry, *The Uneasy Conscience of Modern Fundamentalism* (Grand Rapids: Eerdmans, 1947), p. 36.

2. Sherwood E. Wirt, *The Social Conscience of the Evangelical* (New York: Harper & Row, 1968), p. 154.

3. Earle E. Cairns, *Saints and Society* (Chicago: Moody, 1960), p. 43. The Clapham Sect was the name given to wealthy Evangelicals, mostly businessmen and politicians, who lived in the London suburb of Clapham Commons. Many Dissenters (those of non-Anglican Protestant denominations) were evangelical in belief and practice.

4. *Ibid., passim.* See also Maldwyn Edwards, *John Wesley and the Eighteenth Century: A Study of His Social and Political Influence* (London: George Allen & Unwin, 1933); and Francis J. McConnell, *John Wesley* (New York: Abingdon, 1939), pp. 231-310.

5. Charles Grandison Finney, *Lectures on Revivals of Religion* (Cambridge: Harvard U., 1960; first published 1835), p. 302 and *passim.*

6. James F. Findlay, Jr., *Dwight L. Moody, American Evangelist, 1837-1899* (Chicago: U. Chicago, 1969), pp. 73-78, 88-90, 178-79, 321-23.

7. William G. McLoughlin, Jr., *Billy Sunday Was His Real Name* (Chicago: U. Chicago, 1955); Jacob Henry Dorn, *Washington Gladden: Prophet of the Social Gospel* (Columbus: Ohio State U., 1967), pp. 378-401.

8. This wording is based upon the writer's notes from his own two hearings. After religion editor George Plagenz of the Cleveland *Press* took Graham to task for this statement in a Dec. 11 column, the evangelist replied: "I will have to be more careful from now on. . . . My true views are that this country is in desperate need of social justice and that includes racial, poverty and environmental. However, I can certainly see how some of my remarks could have been misinterpreted. I really did not mean the way they apparently came out" *(The Arizona Republic* [Phoenix], Jan. 1, 1972, p. 13).

9. *Gallup Opinion Index*, Report No. 67 (Jan. 1971), pp. 8-12; *The Arizona Republic* (Phoenix), Jan. 2, 1972, p. 18.

10. *Time* 94 (Oct. 4, 1968): 92, *Christian Century* 85 (Oct. 30, 1968): 1359. For another example of Nixon's reliance on the evangelist, see Garry Wills, "How Nixon Used the Media, Billy Graham, and the Good Lord to Rap with Students at Tennessee U," *Esquire* 74 (Sep. 1970): 119-22, 179-80.

11. Billy Graham, *World Aflame* (New York: Pocket Books, 1966; first published 1965), p. 156.

12. W. David Lockard, *The Unheard Billy Graham* (Waco: Word, 1971), pp.

126-50, 164; *Protest and Politics*, p. 116. For his latest social views, see Billy Graham, *The Jesus Generation* (Grand Rapids: Zondervan, 1971).

13. John Pollock, *Billy Graham* (Grand Rapids: Zondervan, 1967), p. 97.

14. *Ibid.*, p. 98; Lockard, p. 118; Samuel Southard, "Segregation and Southern Churches," *Journal of Religion and Health* 1 (Apr. 1962), pp. 214-15.

15. George M. Wilson, ed., *20 Years Under God: A Pictorial Review of the Billy Graham Ministries* (Minneapolis: World Wide Publications, 1971), pp. 138-41. Some years later in 1965 Graham held several meetings in Southern trouble spots at the special request of President Lyndon Johnson. *Ibid.*, p. 144; Leighton Ford, *One Way to Change the World*, p. 62; Lockard, pp. 117-26; Pollock, pp. 223-29.

16. Billy Graham, "Billy Graham Makes Plea for an End to Intolerance," *Life* 41 (Oct. 1, 1956), pp. 138-51; "A Round Table Has Debate on Christian's Moral Duty," *ibid.*, pp. 139-62.

17. *Newsweek* 55 (Mar. 28, 1960), p. 86; Howard O. Jones, *Shall We Overcome? A Challenge to Negro and White Christians* (Westwood, N. J.: Revell, 1966), pp. 129-30.

18. In the fall of 1971 the writer sent four-page questionnaires on evangelism and social concern to 170 American evangelists, evangelistically oriented pastors, and Christian educators experienced in evangelism. The sampling included the most prominent persons in these fields from every region and represented three races, eighteen denominations, and several interdenominational ministries. The data and quotations used in the following pages are drawn from the eighty-five questionnaires that were returned (50 percent of those sent) which are in the writer's files.

19. Bernard Ramm, "Watch Out for False Spirituality," *Eternity* 15 (Apr. 1964), p. 27.

20. David O. Moberg *Inasmuch: Christian Social Responsibility in the Twentieth Century* (Grand Rapids: Eerdmans, 1965), p. 94.

21. Henry, *A Plea for Evangelical Demonstration*, p. 66.

22. *Ibid.*, p. 18.

23. "Evangelism: How to Get Involved," *Christianity Today* 15 (Aug. 27, 1971), p. 1041.

24. Leighton Ford, "Evangelism in a Day of Revolution," *Christianity Today* 14 (Oct. 24, 1969), p. 67.

25. Gilbert James, "Christians as Agents of Social Change," *Good News* 5 (Oct. 1971), p. 80.

Chapter Nine

1. Richard B. Morris, *Government and Labor in Early America* (New York: Columbia U., 1946), p. 16.

2. Russell H. Conwell, *Acres of Diamonds* (New York: Harper, 1915), p. 18.

3. William Lawrence, "Relation of Wealth to Morals," *World's Work*, (1901): p. 287.

4. See the excellent treatment of these attitudes in Irvin G. Wyllie, *The Self-Made Man in America: The Myths of Rags to Riches* (New Brunswick, N. J.: Rutgers U., 1954).

5. Quoted in Robert Bremner, *From the Depths: The Discovery of Poverty in the United States* (New York: New York U., 1956), p. 26. Herron, for a time a

Congregationalist minister, was one of the early leaders of the Social Gospel movement in America.

6. Quoted in Bremner, p. 27.

7. Rauschenbusch was even willing to make the right use of property one of the tests of church membership. Clyde C. Griffen, "Rich Laymen and Early Social Christianity," *Church History* 36 (Mar. 1967), p. 55.

8. John Spargo, *The Bitter Cry of the Children* (Chicago: Quadrangle, 1968), p. 174.

9. Robert Hunter, *Poverty* (New York: Harper & Row, 1965), p. viii.

10. Irving Bernstein, *The Lean Years: A History of the American Worker, 1920-1933* (Boston: Houghton Mifflin, 1960) gives information on the 1920s. Hoover's speech can be found in the *New York Times*, Aug. 12, 1928, p. 2.

11. Paul A. Carter, *The Decline and Revival of the Social Gospel: Social Political Liberalism in American Protestant Churches, 1920-1940* (Ithaca: Cornell U. 1954), p. 56.

12. Robert M. Miller, *American Protestantism and Social Issues, 1919-1939* (Chapel Hill: U. North Carolina, 1958), pp. 122-23.

13. *New York Times*, Oct. 19, 1954, p. 17.

14. Michael Harrington, *The Other America* (Baltimore: Penguin Books, 1962), pp. 9, 158.

15. Quoted in Sidney Lens, *Poverty: America's Enduring Paradox* (New York: Crowell. 1971). pp. 311-12.

16. *U.S. News and World Report* 71 (July 12, 1971), p. 55; and Lens, pp. 303-4.

17. Edward Banfield, *The Unheavenly City* (Boston: Little, Brown, 1968); and NLC and USCM Staff, "Banfield Dissected," *Nation's Cities*, Jan. 1971, pp. 18-22.

18. Harrington, p. 155.

19. Lens, p. 330.

20. Alan Keith-Lucas, *The Church and Social Welfare* (Philadelphia: Westminster, 1962), p. 5.

21. "Church Money for the Slums," *America* 119 (Nov. 9, 1968), p. 425; "Churchmen United Against Poverty," *America* 115 (July 30, 1966), p. 105; and Haskell H. Miller, *Compassion and Community: An Appraisal of the Church's Changing Role in Social Welfare* (New York: Harper & Row, 1959), pp. 225-26.

22. Keith-Lucas, pp. 25, 10-11, 15-16.

23. Edward Duff, "The Scandal of Squalor," *Commonweal* 81 (Nov. 13, 1964), pp. 223-25.

24. John J. Dougherty, "Voice for the Poor," *America* 118 (Feb. 24, 1968), p. 252.

25. Barbara Ward, "A Claim Against the West," *Commonweal* 81 (Nov. 13, 1964), p. 222.

26. Reginald H. Fuller and Brian K. Rice, *Christianity and the Affluent Society* (Grand Rapids: Eerdmans, 1966), p. 179.

27. "Church and Society," *Christian Century* 83 (Apr. 20, 1966), p. 485; and Harold Lindsell, ed., *The Church's Worldwide Mission* (Waco: Word, 1966), pp. 2-3.

28. Samuel Escobar, "Social Concern and World Evangelism" in *Christ the Liberator* (Downers Grove, Ill.: Inter-Varsity, 1971), p. 104.

29. The incident is described in James E. Johnson, "The Christian and the Emergence of the Welfare State" in *Protest and Politics*, p. 116.

30. David O. Moberg, *Inasmuch* (Grand Rapids: Eerdmans, 1965).

31. For assistance in sensitizing others to the needs of the poor and to receive guidance as to where to begin in combating poverty, consult William M. Pinson, Jr., *Resource Guide to Current Social Issues* (Waco: Word, 1968), pp. 191-95 (poverty) and pp. 218-24 (social action and welfare).

Chapter Ten

1. Frank Graham, *Since Silent Spring* (Greenwich, Conn.: Fawcett, 1970), p. 14.

2. Herbert C. Hanson, *Dictionary of Ecology* (New York: Philosophical Library, 1962), p. 121.

3. Lynton Keith Caldwell, *Environment: A Challenge for Modern Society* (Garden City, N.Y.: Doubleday, 1970), p. 19.

4. *Ibid.*, pp. 80-81.

5. Donald E. Carr, *Death of Sweet Waters* (New York: Norton, 1966), p. 29.

6. *Ibid.*, p. 39. See also Philip Ziegler, *The Black Death* (New York: Day, 1969).

7. *Ibid.*, p. 42.

8. *Ibid.*, p. 48.

9. *Ibid.*, pp. 139, 149.

10. Paul R. Ehrlich and John P. Holdren, *Global Ecology: Readings Toward a Rational Strategy for Man* (New York: Harcourt, Brace, Jovanovich, 1971), p. 67.

11. Graham, p. 239.

12. Ehrlich and Holdren, p. 68.

13. Carr, *The Breath of Life* (New York: Norton, 1965), p. 28.

14. *Ibid.*, p. 33.

15. Ehrlich and Holdren, p. 66.

16. Carr. *Breath of Life*, pp. 44, 46-49.

17. *Ibid.*, p. 51.

18. Ehrlich and Holdren, p. 68.

19. Victor Gruen, *The Heart of Our Cities* (New York: Simon & Schuster, 1964), pp. 63-64.

20. Lewis Mumford, *The Urban Prospect* (New York: Harcourt, Brace & World, 1968), pp. 82-83.

21. Caldwell, p. 139.

22. *Ibid.*, p. 149.

23. *Ibid.*, pp. 36, 75-76.

24. *Ibid.*, pp. 192, 229.

25. "The Historical Roots of Our Ecologic Crisis," *Science* 155 (Mar. 10, 1967), pp. 1203-7. This article is included in its entirety as an appendix in Francis Schaeffer, *Pollution and the Death of Man: The Christian View of Ecology* (London: Hodder & Stoughton, 1970), pp. 70-85. The American edition has been published by Tyndale House, Wheaton, Ill.

26. *Ibid.*, p. 1206.

27. *Saturday Review* 50 (Dec. 2, 1967), pp. 13-15. It is also an appendix in Schaeffer, pp. 86-93.

28. Schaeffer, p. 15.

29. *Ibid.*, pp. 19, 22-23.

30. *Ibid.*, p. 27.

31. *Ibid.*, pp. 30-31, 46.

32. *Ibid.*, p. 57.

33. Caldwell, p. 129.

34. Schaeffer, p. 60.

35. *Ibid.*, p. 59.

36. Some recent works which approach the ecological crisis from a Christian perspective include Walter Brueggemann, "King in the Kingdom of Things," *Christian Century* 86 (Sept. 10, 1969), pp. 1165-66; Ron Widman, "When You've Seen One Beer Can, You've Seen Them All," *Eternity* 20 (May 1970), pp. 12-14, 16, 29; John N. Oswalt, "Is Christianity Responsible for This Mess?" *Eternity* 22 (Sept.

1971), pp. 16-18; Allen Harder, "Ecology, Magic, and the Death of Man," *Christian Scholar's Review* 1 (Winter, 1971), pp. 117-131; and H. Paul Santmire, *Brother Earth* (New York: Nelson, 1971).

Chapter Eleven

The author wishes to express his gratitude to the American Institute of Holy Land Studies, Jerusalem, for making available its facilities and library so that this essay could be completed.

1. Geerhardus Vos, *The Teaching of Jesus Concerning the Kingdom and the Church* (Grand Rapids: Eerdmans, 1958 reprint), p. 78.
2. Unfortunately, it is difficult to change common expressions. Since Arabs are also Semitic, it would be better to use the phrase *Anti-Jewishness* instead of *anti-Semitism*, unless one wishes to include all the Semitic-speaking peoples.
3. Address of Prime Minister Golda Meir at the University of the Negev, Beersheba, Israel, reported in the *Jerusalem Post*, Mar. 12, 1972.
4. These statistics were taken from Israeli government publications and may not always be exactly correct. However, they do at least show the trends.
5. Collectivized agricultural communities which operate on a communal philosophy.
6. *The Israeli Economy: 1950, 1960, and 1980* (Jerusalem: Department of the Treasury, 1972). This is an official government publication which contains 68 pages of figures.
7. This has become evident by the number of conferences sponsored by the American Jewish Committee to encourage dialogue between Christians and Jews. The author took part in one at Westmont College, Santa Barbara, California, in December, 1970.
8. In 1947 the United Nations Special Commission on Palestine recommended that Palestine be divided into two states—Israel and Arab Palestine. Each state was to be subdivided into three sections.
9. An organization called "Christians Concerned for Israel" issued a statement on June 10, 1971, favoring Israeli government control over Jerusalem.
10. Editorial in *The Tablet* (London), Apr. 10, 1971.
11. William G. Oxtoby, "The Middle East: From Polemic to Accommodation," *Christian Century* 88 (Oct. 13, 1971), pp. 1192-97.
12. *Ibid.*, pp. 1195-97.
13. A. Roy Eckardt, "The Fantasy of Reconciliation in the Middle East," *Ibid.*, p. 1199.
14. Alice and Roy Eckardt, *Encounter with Israel: A Challenge to Conscience* (New York: Association, 1970), p. 219.
15. American Friends Service Committee, *Search for Peace in the Middle East* (New York: Fawcett World Library, 1970).
16. *Truth and Peace in the Middle East* (New York: B'nai B'rith and the American Jewish Congress, 1971).
17. Elisabeth Elliot, *Furnace of the Lord* (Garden City, N. Y.: Doubleday, 1969).
18. "American Evangelical Support of Israel Blunts Gospel Thrust in Middle East," *Urbana &* 1, no. 4 (Feb. 1, 1971).
19. John F. Walvoord, *The Millennial Kingdom* (Findlay, O.: Dunham, 1959) Also, Charles Lee Feinberg, *Israel in the Spotlight* (Wheaton, Ill.: Scripture Press, 1956).
20. Hal Lindsey, *The Late Great Planet Earth* (Grand Rapids: Zondervan, 1970).
21. *Ibid.*, pp. 51-52.

22. *Ibid.*, p. 112. The false prophet is described in Rev. 13:11-18.

23. J. Dwight Pentecost, *Things to Come: A Study in Biblical Eschatology* (Findlay, O.: Dunham, 1958), pp. 336-37.

24. The papers presented at this conference have been published in Carl F. H. Henry, ed., *Prophecy in the Making* (Carol Stream, Ill.: Creation House, 1971).

25. George Giacumakis, Jr., "The Israeli-Arab Conflict in the Middle East," in *Protest and Politics*, pp. 227-50.

26. King Hussein of Jordan issued a statement on March 15, 1972, calling for the establishment of a twin kingdom that would encompass both sides of the Jordan River. With the suggested name, The United Arab Kingdom, this new political entity would include a semiautonomous state for the Palestinians.

Chapter Twelve

1. "War Finance," *Encyclopedia Britannica* 23 (1970), pp. 215-17; and Quincy Wright, *A Study of War*, 2d ed. (Chicago: U. Chicago, 1965), p. 1503.

2. *New York Times*, Apr. 17, 1953, p. 4.

3. David M. Shoup, "The New American Militarism," *Atlantic Monthly* 223 (Apr. 1969), p. 52.

4. *Ibid.*

5. There is a voluminous literature on My Lai, but not much has been contributed by Evangelicals. Among the more important works are: Richard Hammer, *One Morning in the War: The Tragedy at Son My* (New York: Coward McCann, 1971); Seymour Hersh, *My Lai 4: A Report on the Massacre and Its Aftermath* (New York: Random House, 1970); and Martin Gershen, ed., *Destroy or Die: The True Story of Mylai* (New Rochelle, N. Y.: Arlington House, 1971).

6. Roland H. Bainton, *Christian Attitudes Toward War and Peace* (Nashville: Abingdon, 1960). Probably the clearest presentation of the just war is by Paul Ramsey, *The Just War, Force and Political Responsibility* (New York: Scribner, 1968). For the pacifist position by one who is not a member of one of the historic peace churches, notice Culbert G. Rutenber, *The Dagger and the Cross* (Nyack, N. Y.: Fellowship, 1958). Also see Thomas Merton, ed., *Breakthrough to Peace: Twelve Views on the Threat of Thermonuclear Extermination* (New York: New Directions, 1968); and Ralph B. Potter, *War and Moral Discourse* (Richmond: John Knox, 1969). Potter contains a valuable forty-page bibliographical essay in which the major contemporary studies on the morality of war are evaluated.

7. John R. Rice, *War in Vietnam: Should Christians Fight?* (Murfreesboro, Tenn.: Sword of the Lord, 1966), p. 18.

8. William E. Nix, "War" in *Our Society in Turmoil*, ed. Gary Collins (Carol Stream, Ill.: Creation House, 1970), p. 262.

9. Ernest J. Sternglass, "The Death of All Children: A Footnote to the ABM Controversy," *Esquire* 72 (Sept. 1969), pp. 1a-1d.

10. Wystan Hugh Auden, *On This Island* (New York: Random House, 1937), Poem 18, p. 47.

11. Summary of Clarence Jordan's sermon contained in Dallas Lee, *The Cotton Patch Evidence* (New York: Harper, 1971), pp. 59-61.

12. Mt. 28:19-20; Lk. 10:29-37; Ac. 17:26; Gal. 3:28; and Eph. 2:11-22.

13. Elisabeth Elliot, *The Liberty of Obedience* (Waco: Word, 1968), pp. 15-17.

14. George Thayer, *The War Business: The International Trade in Armaments* (New York: Simon & Schuster, 1969).

15. For a good discussion of this problem, see William W. Adams, Jr., "Com-

munism, Realism, and Christianity" in *Protest and Politics*, pp. 203-25.

16. H. S. Vigeveno, *Jesus the Revolutionary* (Glendale, Calif.: Gospel Light, 1966).

17. Harold O. J. Brown, *Christianity and the Class Struggle* (New Rochelle, N. Y.: Arlington House, 1970), pp. 61-62.

18. Vernon C. Grounds, *Revolution and the Christian Faith* (Philadelphia: Lippincott, 1971), pp. 213-14.

19. *Ibid.*, pp. 218-19.

20. "Gospel and Revolution" in *New Theology No. 6*, ed. M. E. Marty and D. G. Peerman (New York: Macmillan, 1969), p. 245.

21. Jacques Ellul, *Violence, Reflections from a Christian Perspective*, trans. C. G. King, (New York: Seabury, 1969).

22. Passages which are used to build this biblical definition of justice include: Jer. 5:27-28; 22:13; Is. 1:23; 10:1-2; Ezek. 7:10-11, 23; 45:9; Mic. 6:10-12; 7:2-3; Amos 5:7-15; 6:12; Jon. 3:8; Hab. 1:3-4; Mt. 6:24; 23:14; Mk. 4:19; 6:34; Lk. 3:7-14; 4:18-19; 7:34; Ja. 5:1-6.

23. A commendable effort in the direction of working out an evangelical doctrine of the just revolution is Paul Steeves, "A Time for Violence." *The Other Side* 6 (Sep.-Oct. 1970), pp. 23-27, 31. The writer, however, does have difficulty accepting Steeves' argument that "a Christian must do no act which is not motivated by love. The love which God requires of the Christian is a universal love extending even to one's enemies. However difficult it may seem to love and kill someone at the same time, it must be recognized that it is possible. One can love the object of his violence only when he recognizes his violence is a form of punishment not of anger or vengeance. Love and chastisement are united in the actions of God and they can be likewise united in the actions of His followers" (p. 26).

24. Robert Taber, *The War of the Flea: A Study of Guerilla Warfare* (New York: Citadel, 1970).

25. Samuel Escobar, "Social Concern and World Evangelism" in *Christ the Liberator* (Downers Grove, Ill.: Inter-Varsity, 1971), p. 105.

On the alliance of evangelical Christianity with conservative political and social thought and action see Richard V. Pierard, *The Unequal Yoke: Evangelical Christianity and Political Conservatism* (Philadelphia: Lippincott, 1970).

INDEX

257